Independent Producers' Guide to Film and TV Contracts

To Theo and Ally

Independent:
'unwilling to be under an obligation to others'

Independent Producers' Guide to Film and TV Contracts

Philip Alberstat B.Sc. BA LL B (London)

Focal Press
OXFORD AUCKLAND BOSTON JOHANNESBURG MELBOURNE NEW DELHI

Focal Press
An imprint of Butterworth-Heinemann
Linacre House, Jordan Hill, Oxford OX2 8DP
225 Wildwood Avenue, Woburn, MA 01801-2041
A division of Reed Educational and Professional Publishing Ltd

℞ A member of the Reed Elsevier plc group

First published 1996 as *Media Production Agreements* by Routledge
First published 2000 by Focal Press

British Library Cataloguing in Publication Data
Alberstat, Philip
    Independent producers' guide to film and TV contracts
    1. Motion pictures – Law and legislation – Great Britain
    2. Television – Law and legislation – Great Britain
    3. Contracts – Great Britain
    I. Title
    343.4'1'09946

ISBN 0 240 51583 8

Library of Congress Cataloguing in Publication Data
A catalogue record for this book is available from the Library of Congress

Composition by Genesis Typesetting, Laser Quay, Rochester, Kent
Printed and bound in Great Britain by Biddles Ltd, www.Biddles.co.uk

Contents

Preface		vii
Author's notice		ix

1	Starting a company	1
2	A beginner's guide to copyright	6
3	Film development agreement	17
4	Option and literary purchase agreement	60
5	Writer's agreement	143
6	Co-production agreement	209
7	Distribution agreement	242
8	Finder/executive producer agreement	296
9	Confidentiality/non-disclosure agreement	311
10	Director's agreement	321
11	Presenter's agreement	386
12	Location agreement	408
13	Production manager's agreement	416
14	Release from a living person	429

Appendix A	List of addresses	439
Appendix B	Definition of gross and net receipts/income/profits	450
Appendix C	Inducement letter/agreement	455
Appendix D	Standard form licence to reproduce still photographs	460
Appendix E	Release form (extras)	465
Appendix F	Name/product/logo release	468

Index		471

Preface

The aim of this book is to make first time film-makers and producers aware of various issues both legal and otherwise associated with film and television production. During the last few years I have given many lectures to novice producers wishing to make their first film. A lot of their questions and concerns I have noted and hopefully the contents of this book will answer some of the problems they face while attempting to get their films off the ground. Making movies is one of the most difficult tasks faced by an individual. Producing a film can sometimes take many years of hard work with constant rejection from potential distributors and financiers. However, the most persistent producers will generally get their film made.

There are numerous issues legal and otherwise associated with film production. The intention of this book is to assist readers to understand specific contractual matters as well as give them the tools to make deals within the film and television industry.

The order of chapters has been arranged chronologically to try and coincide with the production process. The first chapter looks at setting up a limited company. Chapter 2 is a basic guide to copyright with the following chapters looking at the various technical and legal aspects of film development, right through to production. The appendices to the book contain details of film-related organizations and sample definitions of net profits.

This book is not a substitute for an experienced film lawyer. The agreements in this book do not offer specific legal advice and producers and others who use these contracts should be aware that in the commercial world all contracts and agreements are different. Specific legal advice should always be obtained where necessary, especially where the facts and circumstances of a particular transaction may be extremely complicated. Furthermore, various case law and statutes are subject to change and differ from country to country.

Regardless of these warnings, users of this book should find the contents both informative and helpful in their pursuit of film-making.

The author of this book would like to thank the following people for their assistance in making this book possible: Louise Wheatland, Julia Foguel, Michael Conradi, Piers Richardson, Kate Hope, Chris Johnstone, Eloise Scotford, Carol Hays and Dr D. T. McVicar.

Author's notice

This book is an introductory guide to some aspects of entertainment law for your general information only as background reading. Law and practice evolve quickly and previous understandings of the law can change radically. This book is not a substitute for legal advice. **Before acting on the sample contracts and documents in this book, you should consult an entertainment lawyer with appropriate qualifications and expertise for advice.** Any given situation will raise a number of legal and commercial concerns, which you may not be able to appreciate. The author, publishers and retailers of this book cannot therefore be held responsible for any losses or claims howsoever arising from the use or reproduction of this book.

Philip Alberstat reserves all rights, including copyright, in this work. No part of this publication may be reproduced, stored in a retrieval system, or transmitted in any way or by any means, including photocopying or recording without the written consent of Philip Alberstat.

Philip Alberstat, as author of this work, asserts his moral rights in accordance with Sections 77 to 80 of the Copyright, Designs and Patents Act 1988.

1 Starting a company

Starting a company

Many 'up and coming' producers frequently ask whether they should start a limited company. There are advantages and disadvantages of being a sole trader compared to a limited company and producers should take proper advice in helping them decide what is best for their purposes. If a producer thinks that their business turnover will be high, then it may be worthwhile to set up a limited company and register for value added tax (VAT). However, limited companies can be quite costly to run and there are specific disclosure requirements that directors of a company must submit to Companies House. In addition, audited accounts must be provided each year and this requires the services of an accountant which can sometimes be very expensive. In some cases, producers may wait to make their first film and use a single purpose company to produce that film.

The following information outlines the two main methods of company formation, which are the creation of a 'tailor-made' company and the purchase of a 'shelf company'.

'Tailor-made' company

A 'tailor-made' company can be created by submitting customized versions of the required documentation to the Companies Registry, namely, the company Memorandum, the Articles, Form 10 and Form 12, along with the present fee of £20. The requirements for these documents are explained below.

A new company can be incorporated on the same day by filing all the required documents at the Companies Registry before the 3 p.m. submission time. This accelerated service requires a higher fee of £100. Companies Registries are located in Cardiff, London, Birmingham, Manchester, Leeds and Edinburgh.

'Shelf company'

Alternatively, it is possible to buy a company which has already been incorporated but which has not traded (a 'shelf company'). This method is convenient and frequently used for speed. Shelf companies' names reflect the fact that they are incorporated for the express purpose of being acquired at a later stage (e.g. 'Alphabeta Trading, No 123').

Once purchased, the company formation agent sends the purchaser of the company the Certificate of Incorporation, along with the Memorandum and Articles (which will generally include standard articles (see below) and an all-purpose objects clause). A board meeting must be held to appoint new directors in place of the nominee directors appointed by the company formation agent, and to transfer the company shares into the names of the intended shareholders. Other matters may also need to be dealt with at the initial directors' meeting, such as whether to issue further shares, who should be the company secretary, and the new name of the company. The directors will need to decide on the location of the registered office (where the company's books must be kept and where legal documents may be served). It is possible to have a director who is the only director of a company, but if so that person cannot also be the company secretary.

If the nominee shelf company directors are resigning and being replaced it is necessary to file Form 288s to record the change.

The shelf company method gives the client the advantage of achieving trading status very quickly but the Memorandum and Articles may still need to be customized.

Documents for incorporation

The Memorandum

This is the document which outlines the objectives of the company, the company name, the nominal capital of the company and whether the members' liability is limited.

The purpose for which the company is in business (objects of the company) must be set out in the Memorandum. A general objects clause is usually adopted allowing the company to operate as a general commercial company, although specific clauses can also be used.

The Memorandum must include the intended company name. The company cannot be registered under an existing company name, so an index of names search at Companies House is required before submitting the intended choice in the Memorandum. A trade marks index search may be required if the new company is to use the company name to trade. This ensures that the name chosen is not already registered as a trade mark. The use of certain words may require written approval from the Secretary of State. The Memorandum also specifies the country of domicile/incorporation (England and Wales, or Scotland).

There are usually two initial shareholders named in the Memorandum. The subscriber's name, address, occupation and number of shares he intends to take in the company must be written in the Memorandum. Once the company is registered, the existing subscribers (usually two) become automatic members of the company. Initially, each subscriber usually takes one share. After incorporation further shares can be issued up to the amount of the nominal capital, and the number of shares the subscribers wish to have allotted to them will be allocated accordingly. Shares are not always issued up to the full amount of the nominal capital.

The final requirements regarding the Memorandum are that the document is dated and the subscribers sign the Memorandum in the presence of a witness.

3

The Articles of Association

The Articles outline the internal rules of the company, such as the extent of delegation of powers from the shareholders to the directors. They deal with directors' voting rights, procedure for proxy voting, procedure for general meetings and board meetings, shares and profits.

Table A articles are a standard set of articles which many companies use (Table A is found in the Companies Act 1985). In most circumstances Table A or a slightly modified version of it will be used, although there is no obligation to modify. However, in some circumstances a company will use a different set of Articles drafted specifically to meet its needs.

Once again, the Articles must be signed by the subscribers to the printed Memorandum. They must be dated and witnessed as for the Memorandum.

Form 10

This is a standard form which specifies the postal address of the registered office of the company. The company's statutory books are kept at the registered office and legal documents can be served at its address. The registered office does not always have to be the place where the company carries out its business (although this is possible). For example, some companies use their solicitor's office or their auditor's office.

Form 10 must also include the details of the first directors and the first secretary of the company. Details will include their names, addresses, business occupations, nationalities, dates of birth and any other directorships held. They must formally consent to acting as director (or secretary) by signing the form. Signatures will also be required by the subscribers to the Memorandum or the solicitor responsible for forming the company on their behalf.

Form 12

This is a statutory declaration confirming, as a formality, that the requirements set out in the Companies Act in relation to the formation of a company have been fulfilled. It must be sworn before a solicitor or commissioner for oaths. The director, secretary or the solicitor involved in the formation of the company can make the statutory declaration.

The Certificate of Incorporation

Once the fee (£20) has been paid and all the documents have been properly prepared and received, the registrar will issue a Certificate of Incorporation. This procedure takes approximately two weeks (alternatively it can be done in one day for £100). The certificate officially brings the company into existence and is evidence that the company has complied with all the necessary requirements. The registrar will allocate a number for the company which the company is legally required to include on its letterhead, along with the address of the registered office. It is an offence not to do so.

Once the certificate has been issued, the company has obtained a separate legal identity which means it can enter into contracts in its own right, and also means the directors' and shareholders' liability is 'limited'. Before incorporation, the company does not exist and contracts entered into by the prospective directors or shareholders may give rise to personal liability on their part.

2 A beginner's guide to copyright

Introduction

A great deal of time, skill, and effort are invested in the writing of books, scripts, lyrics, compositions and other creative works. Whether created in minutes or over a period of years, these works are all a result of a creator's hard work.

These efforts are rewarded, hopefully, by financial receipts and, in some cases, the fame or notoriety of being known as the writer, producer or creator of the work in question. But what happens if someone attempts to copy the work, pass it off as their own and reap the rewards, financial or otherwise, without having put in that effort? This is where the creator or author needs to look to their legal rights.

A book on copyright can run into thousands of pages. This chapter explains only the basic concepts of copyright and gives some ideas and recommendations on how to ensure copyright protection. The chapter also looks briefly at how to exploit your copyright and license or assign your rights.

Questions:

What is copyright?

Which works 'attract' copyright?

Who is the author/owner?

When does copyright start and end?

How is it protected?

Why are there allowable acts?

---

1 What is copyright?

Under English law, copyright is a legal property right that can be used to stop others from copying works without their creator's permission. Unlike the equivalent continental right, which has as its basis the 'right of an author', the English concept is economic. It is the right to prevent copying without permission. Although copyright has existed in English law since manuscripts were first created and plays first performed, one particular statute, **The Copyright, Designs and Patents Act 1988 (CDPA)**, sets out the current law on copyright. It is here that an author or owner of copyright must look to determine, first, whether their work qualifies for protection and, if so, how they can protect or exploit it.

2 Which works 'attract' copyright?

Section 1(1) of the CDPA provides that copyright may exist in three different categories of works:

(a) original literary, dramatic, musical and artistic works;
(b) sound recordings, films, broadcasts or cable programmes; and
(c) typographical arrangement of published edition (i.e. the page layout of a novel or telephone directory).

The first two categories (a) and (b) are most relevant to those in the film and television industry. The length of copyright protection differs according to the nature of the work. These different categories show how wide the scope of copyright protection can be. However, it is important to note a number of particular requirements for copyright:

● The work **must** be original. In contrast to the laws in other European countries, the test of originality is not difficult to pass under English law. All you have to prove is that the work is original to the author and has not been copied. A certain degree of effort on the part of the author is required. This is called the 'sweat of the brow' test; there is no aesthetic requirement. A work is considered literary whether trash novel or Trollope and artistic whether by 'Lucy age 6' or Lucian Freud.

- The work must be permanent, mere transitory marks, irrespective of whether they are used again and again, are not enough.

Despite the wide scope of copyright, these are some limitations which should be noted:

- There is a *de minimis* principle which means that copyright will probably not be available to titles, names or parts of sentences.
- Copyright is not available to protect ideas. It is only available to protect the expression of ideas. For example, where two authors come up with an identical or similar storyline for a novel, both novels will qualify for protection. One author could not stop the other from using the storyline. The question of when idea ends and expression begins is not always easy to resolve.

3 Who gets the copyright?

The creator or writer of the work (the author) is automatically the first owner of the copyright (unless the work is done in the course of their employment). If the work is done in the course of employment rather than on a consultancy basis, it belongs automatically to the employer. However, contracts can vary the position, allowing persons who commission a work to own the copyright in it.

For English copyright protection the author must be a British Citizen, domiciled or resident in the UK, or a company incorporated here. To qualify for protection, the author must have used their own skill and effort to create the work. Sometimes, there may be difficulty in proving who did what in respect of a particular work. For example, two people working on one work may both have copyright in that work if their contributions occurred at the same time (i.e. cartoonist and caption writer or any jointly written novel). However, if one party's contribution is made at a later stage, there may be no joint authorship, but two different copyright works, each with its own protection. In some cases the later work may be an infringement of the earlier work.

An author may choose to assign the copyright in their work to a third party, such as a publisher, who will then become the owner of the work. This is considered further below when we look at how to exploit a work.

In addition to copyright, an author has certain moral rights he can exercise in respect of his works. These include: the right to be identified as the author or director of a work (also known as the 'paternity right'); the right not to have the work subjected to derogatory treatment (also known as the 'integrity right'); and the right to object to false attribution of a work. These moral rights were introduced to bring the UK law into line with the terms of the Berne Copyright Convention.

4 When does the copyright start and finish?

If a work qualifies for copyright protection, the protection lasts for 70 years from the end of the calendar year in which the author dies (for literary, dramatic, musical and artistic copyright works); or 50 years from the end of the calendar year in which it was made (for sound recordings, broadcasts and cable programmes); and 70 years from the death of the last to survive of the principal director, the author of the film screenplay, the author of the film dialogue, and the composer of the film music (for a film).

Table 2.1

Type of work	Example	Length of protection
1. Literary Dramatic Musical Artistic	Book Dance performance Music score Picture, sculpture, photograph	70 years from the end of the calendar year in which the author dies.
2. Sound recordings	CD/tape (of music or sounds)	50 years from the end of the calendar year in which it is made OR if not immediately released – from the end of the calendar year in which it is released.
3. Films	Feature films	70 years from the death of the last to survive of: the principal director, the author of the film screen play, the author of the film dialogue and the composer of the music for the film.
4. Broadcast/cable programme	TV quizshow, cable show	50 years from the end of the calendar year in which the broadcast is made/the programme is included in a cable programme service.
5. Typographical arrangements	Book layout	25 years from the end of the calendar year in which the edition is first published.

5 How is the copyright protected?

The CDPA sets out in detail those acts which infringe copyright. If a third party does any of those acts without permission, whether knowing the work is protected by copyright or not, the copyright owner may bring proceedings to prevent such acts and/or claim damages for losses suffered by such unauthorized use. These restricted acts (also known as 'primary infringements') are:

- copying the work;
- issuing copies of the work to the public;
- renting or lending copies of the work to the public;
- performing, showing or playing the work in public;
- broadcasting the work or including it in a cable programme service; and
- making an adaptation of the work or doing any of the above acts in relation to an adaptation.

It is not necessary for the infringer to do any of the above to all of the work in question. Copying 'a substantial part' of a work is sufficient to breach the copyright in it. What is substantial is a question of quality not quantity. It is necessary to look at what is taken from the work, rather than how much. In the case of well-known works, such as a famous song, copying a few highly recognizable bars may be sufficient to be considered 'substantial'. With less recognizable works, a longer extract may need be to be copied before it can be said that a 'substantial' part has been copied. The question of what is substantial will be looked at objectively in light of all of the circumstances.

In addition to the 'primary' infringements, there are other acts (known as 'secondary infringements') which, if done deliberately knowing that there is an infringement of the copyright, would constitute an infringement. These include:

- importation of an infringing copy;
- possession or dealing with an infringing copy;
- provision of means for making infringing copies;
- permitting use of premises for infringing performances; and
- provision of apparatus for infringing performances.

From a cursory view of what the copyright holder may prevent, it is clear that copyright is a right to prevent the unauthorized economic exploitation of effort. However, copyright is not always a monopoly right and in certain circumstances use of a copyright work may be permitted by law even where such use is not authorized.

6 Why are there allowable acts?

The CDPA permits the unauthorized use of copyright works in certain limited circumstances, mainly where no economic hardship is caused to the author or creator.

The 'fair dealing' defence permits use of a work for research, private study, criticism, review and news reporting. There is also the right of incidental inclusion of work and rights of use by libraries and public administrations. Such uses are clearly for the 'public benefit' and would not usually have adverse financial consequences for the copyright works.

7 Remedies

If infringement of copyright occurs, the copyright owner may avail themselves of both civil and criminal remedies.

Usually, the copyright owner or (exclusive) licensee can bring a civil claim for breach of copyright, claiming damages or account of profits, an injunction, delivery up, destruction or seizure of infringing articles. In many cases, however, authors and independent producers lack sufficient financial backing to take legal action, which can be lengthy and expensive.

- **Damages**: a remedy only when the loss to the copyright owner can be valued. Innocent infringers may be required to give an account of profits but not damages. Where a licence could have been granted to make copies, the level of damages is generally only the licence fee.
- **Account of profits**: the purpose of this remedy is to prevent unjust enrichment of the infringer. The amount is the gain made by the infringer by the infringement (i.e. their profits). This remedy is often more difficult to obtain since it is left to the discretion of the court. A copyright owner seeking an account of profits from a third party will have to show their entitlement.

- **Injunction**: an order of the court which prohibits an act or the continuance of an act. Injunctions can be expensive and difficult to obtain as they are a discretionary remedy and if damages would compensate the potential loss, an injunction will not generally be granted.
- **Delivery-up/destruction/seizure**: a court may order that the infringing copies are delivered up to the copyright owner, destroyed or seized.

Summary – scope of copyright

Owners of copyright works should be aware that copyright is not necessarily always an exhaustive protection since:

- some dealing with the work may be allowed;
- copyright protects merely an expression of an idea, not the idea itself;
- only original works are protected;
- the work must have involved skill and effort;
- the work must be in a permanent form;
- it may be necessary to show definitively the precise date a work is created;
- the protection is not eternal;
- it is an economic right.

Protecting your position

Protecting the work

To get the most from copyright protection, an author or creator should:

- keep confidential all new ideas for screenplays, scores, articles etc. until they are in a permanent form. For example, a script should be finalized even if it is only a working draft prior to discussions with producers or broadcasters;

- keep a dated copy of the work in permanent form in a safe place. A computer readable form is acceptable, although it is advisable to retain a hard copy as well;
- apply a prominent copyright notice to all copies of the work, to ensure infringers cannot claim to be ignorant of the subsistence of copyright in the work.

Exploiting the work

Copyright is useful not only to prevent unauthorized exploitation but also to ensure an author can make the most from their work. Figure 2.1 shows how many different works can be created from one underlying work – each with their own rights. The rights in each of those works may belong to different people.

For example, the author of a book will own copyright in the book and can prevent people from copying it. If the

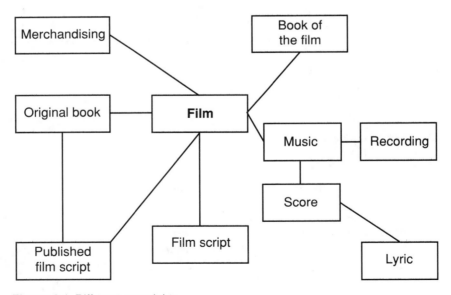

Figure 2.1 Different copyrights

author has licensed to a third party the right to make a film of the book then that third party will own a new copyright in the film. It should not always be assumed that all rights in a work should be licensed or sold to a third party who is going to exploit the work in a different medium. For example, an author may want to retain television rights, merchandising, radio rights, etc. when licensing film rights. In all cases, a written contact should be signed, clearly setting out what rights are being sold and what rights are retained.

Assignments and licences

Owners of the rights in a book or script should consider the various means of exploitation of those rights. An assignment of rights is usually a complete sale of those rights. A licence is a contractual arrangement which permits someone else to exploit or use the work or part of the work in the licence. With a licence, the author or creator retains ownership of the rights in the work in question. Under a licence, if the licensee does not perform its obligations, the licence can be terminated. An assignment of copyright must be in writing and signed by or on behalf of the assignor (i.e. the seller of the rights). For example, the author of a book may enter into an agreement with a publishing company to exploit all of the rights in a specific novel. Alternatively, the author may decide to set up separate deals with several different publishers who may have specialist abilities in selling hardback or softback versions of the novel. Similarly the author may do separate deals in respect of the film and television rights. In each case, the rights could be granted by assignment (sale) or by licence. Licences are generally used by publishers and distributors to exploit specific rights in a book.

Licences may be exclusive or non-exclusive. An exclusive licence must be in writing.

15

In the absence of specific wording, it may not always be clear whether the parties intended an assignment or a licence. In those cases, the court would attempt to determine the intention of the parties from the words used. For example, the payment of a one-off lump sum rather than a regular royalty is indicative of an assignment rather than a licence.

3 Film development agreement

For many producers the earliest opportunity to begin financing a film project is at the acquisition/development stage. The term 'development' refers to the initial stage in the preparation of a film. Development comprises those activities which relate specifically to taking a concept or idea and turning it into a finished screenplay. The development process involves formulating and organizing the concept or idea for a film, acquiring rights to any underlying literary work or screenplay, preparing an outline, synopsis and/or treatment, and writing, polishing and revising the various drafts of the screenplay.

The development process is either initiated by a writer, director or producer, or by a film studio in conjunction with one or more of such persons. The development deal typically begins with the pitching of an idea or film concept or submitting a synopsis, treatment, outline or draft screenplay to creative executives. If a creative executive is interested then the next step will be some form of development deal. In most cases, executives will not commit themselves to production financing until a substantially developed package exists. This usually includes the first draft of a screenplay as well as a budget and the commitment of a director and actors to the project.

There is common consensus that European films suffer from a lack of crucial investment at the development stage. Whilst American studios are able to fund development of a large number of projects at any one time by virtue of their vertically integrated production/distribution and financing systems, European producers find it difficult to raise the necessary finance for this uncertain and hazardous period of the film making process. Europe does not have the kind

17

of studio infrastructure that exists in the United States, and so, European producers, screenplay writers, and directors are often unable to devote sufficient time and resources to the various activities that precede production. The development process has been a source of problems for the European film industry for many decades.

Outside the American studio system, most non-American film producing countries have national/regional funds available to film producers who wish to develop stories and other literary materials into screenplays. These funds may be funded by governments or by broadcasters or by a mixture of both. If a development fund is not publicly funded then it is likely to be more commercially minded and will insist on more onerous loan repayment terms.

European producers now have the option to apply to various pan-European, national and regional funds. In particular, the new European Media Development Agency has recently taken up where the European Script Fund left off. The European Media Development Agency comes within the framework of the new Media II programme of the European Commission. In general, Media II financial support will be given in the form of reimbursable loans to encourage the development of fiction/drama (cinema and television), animation, documentaries with a creative input, and productions enhancing Europe's audio-visual heritage. One of the conditions is that programmes must be aimed at the European and wider international markets. As set out in their guidelines, this is assessed on the basis of the amount of interest shown and commitment made by European distributors and broadcasters. Assistance is given in the form of loans which may not exceed 50 per cent of the development budget and which, in turn, is restricted to 15 per cent of the production budget or 35,000 ECU per project, whichever is the lower. In recognition of the fact that developing a production is a process, the loan will be paid in two equal instalments, the first at the start of the project and the second as it progresses.

This new fund has given priority to production companies with 'packages' of projects. This means that production companies can have up to eight projects and apply for up to 100,000 ECU.

In addition to this pan-European funding, agencies such as British Screen, The Scottish Film Production Fund, and Aide Au Development, a French screenwriting fund, are further examples of national funding agencies available to producers for the development of feature films.

Outside the government subsidy bandwagon, the lucky producer may manage to secure private finance for development, but this is uncommon. The money spent pursuant to a development agreement procures a screenplay which may or may not have a value and may not ever be made into a film which makes an extremely risky investment. A private individual may invest in development for such reasons as generosity, a sense of altruism or (most likely) a need to create a tax loss.

It has been said that those working in the media industries are notoriously reluctant to record the arrangements they make with each other in contract form in any kind of detail. This reluctance is usually evident at the development stage. In most cases, cost is a major factor. Creative individuals generally do not like spending money on lawyers to draw up contracts since they may feel that this is an unjustified expense. If one cannot afford a lawyer, then a costly dispute can be avoided by initially setting out the terms of agreement between two parties in a letter. Although this course of action may help alleviate a future dispute, it is always better to spend some money on a lawyer to initiate a legally enforceable agreement covering all the critical issues than to spend even greater sums resolving disputes through litigation.

What follows is an outline development agreement or (more properly) a loan agreement and security assignment which is intended to demonstrate the type of relationship usually struck between a producer and a development financier. In particular, the agreement sets out how a development financier protects himself against paying for a piece of work he does not like, and attempts to ensure that he recoups his money in the event that the script is produced by or with a third party. It is not weighted particularly in favour of either party to the agreement but obviously it is in the producer's interest that he is allowed to get the screenplay he wants without undue interference by the financier and that the terms of the security assignment are not so onerous as to make the project impossible to finance.

Film development agreement

FILM DEVELOPMENT AGREEMENT

A DATE

THIS AGREEMENT is made   200 .

B PARTIES TO THE CONTRACT

BETWEEN:

1. [Company name/name of individual] of [   ]/a company registered in England under No [   ] whose registered office is at [address]
2. [Company name/name of individual/] of [   ]/a company registered in England under No [   ] whose registered office is at [address]

C PREAMBLE

WHEREAS:

1. The Borrower is entitled to certain rights in and to the Work [by virtue of the Title Documents].
2. The Borrower has requested and the Lender has agreed to make available to the Borrower the Loan for the development of the Development Work according to the Development Schedule for the Development Period.

D DEFINITIONS

In the Agreement, the following words shall have the following meanings:

Borrower's Indebtedness
the Premium, Loan and Profit Participation.

Budget
the development budget and cashflow as set out in the Third Schedule;

FILM DEVELOPMENT AGREEMENT: NOTES

A   DATE

The date should not be inserted until both parties have agreed and signed a final version of the agreement.

B   PARTIES TO THE CONTRACT

The full name, legal description, address (or registered office if a company) and official registration number (if a company) should be indicated here. Each party to the agreement is given an identifiable shortened name which will be a defined term in the agreement and which will be used in these notes.

C   PREAMBLE

The preamble sets out the background to the agreement and describes generally the purpose of the agreement.

D   DEFINITIONS

The definition of 'net profits' is very difficult and beyond the scope of this article. It is often a focus for negotiation between the parties, and it is strongly recommended that legal advice be sought before agreeing to the details of profit participation.

Note that the Lender requires the Borrower to prove that he has legal Title to the underlying work through the necessary title documents and note also that the money is paid in tranches according to a schedule.

Commencement Date
[   ][weeks/days] after signature of this Agreement or the
date of first drawdown of the Loan, whichever is earlier;

Development Period
the period of time stated in the Development Schedule;

Development Schedule
the timetable for production of the Development Work as
set out in the Second Schedule, or as the same may be
varied from time to time by consent in writing of the
Lender;

Development Work
all materials produced at an intermediate stage between
the Work and completion of a Production, further details
of which are set out in the Development Schedule.

Loan
the principal sum of £[   ] to be made available in
stages by the Lender to the Borrower under the terms of
this Agreement;

Premium
a premium equal to [   ]% of monies advanced under the
Loan;

Production
a production based on the Development Work including,
but not limited to a cinematograph film, television
programme, television series or mini series;

Profit Participation
a sum equal to [   ]% of the ['net profits'/'producer
profits'] of a given Production where such term is defined
as in the principal production, financing and
distribution agreements for the Production.

Screenplay
the screenplay based on the Work, setting out the script
for a final full length feature film [or other Production];

Other definitions can, of course, be added depending on the circumstances of any particular deal. These ones are by no means 'set in stone' and can be changed to suit what is needed.

Title Documents
>   the documents, particulars of which are contained in the First Schedule, which evidence the Borrower's title to the Work;

Work
>   a work provisionally entitled [   ], the rights in which are owned by the Borrower [by virtue of the Title Documents];

Writer   [   ] of [   ];

E   INTERPRETATIONS

Clause headings are solely for ease of reference and do not form part of or affect the interpretation of this Agreement.

Where the context so admits or requires, words denoting the singular include the plural and vice versa and words denoting any gender include all genders.

References to Clauses and Schedules are to Clauses in and Schedules to this Agreement.

IT IS AGREED:

F   LOAN

1. The Lender agrees to provide the Loan to the Borrower and the Borrower agrees to use reasonable endeavours to complete the Development Work diligently with care and skill in accordance with the Development Schedule.
2. The obligations of the Lender under the Agreement are conditional upon its receipt and approval of:
    (i)   the Title Documents, including at the Lender's request, signed originals or certified copies.
    (ii)   the Budget.
    (iii) an executed inducement letter from [name of producers] in the form set out in the Fourth Schedule.

E INTERPRETATIONS

These clauses are inserted in order to try and avoid any possible confusion over the interpretation of the agreement.

F LOAN

The Lender will not wish to pay over any money to the Borrower unless he has all the supporting documents in his possession. Note that an inducement letter will only be necessary if the Borrower is a company which will employ the services of a named Producer, as is often the case.

(iv) an executed service agreement in respect of the Writer to write the screenplay.

3. The Loan will be advanced in stages in accordance with the Budget and the Development Schedule.

G THE SCREENPLAY

4. The agreement referred to in sub-clause 2(e) above will provide:

(i) that the Writer shall be available to commence work on the Screenplay no later than the Commencement Date; and

(ii) that the Lender shall have the right to require the Writer to execute all and any documents reasonably required by it in order to ensure that it has absolute title to the Work, Development Work and future such works as provided for in Clause 11 to this Agreement.

5. The Borrower shall produce or procure the production of the Screenplay and the first draft of the Screenplay shall be delivered to the Lender no later than [ ] weeks following the Commencement Date [time being of the essence].

6.

6.1 Payment of each stage of the Loan will be made upon written application (with the Borrower's invoice addressed to the Lender with copy supporting invoices/receipts attached) by the Borrower to the Lender in accordance with the Development Schedule and the Budget, [subject to the Lender's approval of each such application for drawdown and] provided that the Borrower is not in breach of this agreement [and that the Lender is satisfied with the progress of the Development Work].

The money being lent is invariably paid in stages and payments are triggered by certain events such as the delivery of drafts or re-writes.

G   THE SCREENPLAY

Clause 4(ii) is inserted to ensure that the Lender has the power to perfect its security in the event that the Writer might otherwise retain some rights in the Development Work.

The Borrower will not want payments to be subject to the Lender's approval nor will he want the Lender to have the right to review progress and withhold advances if dissatisfied with progress. Whether or not the Lender becomes entitled to such rights will be influenced by the nature of the Lender: if it is a commercial financial entity then it may well intend to become involved in production of a film based on the screenplay and it is therefore important for such entity to make sure it is getting the kind of screenplay it wants.

6.2 Each stage of the Loan shall be used for the purpose for which it is drawn down and in accordance with the Budget and the Development Schedule and any amount of the Loan advanced but not so utilized shall be repaid to the Lender forthwith without demand.

H   PREMIUM AND PROFIT PARTICIPATION

7. The Premium shall be payable immediately upon repayment of the Loan.
8. Upon commencement of a Production the Borrower shall procure that the Lender is contractually entitled to receive the Profit Participation.

I   REPORTING

9.

9.1 The Borrower will:

(i)   fully report to and consult with the Lender and have due regard for – but not be bound to accept – the Lender's comments at all stages of the Development Work; and

(ii)   prepare and submit to the lender – not less than monthly – reports of progress and expenditure until completion of the Development Work; and

(iii)   promptly upon receipt provide the Lender with copies of all documents, receipts, vouchers etc. relating to the Development Work and all such other information as the Lender may reasonably require.

H   PREMIUM AND PROFIT PARTICIPATION

This premium represents the element of risk taken on by the Lender. It is obviously in the Borrower's interest to keep it low or keep it out altogether. In the event that the Lender is only involved at the development stage, then the production financier will generally have the job of repaying the loan made, together with the premium, before he can remove the Lender's charge and take the project further. A high premium, therefore, makes the film harder to finance.

It is normal for a lender to require a net profit participation as further reward for the risk involved in the loan. Once again, the Borrower becomes contractually obliged to procure that the Lender gets this participation and so it therefore becomes a point to be agreed with production financiers as a precondition to a productions deal.

I   REPORTING

It will be important to the Lender that it is provided with regular financing information during the period of development so that it can keep an eye on what is being paid for. Preparation of statements can be time consuming and the regularity of statements is a matter for negotiation between the parties.

9.2 Without limiting the foregoing, the Borrower shall keep separate, complete, true and accurate books of account and the Lender shall have the right, exercisable on not less than 24-hours' prior written notice during business hours, to inspect and/or to audit all such books receipts vouchers and other documents relating to the Development Work.

9.3 Within six weeks of completion of the Development Work, the Borrower shall deliver to the Lender a statement [which need not be audited] detailing expenditure of the Loan on the Development Work, together with all supporting documents receipts vouchers etc. relating to such expenditure not previously submitted under Clause 9(a).

J REPAYMENT

10.

10.1 The Loan and the Premium shall be payable immediately by the Borrower to the Lender:

(i) upon written demand on the occurrence of any of the following events:

(a) A breach by the Borrower of any of the terms and conditions of this Agreement or of any of the representations, warranties or undertakings contained in Clause 14, where such breach has not been remedied within [30] days of service of written notice to do so from Lender; or

(b) The Borrower is declared bankrupt or ceases to do business, becomes unable to pay its debts as they fall due, becomes or is deemed insolvent, has a receiver, manager administrator, administrative receiver or similar officer appointed in respect of the whole or any part of its assets or business, makes any composition or arrangement with its creditors, takes or suffers any similar

J REPAYMENT

Alternatively, a stronger 'termination' clause could be inserted into the contract, which would provide for the contract to be terminated on the occurrence of certain events. The consequences of such termination would be a matter for negotiation between the parties. In addition to payment of the full extent of the Borrower's Indebtedness these provisions might include, for example, the loss of the Borrower's right to recover (under clause 13) its interest in the various works charged to the Lender under Clause 11.

The first sub-section of clause 10.1 protects the Lender as far as possible from losing out in the event of the Borrower becoming insolvent or breaching the terms of the agreement. The second and third sub-section ensure that the Lender is repaid the loan and premium before the film can be made or sold on for further development and/or productions.

action in consequence of debt or an order or resolution is made for its dissolution or liquidation (other than for the purpose of solvent amalgamation or reconstruction), or any equivalent or similar action or proceeding is taken or suffered in any jurisdiction [and the same is not dismissed or discharged within thirty (30) days thereafter].

(c) an order being made or an effective resolution passed to wind up the Borrower (other than for the purpose of solvent reconstruction or amalgamation of the Borrower); or

(ii) in the event of commencement of a Production whereupon such sums shall be repayable not later than the first day of principal photography; or

(iii) in the event of the Borrower selling or otherwise disposing or purporting to sell or otherwise dispose of all or any of the rights in the Work or the Development Work or in the event of the Borrower being forced or required to sell or dispose of or relinquish all or any of those rights. Such sums shall be repayable in any such event, out of the proceeds thereof without demand.

10.2 For the avoidance of doubt, repayment of the Loan and Premium under Clause 10.1 shall be without prejudice to the Lender's right to receive Profit Participation under Clause 8. Once the full extent of the Borrower's Indebtedness has been satisfied, this Agreement shall terminate.

10.3 In addition to the provisions set out at Clause 10.1, the Borrower may make payment in full of the Borrower's Indebtedness at any time during the term of this Agreement.

Film development agreement: Notes

K LEGAL MORTGAGE

11.

11.1 The Borrower with full title guarantee ASSIGNS to the Lender absolutely:

(i)   all the Borrower's right, title and interest in and to the Work and the Development Work for the full period of such rights [together with the benefit of all subsisting undertakings warranties representations covenants agreements and acknowledgements therein contained]; and

(ii) by way of present assignment of future copyright all and any other rights and properties acquired by the Borrower in connection with the Work and/or the Development Work.

PROVIDED THAT the Borrower shall have the right of re-assignment contained in Clause 13.

11.2 The Lender grants the Borrower a licence to use the rights assigned to it under Clause 11.1 for the sole purpose of the development of the Development Work. The Borrower may sub-licence third parties to use those rights for the same purpose. The licence will terminate immediately when the Loan and Premium become payable pursuant to Clause 10.1, when they are paid pursuant to Clause 10.3, or as provided for in Clause 18.

12. The Borrower will not, without the prior written consent of the Lender, create any mortgage, charge, lien, pledge or other security interest over the whole or any part of the Work and the Development Work [such consent not to be unreasonably withheld].

K   LEGAL MORTGAGE

This important clause grants the Lender a security over copyright and other rights relating to the Development Work which effectively prevents them being sold on or dealt with in any way until the Lender is repaid the loan and premium. This is therefore the clause which actively protects the Lender in relation to the loan.

Clause 11.2 is inserted to give the Borrower the legal right to continue to use the Work and the other materials for the purposes of developing a film, even though they have been assigned to the Lender under Clause 11.1. The licence will terminate when the Loan and Premium are payable, which means, for example, that once photography of a Production has started (Clause 10.1(ii)), the Borrower will be in breach of copyright to continue with the Production if it has not repaid the loan.

The effect of this clause is that the producer is prohibited from granting anybody else a secondary charge without the Lender's permission. The second half of the clause which has been placed in square brackets will be useful if the producer requires further funds from another financier at a later stage who will want to take what security is available in order to protect his loan.

13. On repayment of the Loan and Premium (including, for the avoidance of doubt, under Clause 10.3) the Lender will reassign the rights assigned to it pursuant to Clause 11 above to the Borrower or as the Borrower may direct, provided that nothing in this clause shall release the Borrower from its obligation to pay or procure payment of the Profit Participation to the Lender and prior to any such re-assignment the Lender shall be entitled to require the Borrower and/or the proposed assignee (if not the Borrower) to enter into such documentation as the Lender may reasonably require to protect, preserve and secure the Lender's right to be paid and to receive the Profit Participation.

L WARRANTIES, OBLIGATIONS AND INDEMNITIES

14. The Borrower hereby represents, warrants and undertakes with the Lender that:
    (i)   the Borrower is the beneficial and legal owner of the copyright in the Work;
    (ii)   the Borrower will observe and perform all of the terms and conditions of the Title Documents on its part to be observed and performed and will continue to observe and perform the same and will indemnify and keep the Lender fully indemnified from and against all claims, proceedings, costs, damages and expenses suffered or incurred by the Lender by reason of the non-performance or non-observance by the Borrower of any of the terms, conditions, warranties and undertakings contained in the Title Documents;
    (iii) the Borrower will, at the Lender's expense, at all times do and execute all such things and documents as may be reasonably required by the Lender to give effect the Lender's rights under this Agreement;

This clause provides for the release of the charge upon repayment to the Lender of the Loan together with the Premium (if any). Note that release of the charge is conditional upon the Lender being made contractually entitled to his profit participation by a new contract drawn up by the Lender and the Borrower or a third party production financier.

L WARRANTIES, OBLIGATIONS AND INDEMNITIES

Note that the credit accorded to the Lender in (iv) is more appropriate to a company providing finance and an individual lender may require a credit as executive producer or associate producer and such credits are a matter for negotiation with the producer.

The producer will want to avoid any limitation on his ability to enter into production agreements with third parties similar to that contained in (viii) unless the Lender is also a production financier who intends to take the project on to production. Otherwise, the Borrower can only enter into a production agreement with the consent of the Lender. If the Lender refuses, another option would be for the Borrower to repay the Loan and Premium and thus release the mortgage created by Clause 11. In this event, there would still be the issue of the Profit Participation for negotiation before the Agreement would terminate (under Clause 10.2).

(iv) until such time as the Lender shall reassign to the Borrower the Borrower's rights assigned pursuant to Clause 11 to the Lender, the Borrower shall ensure that all copies of any synopsis, treatment or screenplay developed under this Agreement shall contain a notice in the following form:

> 'Developed in association and with the assistance of [name of Lender's company/Lender]'

and in addition shall contain a copyright notice in the following form:

> '©200[0] [Name of Lender]'

The Borrower will also ensure that all copies issued by the Borrower or under its control of the first or any Production (and all paid advertisements for any such Production) will accord the Lender a prominent front screen credit – unless there are no front screen credits when it shall be a prominent end screen credit – in the following form:

> 'Developed in association and with the assistance of [Name of Lender]'
> OR
> 'Developed by [Lender]'

(v) it is the Borrower's intention that the Development Work will result in a full length feature film for exhibition and world wide commercial exploitation in all media;

(vi) the Borrower shall comply with all relevant union and industry agreements and all statutory obligations in producing the Development Work;

(vii) the Development Work will be executed with reasonable skill and care;

(viii) the Borrower shall not [prior to repayment of the Loan and Premium], without the prior written consent of the Lender, enter into any agreement with any third party for any Production [which would diminish or derogate from the Lender's rights hereunder];

(ix) it will give between four and eight weeks' written notice to the Lender of the expiry of the option period referred to in the Option Agreement dated [   ] and referred to in the First Schedule hereto.

(x) it will meet the obligations and deadlines set out in the Development Schedule.

M   RECEIVER

15. The Lender shall be entitled at any time after the Loan and Premiums have been payable in accordance with Clause 10 to appoint in writing a receiver or a receiver and manager of all or any part of the rights assigned to the Lender under this Agreement and further from time to time to remove such receiver and appoint another in his place.

16. The Borrower hereby irrevocably appoints the Lender and any and every receiver or receiver and manager appointed by the Lender under this Agreement to be the Borrower's attorney unless and until the Borrower is made bankrupt or goes into liquidation, after which he will act as principal and will not become the agent of the Lender. The receiver, in the Borrower's name and on the Borrower's behalf and as the Borrower's act and deed will be authorized to execute seal and deliver any document or do any act which may be required for the purpose of raising funds to repay the Borrower's Indebtedness to the Lender. For the avoidance of doubt, the Receiver is empowered to assign the licence granted by Clause 11.2, or to terminate or assign sub-licences granted under it.

M   RECEIVER

Clauses 15, 16 and 17 give the Lender power to appoint a receiver to enforce his security, in other words allows him to come in and take possession and control of the Development Work in the event that, for one reason or another, he is not repaid his loan and premium. A Lender will insist on provisions similar to these as they form the backbone of the agreement from his point of view. Note that Clause 17 is specific to the UK. Other jurisdictions should insert the appropriate legislation.

17. The statutory power of sale shall be exercisable at any time after the Borrower's Indebtedness becomes repayable in accordance with Clause 10 hereof [and s.103 and s.109 of the Law of Property Act 1925 shall not apply to this security].

N CONTROL OF THE DEVELOPMENT WORK

18. If either:
    (i)   [Name of Producer] for any reason – including death, sickness or injury – ceases to have day to day control of or becomes detached from the Development Work; or
    (ii) the Borrower fails to meet the deadlines imposed by the Development Schedule after having been given [30] days' notice in writing by the Lender that it should do so;
    at the option of the Lender, either:
    (i)   the Borrower will repay or procure the repayment of the Loan and Premium and secure payment of the Profit Participation to the Lender; or
    (ii) the licence granted by Clause 11.2 will terminate immediately and the Borrower will be required to execute all documents reasonably required by the Lender to enable it to take charge of the development of a Production (whether actual or proposed), including to assign all rights and interests which the Borrower has in the Development Work, or in any other contracts or rights which relate to any proposed or actual Production to the Lender. [Upon such assignment(s) the Lender shall endeavour to preserve ['name of Producer'] right to receive a sum equal to [   ]% of net profits of a Production].]
19. The Borrower shall not be entitled to assign this Agreement either in whole or in part [without the Lender's consent].

N   CONTROL OF THE DEVELOPMENT WORK

The Producer will obviously wish to resist vigorously any ability by the Lender to call in his debts or take over the project merely because he feels the producer is unable to complete his job. On the other hand, the Lender will probably wish to protect his investment in this way and this will become a matter for negotiation between the Producer and the Lender. In practice, the Development Schedule will often be changed or rewritten by mutual agreement, and most lenders will be reluctant to step into the shoes of the Borrower in the way envisaged by this section.

The Lender will not want the Producer to assign this agreement unless he can fully satisfy himself that the assignee is someone capable of completing the development work on budget and in accordance with the development schedule.

O BOILERPLATE CLAUSES

20. No waiver by either party of any breach of any of the terms or conditions of this Agreement shall be deemed or construed to be a waiver of any preceding or succeeding breach of the same or any other terms or conditions of this Agreement. All rights, remedies, undertakings and obligations contained in this Agreement shall be cumulative and none of them shall limit any other right, remedy, or obligation.

21. Nothing in this Agreement shall be construed or deemed to constitute a partnership or joint venture between the parties hereto and save as expressly herein provided, neither party shall hold itself out as the agent of the other.

22. If any clause or any part of this agreement or its application to either party shall, for any reason, be adjudged by a court or tribunal or other lawful authority of competent jurisdiction or rendered under any applicable law to be invalid, illegal or unenforceable, the remainder of this Agreement shall continue in full force and effect.

23. Any notices required to be given under the provisions of this Agreement shall be in writing and shall be deemed to have been duly served if delivered by hand or sent by facsimile or within the United Kingdom by first class registered or recorded delivery mail and any notice so given shall be deemed to have been served:
    (i)   if hand delivered at the time of delivery
    (ii)   if sent by facsimile or print out communication mechanisms within eight hours of transmission during business hours at its destination or within twenty-four hours, but subject to receipt by the sender of confirmation of transmission
    (iii) if sent by prepaid post as aforesaid within forty-eight hours of posting (exclusive of the hours of Sunday) if posted to an address within the country of posting and seven days of posting if posted to an address outside the country of posting.

O   BOILERPLATE CLAUSES

Clauses 20–25 are representative of the standard 'boilerplate' clauses to be found at the end of most contracts made under English law. Note that the Agreement specifically states that no partnership or joint venture has come into being between the parties as this would have unfavourable financial and tax implications. Note also that the Agreement is made expressly subject to English law which is obviously only relevant where one or both of the parties are English. An English producer should certainly request that the Agreement be made subject to English law and the jurisdiction of the English Courts as this will in almost all cases prove more convenient both financially and pragmatically.

24. This Agreement replaces, supersedes and cancels all previous arrangements, understandings, representations or agreements between the parties whether oral or written with respect to its subject matter of and expresses and constitutes the entire Agreement between the Borrower and the Lender and no variation of any of the terms or conditions of this Agreement may be made unless such variation is in writing and signed by duly authorized representatives on behalf of each of the parties. The parties exclude their rights to sue for pre-contractual misrepresentation, unless such misrepresentation was made fraudulently.

25. This agreement is made in England and shall be construed in all respects in accordance with and governed by English Law and the parties irrevocably submit to the exclusive jurisdiction of the English Courts.

FIRST SCHEDULE
(the Title Documents)

DATE	DESCRIPTION	PARTIES

The First Schedule contains the documents which entitle the Borrower to use whatever underlying works he is using as the basis of the screenplay. The Lender will insist on seeing these not only to show that the Borrower is not wasting his time but also so that the Lender can itemize these documents which form part of the security for his loan.

SECOND SCHEDULE
(the Development Schedule)
(the Development Work)

DATE   EVENT

The Second Schedule specifies all things to be done by the Producer and the Writer he contracts with and the dates by which these things are to be done.

THIRD SCHEDULE
(the Development Budget and Cashflow)

This Budget itemizes the amounts that are being spent on different items such as option fees, overheads, secretarial costs, telecommunications, photocopying and legal.

FOURTH SCHEDULE (Inducement Letter)

FROM: **[Name of Producer]**
TO: **[Name of Lender]**

Dear Sirs

RE: [   ] ('the Work')

In consideration of your entering into the attached loan agreement and security assignment (the 'Loan Agreement') with [   ] ('the Borrower') which I have read and fully understand and pursuant to which you have agreed to provide certain funds to the Borrower to enable the Borrower to carry out certain Development Work as set out and described in the Loan Agreement, I represent and undertake as follows:

1. I am a director of the Borrower.
2. I will be personally involved in either carrying out or supervising the Development Work.
3. I will use all reasonable endeavours to ensure that the Borrower carries out the Development Work to the highest standards and honours its agreement with you in all respects.
4. I hereby warrant that (a) all the products of my services will be original to me and will not be defamatory of any person, firm or company, (b) all necessary waivers of any moral rights relative to any material or work created or otherwise contributed to the Work by me are hereby given insofar as the same are necessary to service the grant of rights under this Agreement; and (c) nothing therein will infringe the copyright or other personal or proprietary right(s) of any person, firm or company or infringe any statutory obligation.

Yours faithfully

. . . .
[Name of Producer]

As indicated earlier on in this chapter, the inducement letter comes from the producer personally if his services are loaned out by a company. In the letter he will make personal representations and undertakings so that he too is contractually bound if the loan company does not fulfil its contractual obligations.

DULY EXECUTED

Signed as a Deed by [Lender]

. . . .
Director

. . . .
Director/Secretary

Signed as a Deed by [Borrower]

. . . .
Director

. . . .
Director/Secretary

The above is how the Agreement should be executed if by a company or companies. In the case where either the Lender or the Borrower or both are individuals then it is sufficient for that individual to put the following:

Signed as a Deed by . . . .

in the presence of [   ]

4 Option and literary purchase agreement

Film and television producers rely upon many sources of material for their films and programmes. This chapter deals with source works which are already in existence and which will form the underlying basis for a film or programme. They may be in the form of a published book, a book still in manuscript form, a script, treatment or a combination of the above materials.

The cost of making films and television programmes is sometimes prohibitive. Instead of paying large acquisition prices up front it is customary for producers to seek an option on an underlying work for a sum, usually around 10 per cent of the eventual purchase price.

An option is an agreement with the rights owner where in return for payment the rights owner grants to the producer for a limited period of time the exclusive opportunity to acquire or license certain rights in the underlying work for a specified price. The benefit of an option is that it is less expensive for a film producer to take out an option than to acquire or license the rights in an underlying work outright. From the perspective of the rights owner if the producer does not exercise the option then the rights owner will be able to sell or re-option these rights to someone else.

Option agreements should always be confirmed in writing. The following points should always be specified in an option agreement:

1 The length of the option
2 Payment in respect of the option
3 The rights being optioned
4 What the payment will be for the underlying rights when the option is exercised.

It is essential that if the option is exercised then the terms and price of the assignment or licence of rights are clearly agreed. The exercise price and terms should always be agreed at the same time as the option. If this is not done there will be confusion, uncertainty and possibly further expense incurred.

Option periods normally run anywhere from six to eighteen months. There can also be an agreement where this period is renewable upon further payment of a fee. The producer should keep in mind that the longer the period of time that rights are tied up the more expensive it will be.

In some circumstances an extension to the option will only be granted if the producer can prove that some progress has been made in trying to produce the project. However, this is something that should be negotiated prior to signing the option.

When trying to acquire or license rights, one should be certain that the work is still in copyright. If work is out of copyright then it will be referred to as in the public domain. The person acquiring the rights in a work should be certain that they are acquiring the necessary rights, from the proper owner.

In the United Kingdom, there is no central registry which sets out who owns a literary work and whether a literary work is still in copyright. In the United States it is possible for producers and others to search the United States Copyright Office at the Library of Congress in Washington, DC, to determine who has proper ownership and whether a specific work is still in copyright. At one time it was a pre-requisite for copyright protection in the United States to register copyright at the United States Copyright Office. Although no longer a requirement, all American literary works and most foreign literary works which are exploited in the United States are still registered at the US Copyright Office. This register contains details of transactions in relation to the recorded literary work and makes reference to any assignments or licences granted regarding rights contained in those works.

Although the US Copyright office does not absolutely ensure that a literary work's chain of title is in order, it will usually indicate whether there is some problem as to who the rightful owner is. A search may show that the copyright belongs to someone else or that certain rights have been previously granted. It is always worth spending money at the outset to determine whether a problem exists.

Since an option is a contract there must be some consideration (i.e. money) for it to be legally binding. It should be noted that consideration is usually in the form of payment, however promising to do something in return for granting an option on the rights can also be considered a form of consideration. Options should never be free, since under US and UK contract law the option may not be enforceable.

Usually the first fee paid in an option agreement is made in advance and on account of the final purchase price which should be set out in the acquisition agreement. The first fee is usually not returnable. The second fee payable is often around 5 per cent of the purchase price and is in most cases not on account of the final purchase price.

The underlying reason for the option period is to enable a producer to put together the creative elements for their production without committing a large amount of money before they can interest distributors and other financiers in backing the project.

In the event that the producer is not successful then their losses are limited to the option fee and perhaps some development costs. If the rights to a book or film script had been sold outright then a producer who was unable to interest any distributors or financiers in the project may be out of pocket for a great deal of money.

It is essential for producers and rights owners to specify which rights are being optioned. The contract found in this chapter offers a typical form of option agreement and shows essential elements which are needed as well as a standard form of assignment. The agreement assumes that the buyer (or producer) will take all available rights whereas some options and assignments will only make reference to one set of rights (i.e. television rights only). I sometimes call this the 'Everything but the kitchen sink assignment' because it assumes that the seller will give up everything. However, in practice, this is seldom the case. This agreement is a combination of a UK and US document and must be adapted according to the circumstances of each transaction. It should be noted that this type of agreement should not be relied on without further specialist legal advice and is for reference purposes only.

OPTION and LITERARY PURCHASE AGREEMENT

THIS AGREEMENT is made and entered into as of
_____ (date), by and BETWEEN:

_____
(name and address of Writer) ('the Writer') and

_____
(name and address of Producer) ('the Producer').

1 WRITER'S REPRESENTATIONS AND WARRANTIES

(a) Sole Proprietor: the Writer represents and warrants to
Producer that the Writer is the sole and exclusive
proprietor, throughout the world, of an original work
written by _____ entitled ('the Work' or
'Literary Property').

(b) The Writer represents and warrants to the Producer that
the following statements are true and correct in all
respects with respect to the said Work:

[(i) [the Writer is the sole author of the Work.]

(ii) The Work was first published on (date) by
_____ under the title [   ] and was
registered for copyright in the name of
_____, [under copyright registration number
_____, in the Office of the United States
Register of Copyrights, Washington, DC] (if
applicable).

No Motion Picture or dramatic version of the Literary
Property, or any part of it, has been manufactured,
produced, presented or authorized; no radio or
television development, presentation or programme based
on the Literary Property, or any part of it, has been
manufactured, produced, presented, broadcast or
authorized, and no written or oral agreements or
commitments at all with respect to the Literary Property
or with respect to any right therein, have previously
been made or entered by or on behalf of the Writer

OPTION AND LITERARY PURCHASE AGREEMENT: NOTES

PREAMBLE (A) WRITER – The Writer will usually be the rights owner or the owner of the copyright in the literary property or work being sold. In most cases this will not usually be the publisher. It should be the author or writer of the literary property or work. Producers should ensure that they are contracting with the proper owner. See notes regarding US copyright office and registration below.

1 WRITER'S REPRESENTATIONS AND WARRANTIES

(a) One of the most essential warranties given by the Writer to the Producer is that the Writer owns all the rights they are selling free and clear of any other obligation and that they own the rights being granted and are in a position to enter into the agreement.

(b) The Writer may not be the sole author of the literary property or work, and therefore it is essential that the identity of the author be stated. For clarity, it should be stated when the literary material or work was first published. Sometimes the title may have changed and therefore the literary material or work was published under a different name. Reference should also be made to the United States copyright office. Copyright law in the United States used to be different in a number of important respects to the copyright law of the United Kingdom. At one time, copyright law in the United States was something of a minefield for copyright materials, particularly since the term of copyright was split into two terms of twenty-eight years and copyright could not be acquired for the duration of the total term of copyright in a straight forward manner. In recent years there have been significant changes in the law and in 1989 the United States joined the Berne Convention. Thus copyright protection in the United States is now much more in line with the protection afforded in the United Kingdom. There used to be a requirement that in order to have protection in the United States, copyright material had to be registered at the Library

(except with respect to the publication of the Work as set forth above).

(c) No Infringement or Violation of Third Party Rights: the Writer represents and warrants to the Producer that the Writer has not adapted the Literary Property from any other literal, dramatic or other material of any kind, nature or description, nor, excepting for material which is in the public domain, has the Writer copied or used in the Literary Property the plot, scenes, sequence or story of any other literary, dramatic or other material; that the Literary Property does not infringe upon any common law or statutory rights in any other literary, dramatic, or other material; that as far as the Writer has knowledge, no material in the Literary Property is libellous or violative of the right of privacy of any person and the full use of the rights in the Literary Property which are covered by the within option would not violate any rights of any person, firm or corporation; and that the Literary Property is not

of Congress in Washington, DC, and carry a copyright notice. Registration can still be made, but it is optional, as is the bearing of copyright notice. In the United Kingdom, copyright exists without having to be recorded in a central register. Producers wishing to exploit any copyright work in the United States should, however, register their work at the US Copyright Office. The advantage undertaking registration is that under certain US laws if there is, at a later date a copyright infringement then an author can prove that the registered work is actually theirs. Producers should be aware that if a literary property or work is eventually fully financed for production, the various financiers, banks and completion guarantors will require a copyright search from the US Copyright Office as well as a full report on title (ownership).

Copyright law in the United Kingdom is based on the Copyright Designs and Patents Act 1988.

The warranty should also specifically state that no other version of the literary property or work has been created. In the event that there has been a previous version and the producer wishes to produce a remake of an earlier film or television programme then this must be specifically stated.

(c) This warranty puts a burden on the author that in the event of any copying, libel or breach of privacy then the responsibility will be on the author or Writer and not on the Producer. This warranty also ensures that the work is in copyright and is not in the public domain. (See later explanation.) Under the 1988 Copyright Act, copyrights subsist in:

(i)　Original literary, dramatic, musical or artistic works;

(ii)　Recordings, films, broadcast or cable programmes; and

(iii)　Typographic arrangements of a published edition.

Copyright is ownership of property (intellectual property) and only the owner of the property is entitled to copy it, issue copies to the public, perform, show or play it in public, broadcast it or adapt it. If anybody does any of these things without acquiring the necessary rights or licence from the owner, he or she is infringing copyright. There are two types of copyright which are of primary concern to the Producer.

in the public domain in any country in the world where copyright protection is available.

(d) No Impairment of Rights: the Writer represents and warrants to the Producer that the Writer is the exclusive proprietor, throughout the world, of the rights in the Literary Property which are covered by the within option; that the Writer has not assigned, licensed nor in any manner encumbered, diminished or impaired these rights; that the Writer has not committed nor omitted to perform any act by which these rights could or will be

One is that the copyright material the producer is commissioning for a film or television programme will generally fall within the scope of (i) above; the other is that the ownership of copyright in the completed programme will fall within (ii) above. The creator of the original literary, dramatic, musical or artistic work is generally the first owner of copyright, except when the work is carried out or created by an employee in the course of his employment, in which case (subject to any agreement to the contrary) the employer is the copyright owner. The term of copyright as a general rule, for literary, dramatic and musical works first published or recorded in the United Kingdom lasts for the lifetime of the creator and seventy years thereafter. Recent European Union directives have harmonized the term of copyright which prior to approval by the United Kingdom government was the lifetime of the creator plus fifty years. The new legislation provides for copyright to last for seventy years after the death of the author of a work. Producers should be aware of lengths of copyright as well as certain exceptions. It is advisable for producers to read the various provisions in the Copyright, Designs and Patents Act 1988.

Public domain applies to materials which no longer qualify for copyright protection and in most cases are freely available for public use, subject to various exclusions.

The warranty also clarifies that the literary property is original to the Writer, has not been copied and does not infringe copyright from another source. Producers should ensure that they receive this warranty in the event that the writer has plagiarized or stolen someone else's material.

(d) This warranty serves two purposes. First, to encourage the Writer to disclose any exceptions to the general nature of this warranty. It is better that the Producer is aware of the difficulties before contracts are signed as this reduces the possibility of any disputes for breach of warranty arising once the option and Literary Purchase is completed. The second and more important reason is to impose liability on the Writer in the event that the literary material is inadequate or encumbered, diminished or impaired; and that there is no outstanding claim or litigation pending against or involving the title, ownership and/or copyright in the Literary Property, or in any part of it, or in the rights which are covered by the within option. The Writer further represents and warrants that no attempt hereafter will be made to encumber, diminish or impair any of the rights herein granted and that all appropriate protections of such rights will continue to be maintained by the Writer.

Without limiting any other rights the Producer may have in the Literary Property, the Writer agrees that if there is any claim and/or litigation involving any breach or alleged breach of any such representations and warranties of the Writer, the option period granted hereunder and any periods within which the Producer may, pursuant to the provisions of Clause 3 hereof, extend the options, shall automatically be extended until no claim and/or litigation involving any breach or alleged breach of any such representation and warranties of the Writer is outstanding, but in any event not for a period more than one (1) additional year. Any time after the occurrence of such a claim and/or litigation until the expiration of the option period, as extended, the Producer may, besides any other rights and remedies the Producer may have in the Literary Property, rescind this agreement and in such event, despite anything else to the contrary contained herein, the Writer agrees to repay the Producer any monies paid by the Producer to the Writer hereunder concerning the Literary Property and any reasonable amounts expended by the Producer in developing or exploiting the Literary Property. Without limiting the generality of the foregoing, the Writer agrees that the Writer will not, any time during the option period, exercise or authorize or permit the exercise by others of any of the rights covered by the option or any of the rights reserved by the Writer under the provisions of Exhibit A which are not to be exercised or licensed to others during any period therein specified.

defective or that the Writer does not have adequate title. In essence, this warranty allocates risk between the Writer and the Producer. The Writer will seek to reduce the risk by making disclosures and limiting its liability for any breach of warranty. Any breach of warranty will give the Producer the right to claim damages from the Writer. During negotiations the Producer should assess the likelihood of any claim arising from the Writer's ability to compensate the Producer if a claim is successful. However, the Writer's ability to pay will depend on the financial status of the Writer.

This warranty goes one step further by stating that if there is any litigation or claim resulting from any breach or alleged breach then the option is extended for an additional year in order to hopefully sort out any problems.

Some literary properties or works can be subject to litigation over who the rightful owner is, thus, it is important to include such a warranty.

2   CONSIDERATION FOR OPTION

In consideration of the payment to the Writer of the sum of
£_____ receipt of which is hereby acknowledged, the
Writer agrees to and does hereby give and grant to the
Producer the exclusive and irrevocable option to purchase
from the Writer the rights in the Literary Property as
described in Exhibit A for the total purchase price specified
and payable as provided in Exhibit A, provided that any
sums paid under this Clause 2 or any other provision of
this agreement with respect to the option shall be credited
against the first sums payable in account of such purchase
price. If the Producer shall fail to exercise this option, then
the sums paid to the Writer hereunder with respect to the
option shall be and remain the sole property of the Writer.

2   CONSIDERATION FOR OPTION

The fee for the initial options and any renewals should be clearly stated. Initial Option payments are usually made on account of the final purchase price (that is, if the option is exercised). For example if the option fee is £1000 and the purchase price is £10,000 then if the Producer exercises the option he must pay £9,000 to purchase the property.

Because an option is a contract there must be consideration for it to be legally binding. As a general rule option payments are equivalent to 10 per cent of the sum to be paid for the rights. However, because this money is at risk, producers should try and negotiate a lower initial payment. In some circumstances instead of monetary consideration other forms of consideration can be made. For example, a promise to do something in return for the rights being granted is also consideration. This type of consideration might be the agreement to grant an option on the basis that the rights owner will have a role in the eventual production of a film or television programme or some financial interest in it. Particular care must be taken with this type of option agreement. Producers must always aim for maximum flexibility in being able to respond to whatever requirements a broadcaster or third party financier may stipulate in order to commit to eventual production. For example, if an option has been granted on the basis that the rights owner will be engaged as director or script writer this may cause serious problems for the project if they are not acceptable to a broadcaster or financier. As a precaution against this the option agreement should provide that such a person will be engaged, subject to financier or broadcaster approval. In these circumstances the option agreement should go on to provide for a fallback position in the form of profit share or a consultancy fee on the production in the event that the financier or broadcaster does not approve their participation.

Care should also be taken when agreeing a financial interest in the eventual production in return for an option. To avoid possible difficulties with eventual financiers who are not prepared to

3 OPTION PERIOD

The option shall be effective during the period commencing on the date hereof and ending _____ ('the Initial Option Period'). The Initial Option Period may be extended for an additional _____ months by the payment of £_____ on or before the expiration date specified above ('the Second Option Period').

accept this obligation, such financial obligation should be defined as the share of the *Producer's* own net profit from the production not 100 per cent of the profits (see later notes on Net and Producer's profits).

Another indicator of what producers should pay for source work rights is somewhere in the region of 1–2 per cent of the eventual production budget. Although this is not a rigid formula (i.e. a major best selling novel would cost much more) it is a useful guide to use when trying to work out a reasonable price to offer a writer for their works.

3 OPTION PERIOD

During the option period the producer can either exercise the option or renew it for a further period. It is important to realize that it is not necessary to exercise the option and pay for the rights until the commencement of production. Because of the length of time it can take to carry out initial work on a project, gain interest from broadcasters or financiers, carry out further development work and secure financing for production, the producer should have a minimum total option period of at least two years. For other types of expensive programming this time period should, ideally be longer. Although two years is the minimum option period, rights owners will likely expect a considerable sum if their rights will be tied up for that length of time. In most circumstances it is usual for options to be staged so that the initial option period runs for twelve months with the producer having the right to extend the option for further consecutive periods of six or twelve months each and with each extension, a further option payment must be made to the rights owner.

A common occurrence is for the rights owner to be prepared to grant extensions to the option, only if it can be proved, that progress is being made towards eventual production. Although a producer may be paying a considerable amount of money for the option, this is not always an unreasonable request for rights owners to make. In these circumstances, producers should take

4 EXERCISE OF OPTION

(a) Notice of Exercise: If the Producer elects to exercise the within option, the Producer _____ (any time during the Option Period) shall serve upon the Writer written notice of the exercise of it by addressing such notice to the Writer at his address as specified in Exhibit A and by depositing such notice addressed by certified or registered post or courier.

(b) The purchase price shall be paid to the Writer according to Exhibit A.

care to ensure that the required demonstration of progress is pinned to a specific action taking place, so that there can be no argument as to whether progress has or has not been made. For example, if the rights that have been optioned are in the form of a book, the commissioning of a screenplay, clearly will be evidence of progress being made toward eventual production. However, producers should avoid such a provision and keep the option based solely on various time periods.

Payments made to extend the option period may or may not be on account of the purchase price. This is an important issue that should be clearly set out in preliminary negotiations between the Producer and the Writer.

4   EXERCISE OF OPTION

This clause sets out the procedure of exercising the option and purchasing the rights in a literary property or work. In this contract the Purchase Agreement is referred to as Exhibit (A), with additional Exhibits (B) and (C) as supporting documentation.

In order to properly exercise the option it must be exercised in writing and sent to the Writer at the appropriate address in the pre-amble of the contracts. To avoid any dispute as to whether the Option was exercised, the Producer should send the notice by registered post, courier or deliver the notice personally by hand.

It is essential that the purchase price set out in Exhibit (A) is paid in order to properly assign the rights stated in the contract.

(a) When the Producer exercises the option, the Writer is under an obligation to deliver to the Producer a signed copy of the Purchase Agreement and other documents to confirm ownership. This clause provides that if the Writer does not sign or deliver the appropriate agreement and other documents then the Producer has the right to sign the agreement on the Writer's behalf. Usually the Writer will sign the Purchase Agreement but leave it undated. Once payment is made then the Producer will date the agreement and send a copy to the Writer.

(c) The option may be exercised only by notice in writing as aforesaid; no conduct or oral statement by the Producer or his agents, representatives or employees shall constitute an exercise of the option.

(d) Additional Documents: If the Producer exercises the option, the Writer, without cost to the Producer (other than the consideration provided for herein or in Exhibit A) shall execute, acknowledge and deliver to the Producer, or shall cause the execution, acknowledgement and delivery to the Producer of such further instruments as the Producer may reasonably require to confirm unto the Producer the rights, licences, privileges and property which are the subject of the within option. If the Writer shall fail to execute and deliver or to cause the execution and delivery to the Producer of any such instruments, the Producer is hereby irrevocably granted the power coupled with an interest to execute such instruments and to take such other steps and proceedings as may be necessary concerning it in the name and on behalf of the Writer and as the Writer's attorney-in-fact. The Writer shall supply all supporting agreements and documentation requested by the Producer.

(e) Failure to Execute Documents: If the Writer shall fail to execute, acknowledge or deliver to the Producer any agreements, assignments or other instruments to be executed, acknowledged and delivered by the Writer hereunder, then the Producer is hereby irrevocably appointed the Writer's attorney-in-fact with full right, power and authority to execute, acknowledge and deliver the same in the name of and on behalf of the Writer, the Writer acknowledging that the authority and agency given the Producer is a power coupled with an interest. If the property has not been published or registered for copyright in the United States Copyright Office, and as a result thereof Exhibits 'A', 'B' and 'C', attached hereto, have not been completed with respect to the publication and copyright data and other data,

(d)/(e) In some agreements a Short Form Copyright Assignment will be attached. In this precedent it can be found as Exhibit B. This precedent also contains a Short Form Option Agreement which is found as Exhibit C. Exhibit B and Exhibit C of this precedent are summaries of the Option and Purchase Agreement. These exhibits are usually signed simultaneously with the main Option and Purchase Agreement. These short form agreements can be sent to the United States Copyright Office which is used as evidence of the assignment of rights. Note the different signature provisions which are used in the US and the UK.

the Producer is authorized and instructed by the Writer to insert the correct publication and copyright data in the appropriate blanks in Exhibits 'A', 'B' and 'C' or after the property has been published and registered for copyright, and in this connection the Writer agrees to notify the Producer promptly in writing of the publication and registration of the Literary Property for copyright, specifying in such notice the name of the publisher, the date and place of publication, the name of the copyright proprietor and the date and entry number of the copy registration in the United States Copyright Office, all of which information may be inserted by the Producer in the appropriate blanks in such documents.

5 EFFECTIVENESS OF EXHIBITS 'A', 'B' AND 'C'

Concurrently with the execution of this agreement, the Writer has executed Exhibits A (Literary Purchase Agreement), B (Short Form Option Agreement for Recordation) and C (Assignment of the Copyright), which are undated, and it is agreed that if the Producer shall exercise the option (but not otherwise), then the signature of the Writer to Exhibits A, B and C shall be deemed to be effective, and these Exhibits shall constitute valid and binding agreements and assignment effective as of the date of exercise of such option, and the Producer is hereby authorized and empowered to date such instruments accordingly. If the Producer fails to exercise the option, the signature of the Writer to Exhibits A, B and C shall be void and of no further force or effect whatever, and the Producer shall not be deemed to have acquired any rights in or to the Literary Property other than the option hereinabove provided for. If the Producer exercises the option, the Producer will execute and deliver to the Writer copies of Exhibit A, dated as of the date of the exercise of the option, and the Writer will, if so requested by the Producer, execute and deliver to the Producer additional copies of Exhibits A, B and C. Notwithstanding the failure or omission

5 EFFECTIVENESS OF EXHIBITS 'A', 'B' AND 'C'

This clause clarifies any ambiguity as to how the rights are assigned once the option is exercised.

of either party to execute and/or deliver such additional documents, it is agreed that upon the exercise of the option by the Producer, all rights in and to the Literary Property agreed to be transferred to the Producer pursuant to the provisions of Exhibit A shall be deemed vested in the Producer, effective as of the date of exercise of the option, which rights shall be irrevocable.

6 RIGHT TO ENGAGE IN PRE-PRODUCTION

The Writer acknowledges that the Producer may, at its own expense, during the option period, undertake pre-production activities in connection with any of the rights to be acquired hereunder including, without limitation, the preparation and submission of treatments and/or screenplays based on the Literary Property.

7 RESTRICTIONS

During the Option Period, the Writer shall not exercise or otherwise use any of the rights herein granted to the Producer and as more particularly described in Exhibit A hereof nor the rights reserved to the Writer pursuant to Clause 2 (Rights Reserved) of Exhibit A, nor shall the Writer permit the use of nor shall the Writer use any other right the Writer has reserved in a way that would in any manner or for any purpose unfairly compete with, interfere with or conflict with the bill and unrestricted use of the rights herein granted to the Producer and as described in Exhibit A.

8 ASSIGNMENT

This Option Agreement and the rights granted hereunder may be assigned by the Producer to any other person, firm or corporation.

7 RESTRICTIONS

This clause is a warranty from the Writer that they will not interfere with the Producer's ability to make use of the property (i.e. by selling or optioning the property to someone else). This would clearly be a breach of contract.

8 ASSIGNMENT

Most producers will insist that they have the right to assign. In English law the Producer will remain liable for their obligations notwithstanding the assignment. The Producer will not be able to escape these obligations unless it is specifically stated in the contract. Sometimes, the Writer will wish to limit the right to

9 OPTION REVERSION AND TURNAROUND RIGHT

(a) If the Producer does not timely exercise the option during its original or extended term and timely pay the purchase price, the option shall end and all rights in the Literary Property shall immediately revert to the Writer. The Writer shall retain all sums therefore paid. The Producer shall immediately execute and deliver to the Writer any assignments and documents required to effectuate the Reversion. If the Producer shall fail or be unable to do so, the Producer hereby grants the Writer a power coupled with an interest to execute and deliver such documents as the Producer's attorney-in-fact.

(b) If the option is timely exercised and the purchase price paid and if a motion picture company does not produce a motion picture based on the Literary Property within [ ] years from purchase of the Literary Property, the Writer shall have a turnaround right to reacquire and set up the Literary Property elsewhere, and upon obtaining such other commitment, to reimburse the Producer or motion picture company for its actual direct out-of-pocket development costs in connection with the Literary Property, such as fees to scriptwriters, but excluding payments to the Writer and any payments to the Producer not directly related to scripting services.

assign. One reason would be that the Writer only wants the specific Producer to make use of the property. However this may cause problems with financiers of a project and therefore a compromise would be to add the words 'the Producer shall not assign the property without the Writer's prior written consent and such consent shall not be unreasonably withheld'.

9 OPTION REVERSION AND TURNAROUND RIGHT

(a) From the writer's point of view, this clause can be used to protect the Writer in the event that the Producer does not exercise the Option or pay the sums due under the contract. This clause specifically sets out that if certain sums are not paid under the contract then the Producer loses any rights he may have over the property and **must** re-assign any rights acquired.

(b) This clause is also known as a turn-around provision. This enables the Writer to re-acquire the rights if the Producer has not done anything with them within a certain period of time.

It is up to the Writer to determine how long a period this should be. The Writer should also determine what sum they are willing to pay in order to re-acquire the property. In addition to the expenses and costs set out in this clause the Producer may insist that for the writer to re-purchase the literary property or work that the Writer must include interest payments on any monies paid. Producers should try and negotiate a provision which enables them to recoup not only interest on monies paid but also any or all development costs.

Note that under the Writers Guild of Great Britain/Producers Alliance for Cinema and Television Agreement, a writer has the right to reacquire all rights in an original script if principal photography of a production based on the script has not commenced within two years after the date of delivery to the

(c) In addition, if the Producer decides not to exercise the option in Clause 1, above, any time before the expiration of the Option Period, or decides not to extend such option, the Producer agrees to notify the Writer of such decision as soon as reasonably possible, but in no event later than the applicable option or extension deadline. When such notice is given, the option granted hereunder to the Producer shall automatically revert to the Writer.

10   FORCE MAJEURE

'Force majeure' means any fire, flood, earthquake, or public disaster; strike, labour dispute or unrest; embargo, riot, war, insurrection or civil unrest; any act of God, any act of legally constituted authority; or any other cause beyond the Producer's control which would excuse the Producer's performance as a matter of law. If because of force majeure, the Producer's performance hereunder is delayed or prevented then the option period provided herein and any performance by purchase shall be extended for the time of such delay or prevention of it.

11   SECTION HEADINGS

The headings of paragraphs, sections and other subdivisions of this agreement are for convenient reference only. They shall not be used in any way to govern, limit, modify, construe this agreement or any part or provision of it.

Producer of the materials the writer has been commissioned to write. In order to re-acquire the rights, the Writer must repay 50 per cent of the fees paid by the Producer to the Writer. Similar provisions are found in the Writers Guild of America agreement. However, this provision only applies if a producer engages a member of the guild.

(c) This clause puts an obligation on the Producer to notify the Writer that they do not wish to exercise the option.

10   FORCE MAJEURE

A force majeure clause is another common provision found not only in option Agreements but in many other contracts concerning the film and television industry. Force majeure means 'superior force', and it refers to certain events beyond the control of the Writer or production company that may force suspension of the contract. If one of these events restricts the Producer's ability to conform with the contract then this will not put the Producer in breach of contract. In some contracts, if the suspension lasts more then five weeks, then each party to the contract will have the right to terminate. Producers should ensure that such a provision is included. Film and television production is a highly unpredictable industry and producers should be prepared for anything.

11   SECTION HEADINGS

This clause is to specifically set out that the headings used in the contract are for reference purposes only and do not affect the substance of the Agreement. There have been cases that suggest section headings may influence the essence of a

12 ARBITRATION

Any controversy or claim arising out of or relating to this agreement or any breach thereof shall be settled by arbitration in accordance with [set out specific details of type of arbitration to be used]. The determination of the arbitrator in such proceeding shall be final, binding and non-appealable.

13 ENTIRE AGREEMENT

This agreement, including the Exhibits attached hereto, contains the complete understanding and agreement between the parties with respect to the within subject matter, and supersedes all other agreements between the parties whether written or oral relating thereto, and may not be modified or amended except by written instrument executed by both of the parties hereto.

contract. This is a common clause found in most commercial agreements and it is recommended to insert such a clause to avoid any confusion.

12 ARBITRATION

This clause is often found in American agreements due to the high costs of litigation. In the United Kingdom these clauses are now being used more frequently.

During negotiations between the Producer and the Writer, each party should determine who they would like to see appointed as Arbitrator. In the United Kingdom, there is an Institute of Arbitrators who will appoint an arbitrator with specialist knowledge of the film and television industry. In some cases, the president of the Writers Guild of Great Britain may be designated as an arbitrator, whose decision is final. There also exists an alternative dispute settlement scheme which was recently set up by various law firms in London. They offer an informal and inexpensive means of solving disputes between those involved in the entertainment industry. The Producers Alliance for Cinema and Television has a full list of members and procedures. In some circumstances, it may be worthwhile using the informal Disputes Settlement Scheme. This scheme offers fast, informal and inexpensive settlement of disputes between authors and publishers.

14 NOTICES

Any notices required to be given under the provisions of this Agreement shall be in writing and shall be deemed to have been duly served if hand delivered or sent by telex or facsimile or other print out communication mechanism or within the United Kingdom by prepaid first class registered or recorded delivery post or outside the United Kingdom by prepaid registered airmail correctly addressed to the relevant party's address as specified in this Agreement or at such other address as either party may hereafter designate from time to time in accordance with this clause with copies in the case of the Writer to [   ] of [   ] and in the case of the Producer to [   ] of [   ] and any notice so given shall be deemed to have been served:

(a) if hand delivered at the time of delivery
(b) if sent by telex or facsimile or other print out communication mechanism within eight hours of transmission during business hours at its destination or within twenty-four hours if not within business hours but subject to proof by the sender that he holds an acknowledgement from the addressee confirming receipt of the transmitted notice in readable form and
(c) if sent by prepaid post as aforesaid [when the same would have reached the addressee in the ordinary course of posting] [within forty-eight hours of posting (exclusive of the hours of Sunday) if posted to an address within the country of posting and [seven] days of posting if posted to an address outside the country of posting].

15 GOVERNING LAW

This Agreement shall be construed and performed in all respects in accordance with and shall be governed by English Law and the parties irrevocably submit to the jurisdiction of the [English courts] [the Writer hereby irrevocably appoints [   ] of [England] to accept service of all proceedings hereunder].

14 NOTICES

One must determine where and how specific notices should be sent. In most agreements notices are sent to the addresses of the parties stated in the agreement. In order to avoid confusion as to whether a notice was actually sent and received, this clause should make specific reference as to how and when a notice is actually served on the other party.

15 GOVERNING LAW

Since the entertainment industry is an international business, the parties to the agreement may not both be situated or resident in the same territory or country and are therefore subject to different laws and different legal systems. If an arbitration clause is not used then it is essential that the parties to the agreement specify which laws and in what jurisdiction these laws will be applied. As

IN WITNESS WHEREOF, the parties hereto have signed this Option Agreement as of the day and year first hereinabove written.

SIGNED by the Writer   }
in the presence of:

SIGNED by the Producer   }
in the presence of:

a general rule the Producer will set out that the governing law will be in the jurisdiction of his country.

It is always advisable to designate a jurisdiction, otherwise in the event of any legal proceedings, the first step in the action may be to determine where the proceedings will take place.

Producers should always insist that the governing law provision is in their own jurisdiction. This will save the Producer from having to travel to another country to initiate or defend a legal action. This may ultimately be much more costly than starting an action in the Producer's own jurisdiction.

Exhibit A (Literary Purchase Agreement)

This Agreement is made on the   day of   (date)

BETWEEN:

(1)
('the Writer') and

(2)
('the Producer').

WITNESSETH

WHEREAS, the Writer is the sole and exclusive Writer throughout the world of all rights in and to the literary work entitled: _____ Written by _____ (which work has been filed in the United States Copyright Office under Copyright Registration Number _____); this work including all adaptations and/or versions, the titles, characters, plots, themes and storyline is collectively called the 'Work'; and

WHEREAS, the Producer wants to acquire certain rights of the Writer in consideration for the purchase price provided herein and in reliance upon the Writer's representations and warranties;

NOW, THEREFORE, the parties agree to as follows:

1 RIGHTS GRANTED

The Writer with full title guarantee hereby sells, grants, conveys and assigns to the Producer by way of assignment of present and future copyright the entire copyright and all other rights title and interest of whatsoever nature including but not limited to all motion picture rights (including all silent, sound dialogue and musical motion picture rights), all television motion-picture and other television rights, with limited radio broadcasting rights and 7,500-word publication rights for advertisement, publicity

EXHIBIT A: NOTES

See earlier note regarding proper legal ownership.

1 RIGHTS GRANTED

The rights set out in this clause are usually included in any grant of rights clause. However the grant of rights is a matter for specific negotiations between the Writer and the Producer and therefore certain rights may be excluded. During negotiations the exclusion of specific rights should be clearly stated and recorded.

These rights are also known in the film and television industry as film, television and allied rights and include but are not limited to some or all of the following rights:

and exploitation purposes, and certain incidental and allied rights, throughout the world, in and to the Work for the full period of copyright and all renewals and extensions thereof and thereafter. Included among the rights granted to the Producer hereunder (without in any way limiting the grant of rights hereinabove made) are the following sole and exclusive rights throughout the world.

(a) To make, produce, adapt and copyright one or more motion picture adaptations or versions, whether fixed on film, tape, disc, wire, audio-visual cartridge, cassette or through any other technical process whether now known or from now on devised, based in whole or in part on the Work, of every size, gauge, colour or type, including, but not limited to, musical motion pictures and remakes of and sequels to any motion picture produced hereunder and motion pictures in series or serial form, and for such purposes to record and reproduce and license others to record and reproduce, in synchronization with such motion pictures, spoken words taken from or based upon the text or theme of the Work and any kinds of music, musical accompaniments and/or lyrics to be performed or sung by the performers in any such motion picture and any other kinds of sound and sound effects.

(b) To exhibit, perform, rent, lease and generally deal in and with any motion picture produced hereunder:

(i) by all means or technical processes whatsoever, whether now known or from now on devised including, by way of example only, film, tape, disc, wire, audio-visual, cartridge, cassette or television (including commercially sponsored, sustaining and subscription or pay-per-view television, or any derivative of it); and

(ii) anywhere whatsoever, including homes, theatres and elsewhere, and whether a fee is charged, directly or indirectly, for viewing any such motion picture.

(a) to adapt the work into a film. This clause tries to cover all forms that films may be found on, as well as future forms of delivery. The wording of this clause should be quite specific whether it is for one film or further films. Further films may include remakes and sequels to the initial film and therefore one should consider whether further payments should be made and how these will be made.

(b) new technology such as CD-ROM, digital video disc and the Internet offer the potential to reap enormous revenues from existing books, films and other forms of creative materials and works. In order for owners of these materials to be confident that they are entitled to exploit their assets in these new formats, they must ensure that the grant of rights will include all forms of delivery now known, or to be invented.

(c) To broadcast, transmit or reproduce the Work or any adaptation or version of it (including without limitations to, any motion picture produced hereunder and/or any script or other material based on or using the Work or any of the characters, themes or plots of it), by means of television or any process analogous thereto whether now known or from now on devised (including commercially sponsored, sustaining and subscription or pay-per-view television), by motion pictures produced on films or by means of magnetic tape, wire, disc, audio-visual cartridge or any other device now known or from now on devised and including such television productions presented in series or serial form, and the exclusive right generally to exercise for television purposes all the rights granted to Producer hereunder for motion picture purposes.

(d) Without limiting any other rights granted to the Producer, to broadcast and/or transmit by television or radio or any process analogous thereto whether now known or from now on devised, all or any part of the Work or any adaptation or version of it, including any motion picture or any other version or versions of it, and announcements about said motion picture or other version or versions, for advertising, publicizing or exploiting such motion picture or other version or versions, which broadcasts or transmissions may be accomplished with living actors performing simultaneously with such broadcast or transmission or by any other method or means including the use of motion pictures (including trailers) reproduced on film or by means of magnetic tape or wire or through other recordings or transcriptions.

(c) Producers should be aware as to how changes in new technology change the concepts of intellectual property law. Clearly the law must be adapted to embrace the various new mediums. Contracts will have to be modified so that the number of rights that must be acquired will increase dramatically. Producers, as well as writers, must become familiar with the culture of the computer industry and technology and how this may affect new mediums of delivery.

Intellectual property in the entertainment industry is currently created and used in forms such as film, video, laser disc, digital video and compact disc, CD-ROM, CD-I, 3DO, Nintendo and Sega. Writers and producers must understand the precedents and definitions within the entertainment industry in describing rights of ownership and usage of intellectual property, and both must adapt to understand the language of computer created and driven intellectual property. As previously noted, the judicial system and the members of the entertainment industry are being challenged to adapt and apply existing laws, cases, rules and regulation as well as enacting new legislation to reconcile the conversions of this computer driven technology for the benefit of all. With regards to intellectual property, its ownership and rights of performance and copying in the entertainment industry, there is a great focus in the following areas:

(i)   Motion picture production for theatrical and television product using digitized imagery and audio data technology to create intellectual property;

(ii) Motion picture production of intellectual property for simulation rides and attractions;

(iii) Motion picture production of intellectual property for cultural theme attractions for the end user at museums and special cultural and historical sites;

(iv) Motion picture production of intellectual property for industry training, motivational, and marketing of employees and products, including the commercial

(e) To publish and copyright or cause to be published and copyrighted in the name of Producer or its nominee in any languages throughout the world, in any form or media, synopses, novelizations, serializations, dramatizations, abridged and/or revised versions of the Work, not exceeding 7,500 words each, adapted from the Work or from any motion picture and/or other version of the Work for advertising, publicizing and/or exploiting any such motion picture and/or other version.

(f) For the foregoing purposes to use all or any part of the Work and any of the characters, plots, themes and/or ideas contained therein, and the title of the Work and any title or subtitle of any component of the Work, and to use said titles or subtitles for any motion picture or other version of adaptation whether the same is based on or adapted from the Work and/or as the title of any musical composition contained in any such motion picture or other version or adaptation.

(g) To use and exploit commercial or merchandise tie-ups and recordings of any sort and nature arising out of or

usage to develop and exploit existing product and new product and/or systems;

(v) Motion picture production of intellectual property for virtual reality attractions, the creation of a state of being in reality in an artificially-created, three-dimensional, multi-sensory environment simulating reality and perceived by the user;

(vi) Motion picture production of intellectual property for computer driven imagery for games testing the skill and competence of the user.

A glossary of words and terms of both cultures has been created in order to examine the various legal issues of multi-media programming for the strategic markets noted above. One should note that these words and terms are still not set in concrete and change along with changes in technology.

(e) Seven thousand five hundred words is an industry standard, which is used in many contracts, in reference to the right to publish synopses, serializations, etc. From the Producer's point of view, this is helpful in the promotion of a film or television programme, since it gives the Producer the ability to substantially utilize the literary material.

(f) Producers should try and acquire all rights to the characters, etc. in order to fully exploit the literary materials by creating spin-offs or other programmes based on the specific characters.

connected with the Work and/or its motion picture or other versions and/or the title or titles of it and/or the characters of it and/or their names or characteristics. All rights, licences, privileges and work herein granted to the Producer shall be cumulative and the Producer may exercise or use any or all said rights, licences, privileges or work simultaneously with or in connection with or separately and apart from the exercise of any other of said rights, licences, privileges and work. If Writer from now on makes or publishes or permits to be made or published any revision, adaptation, sequel, translation or dramatization or other versions of the Work, then the Producer shall leave and the Writer hereby grants to the Producer without Payment therefore all of the same rights therein as are herein granted the Producer. The terms 'Picture' and 'Pictures' as used herein shall be deemed to mean or include any present or future kind of motion picture productions based upon the Work, with or without sound recorded and reproduced synchronously with it, whether the same is produced on film or by any other method or means now or from now on used for the production, exhibition and/or transmission of any kind of motion picture productions.

2 RIGHTS RESERVED

The following rights are reserved to the Writer for the Writer's use and disposition, subject, however, to the provisions of this agreement:
(a) Publication Rights: The right to publish and distribute printed versions of the Work owned or controlled by the Writer in book form, whether hardcover or softcover, and in magazine or other periodicals, whether in instalments or otherwise subject to the Producer's rights as provided for in Clause 1 above.

GENERAL NOTE (a)–(g)

What are known as secondary rights or spin-off rights are the rights, to exploit the literary property, programme, or film which it is based on, in other media such as publishing, cinema, stage, radio, merchandising, records etc. A producer must give careful thought to the extent to which the secondary rights might have commercial value. The provision for ownership and control of the secondary rights should be negotiated at the time of acquiring the literary property and be included within the rights agreement. This clause (a)–(g) encompasses all rights which a producer should try and acquire. For some source materials, the agreement can simply provide for the acquisition of specific rights such as television rights or feature film rights. If a limitation is placed on the type of right required for exploitation, then this will reflect in the price paid for those rights. Film producers should always keep in mind that a specific character could be spun-off into an animated or live action television series. Therefore, secondary or spin-off rights can be very valuable.

2 RIGHTS RESERVED

(a)/(b)/(c) Sometimes the Writer may wish to hold back certain rights which the Producer may be interested in. This clause sets out various holdbacks, which are agreements not to exercise certain rights which the Writer has retained but if were exercised, would have some form of negative effect on the rights granted to the producer. Note that holdbacks do

(b) Stage Rights: The right to perform the Work or adaptations of it on the spoken stage with actors appearing in person in the immediate presence of the audience, provided no broadcast, telecast, recording, photography or other reproduction of such performance is made. The Writer agrees not to exercise, or permit any other person to exercise, said stage rights earlier than _____ years after the first general release or telecast, if earlier, of the first Picture produced hereunder, or _____ years after the date of exercise of the Producer's option to acquire the work, whichever is earlier.

(c) Radio Rights: The right to broadcast the Work by sound (as distinguished from visually) by radio, subject however to the Producer's right always to:

   (i) [exercise its radio rights provided in Clause 1 above for advertising and exploitation purposes by living actors or otherwise, by using excerpts from or condensations of the Work or any Picture produced hereunder; and];

   (ii) in any event to broadcast any Picture produced hereunder by radio. The Writer agrees not to exercise, or permit any other person to exercise, Writer's radio rights earlier than _____ years after the first general release or initial telecast, if earlier, of the first Picture produced hereunder or _____ years after the date of exercise of Producer's option to acquire the work, whichever is earlier.

(d) Author-Written Sequel: A literary work (story, novel, drama or otherwise), whether written before or after the Work and whether written by the Writer or by a successor in interest of the Writer, using one or other of the characters appearing in the Work, participating in different events from those found in the Work, and whose plot is substantially different from that of the Work. The Writer shall have the right to exercise publication rights (i.e. in book or magazine form) any time. The Writer agrees not to exercise, or permit any

not last forever and as a usual practice, are restricted to a maximum of seven years from the date of either when the rights were acquired or from the first release of either a film or television programme.

Where the owner of a literary property or work grants only the film rights in that work, the acquirer of those rights (the producer) should insist on a lengthy holdback of the television rights. From the rights owner's perspective, they should insist on a shorter holdback period, in case the film version of their work, is a success and they subsequently wish to exploit the more valuable television rights.

other person to exercise, any other rights (including but not limited to motion picture or allied rights) of any kind in or to any author-written sequel earlier than _____ years after the first general release of the first Picture produced hereunder, or _____ years after the date of exercise of the Producer's option to acquire the work, whichever is earlier, provided such restriction on the Writer's exercise of said author-written sequel rights shall be extended to any period during which there is in effect, in any particular country or territory, a network television broadcasting agreement for a television motion picture, (i) based upon the Work, or (ii) based upon any Picture produced in the exercise of rights assigned herein, or (iii) using a character or characters of the Work, plus one (1) year, which shall also be a restricted period in such country or territory, whether such period occurs wholly or partly during or entirely after the _____ year period first referred to in this clause. Any disposition of motion picture or allied rights in an author-written sequel made to any person or company other than the Producer shall be made subject to the following limitations and restrictions:

(e) Since the characters of the Work are included in the exclusive grant of motion picture rights to the Producer, no sequel rights or television series rights may be granted to such other person or company, but such characters from the Work which are contained in the author-written sequel may be used in a motion picture and remakes of it whose plot is based substantially on the plot of the respective author-written sequel.

It is expressly agreed that the Writer's reserved rights under this subclause relate only to material written or authorized by the Writer and not to any revision, adaptation, sequel, translation or dramatization written or authorized by the Producer, although the same may contain characters or other elements contained in the Work.

Option and literary purchase agreement: Notes

3   RIGHT TO MAKE CHANGES

The Writer agrees that the Producer shall have the unlimited right to vary, charge, alter, modify, add to and/or delete from the Work, and to rearrange and/or transpose the Work and change the sequence of it and the characters and descriptions of the characters contained in the Work, and to use a portion or portions of the Work or the characters, plots, or theme of it with any other literary, dramatic or other material of any kind. The Writer hereby waives the benefits of any provisions of law known as the 'droit moral' or any similar law in any country of the world and agrees not to permit or prosecute any action or lawsuit on the ground that any Picture or other version of the Work produced or exhibited by the Producer, its assignees or licensees, in any way constitutes an infringement of any of the Writer's droit moral or is in any way a defamation or mutilation of the Work or any part of it or contains unauthorized variations, alterations, modifications, changes or translations.

3 RIGHT TO MAKE CHANGES

This clause gives the Producer the right to make changes, modify and rearrange the literary property being purchased. Producers and writers should also be aware of moral rights.

Moral rights were introduced into English law in the Copyright Design and Patent Act 1988 to bring English law into line with that of many European countries which have long had protection for authors' moral rights. In many countries moral rights are an inalienable right whereas in the United Kingdom they can be waived. There are two types of moral rights; the right of integrity and the right of paternity.

Rights of integrity give the authors of copyright works the right not to have their works subjected to derogatory treatment. Treatment means any addition to, deletion from, alteration to or adaptation of their work. Derogatory treatment involves distortion or mutilation of the work, or treatment otherwise prejudicial to the honour or reputation of the author or director. Producers should insist that moral rights waivers are secured in each and every production contract involving an assignment or licence of copyright material. Without a waiver, there is a risk of overall editorial control being challenged by unhappy authors. Sometimes, television programmes or films cannot be sold unless purchasers, such as broadcasters, are allowed to adapt the material to fit the schedules and other requirements of their markets. In these circumstances, a Moral Rights Waiver is essential. Productions could be put at risk if an author were to claim that even very minor cuts or additions to his work constituted derogatory treatment and then took the matter up in court. A moral rights waiver must be given in writing and signed by the proper owner.

The Right of Paternity gives the author or director the right to be identified as the creator of the work or the director of the film. This right must be specifically asserted usually in writing and signed by the author. Once this right has been asserted the author or director has the entitlement to receive credit. This is covered by standard credit provisions in most industry agreements.

4   DURATION AND EXTENT OF RIGHTS GRANTED

The Producer shall enjoy, solely and exclusively, all the rights, licences, privileges and work granted hereunder throughout the world, in perpetuity, as long as any rights in the Work are recognized in law or equity, except as far as such period of perpetuity may be shortened due to any now existing or future copyright by the Writer of the Work and/or any adaptations of it, in which case the Producer shall enjoy its sole and exclusive rights, licences, privileges and work hereunder to the fullest extent permissible under and for the full duration of such copyright or copyrights, whether common law or statutory and any renewals and/or extensions of it, and shall after that enjoy all such rights, licences, privileges and work non-exclusively in perpetuity throughout the world. The rights granted herein are in addition to and shall not be construed in derogation of any rights which the Producer may have as a member of the public or pursuant to any other agreement. All rights, licences, privileges and work granted herein to the Producer are irrevocable and not subject to rescission, restraint or injunction under any circumstances.

5   CONSIDERATION

As consideration for all rights granted and assigned to the Producer and for the Writer's representations and warranties, the Producer agrees to pay to the Writer, and the Writer agrees to accept:
(a) For a theatrical or television motion picture £_____ in addition to any sums paid in connection with the option

4 DURATION AND EXTENT OF RIGHTS GRANTED

This clause grants the buyer all rights in perpetuity. In the event that certain laws do not recognize that copyright may be assigned in perpetuity then this clause enables the buyer to own the property for the longest permissible time that copyright may be granted. It is important for a seller of rights to realize that he does not necessarily have to assign all rights for the full period of copyright. It may be preferable to grant a licence for a shorter period of time (i.e. fifteen or twenty years). If a licence is granted then the licence should be clear as to which rights are granted and how those rights can be exploited. If a licence is granted it must clearly state that it is either capable or incapable of being terminated.

An assignment of rights is preferable to a licence since assignment generally means that the assignee acquires the rights for the full term of copyright. Licences are usually for a fixed term after which the rights revert to the licensor. Most companies that take a licence prefer a period of time of at least ten to twenty-five years. This gives them ample opportunity to exploit a finished television programme or film based on those rights.

From the writer's or rights owner's perspective they should try and negotiate a licence period which will enable the rights to be exploited by the Producer but will eventually revert back to the Writer or rights owner. Writers and rights owners should think of their rights as their pension. If they can renew their rights they can continue earning revenues from their exploitation.

5 CONSIDERATION

There are various ways of setting out how payment is made. In this clause, payment will be made according to the form of exploitation of the literary property or work. A credit will be given against the payments made in the option. Payments may also be staggered, either upon exercise of the option or on the first day of principal photography.

periods so payable upon exercise of the option to acquire the Work.

(b) For any mini-series, £_____ per hour, pro-rata for part hours.

(c) For any sequel or remake of a theatrical or television motion picture based on the Work, one-half ($\frac{1}{2}$) and one third ($\frac{1}{3}$), respectively, of the amount paid for the initial motion picture, payable upon commencement of principal photography of the subsequent production.

(d) For any television series produced, based on the Work, the Producer will pay the following royalties per initial production upon completion of production of each programme: up to 30 minutes £_____ ; over 30, but not more than 60 minutes £_____ ; over 60 minutes £____; and in addition to the foregoing, as a buy-out of all royalty obligations, one-hundred per cent (100%) of the applicable initial royalty amount, in equal instalments over five (5) re-runs, payable within thirty (30) days after each such re-run.

As and for contingent compensation _____ per cent of one-hundred (100%) of the net profits (including allied and ancillary rights) of each motion picture and television program or series based on the Work, in whole or in part, with profits defined according to the same definition obtained by the Producer; provided, however, that the Writer's percentage shall not be subject to any reductions or preconditions whatsoever.

6   REPRESENTATIONS AND WARRANTIES

(a) Sole Proprietor: The Writer represents and warrants to the Producer that the Writer is the sole and exclusive proprietor, throughout the universe, of that certain original work written by the Writer entitled _____.

Sometimes, principal photography may never start and therefore payment will never be made. From the writer's or rights owner's perspective if they do not believe that a producer can eventually make a film or television programme then they should try and get as much money as they can up front. Some writers make a very good income by continually optioning their materials to producers without their work ever being produced. Great care should be taken regarding share of profits. It is essential to be clear on what the definition of profits is. The definition of profits should be made according to the circumstances of each project. When negotiating net profits individuals should take professional advice. Net profits or what is known throughout the industry as the 'back end' are used by producers to encourage others who work on the film. There is a substantial difference between net profits and producers net profits. In general, net profits will be all the proceeds realized by exploiting a film or television programme after deducting various distribution expenses, sales agency commissions, the cost of actually producing the film or TV programme and any deferred fees that have not been paid. The Producer's net profits will be the funds realized after exploitation of the film, after the deduction of any of the above expenses and any share of net profits have been paid to other third parties. Once these payments have been made then the producer will be able to realize his share of net profits. In some net profit definitions there is usually a right for an individual to inspect the books of account of a production company or distributor as well as the right to receive statements setting out whether a film is in net profits. This is an area where professional advice is highly recommended. Some of the highest grossing films in Hollywood have never shown a profit because of creative accounting and the studio's high distribution and overhead costs.

6 REPRESENTATIONS AND WARRANTIES

This clause is always repeated in the Exhibit because the Exhibit is a separate agreement.

(b) The Writer represents and warrants to the Producer as follows:

   (i)   The Writer is the sole author and creator of the Work.

   (ii)   The work was first published in [   ] by [   ] (publisher) under the title [_____] (and was registered for copyright in the name of _____, under copyright registration number _____ in the Office of the United States Register of Copyrights, Washington, DC)

   (iii) No motion picture or dramatic version of the Work, or any part of it, has been manufactured, produced, presented or authorized; no radio or television development, presentation, or programme based on the Work, or any part of it, has been manufactured, produced, presented, broadcast or authorized; and no written or oral agreements or commitment at all with respect to the Work, or with respect to any rights therein, have been made or entered by or on behalf of the Writer (except with respect to the publication of the Work as set forth above).

   (iv) None of the rights therein granted and assigned to the Producer have been granted and/or assigned to any person, firm or corporation other than the Producer.

(c) No Infringement or Violation of Third-Party Rights: the Writer represents and warrants to the Producer that the Writer has not adapted the Work from any other literary, dramatic or other material of any kind, nature or description, nor, except material which is in the public domain, has the Writer copied or used in the Work the plot, scenes, sequence or story of any other literary, dramatic or other material; that the Work does not infringe upon any common law or statutory rights in any other literary, dramatic or other material; that the Work does not infringe upon any common law or statutory rights in any other literary, dramatic or other material; that no material contained in the Work is

Option and literary purchase agreement: Notes

libellous or violative of the right of privacy of any person; that the full utilization of any and all rights in and to the Work granted by the Writer pursuant to this Agreement will not violate the rights of any person, firm or corporation; and that the Work is not in the public domain in any country in the world where copyright protection is available.

(d) No Impairment of Rights: the Writer represents and warrants to the Producer that the Writer is the exclusive proprietor, throughout the universe, of all rights in and to the Work granted herein to the Producer; that the Writer has not assigned, licensed or in any manner encumbered, diminished or impaired any such rights; that the Writer has not committed or omitted to perform any act by which such rights could or will be encumbered, diminished or impaired; and that there is no outstanding claim or litigation pending against or involving the title, ownership and/or copyright in the Work, or in any part thereof, or in any rights granted herein to the Producer.

The Writer further represents and warrants that no attempt shall be made hereafter to encumber, diminish or impair any of the rights granted herein and that all appropriate protection of such rights will continue to be maintained by the Writer.

7 INDEMNIFICATION

(a) The Writer agrees to indemnify the Producer against all judgments, liability, damages, penalties, losses and expense (including reasonable legal fees) which may be suffered or assumed by or obtained against the Producer by reason of any breach or failure of any warranty or agreement herein made by the Writer.

(b) The Producer shall not be liable to the Writer for damages of any kind in connection with any picture it may produce, distribute or exhibit, or for damages for

7 INDEMNIFICATION

Each party to the Agreement should try and give an indemnity against losses which may be suffered by either party as a result of a breach of the warranties or representations in the contract. The Producer will want the Writer to stand behind their warranties and indemnify them in case a warranty is breached. When the Writer indemnifies the Producer, the Writer agrees to reimburse the Producer for any losses, including legal costs. An indemnity however is only worth as much as the person standing behind it. It may be a waste of time for a producer to seek

117

any breach of this Agreement (except failure to pay the money consideration herein specified) occurring or accruing before the Producer has had reasonable notice and opportunity to adjust or correct such matters.

(c) All rights, licences and privileges herein granted to the Producer are irrevocable and not subject to rescission, restraint or injunction under any circumstances.

8 PROTECTION OF RIGHTS GRANTED

The Writer hereby grants to the Producer the free and unrestricted right, but at the Producer's own cost and expense, to institute in the name and on behalf of the

reimbursements from an impoverished writer. It is essential for producers to purchase Errors and Omission Insurance (E&O) prior to production of a film or television programme. While negotiating an indemnity, the representative of the Writer may ask that the Writer be named as an insured on the E&O policy. This will ensure that the insurance company defends the writer in addition to the Producer if a claim arises.

E&O insurance protects the policy holder from various claims, such as defamation, invasion of privacy, trademark and copyright infringements. For example, if a producer (the policy holder) carelessly infringed someone else's copyright when producing a film, the producer may be liable for damages. E&O insurance should, in most circumstances, pay for any liability incurred as well as legal defence costs. Like other insurance policies, there is usually a deductible, usually in the range of £5,000–£10,000 depending on the type of claim. E&O insurance does not cover intentional wrong-doings. The insurance broker or carrier often requires that the applicant's lawyer review and approve a script and other documents before a policy is issued. In addition, a copyright report and title report may be needed and all employment agreements must be in writing and signed. If music is to be used, then all of the proper clearances must be checked. Rights of privacy and publicity are not always a major concern in the United Kingdom film and TV industry, however, any American distributors or broadcasters will ask that these areas have been properly cleared before purchasing a film or television programme from a producer.

A policy will usually last between three and five years and can be renewed if a further payment is made. In most cases the insurance will cover not only the producer but also the financiers and others who may have an interest in the production.

8 PROTECTION OF RIGHTS GRANTED

This clause gives the Buyer the right to protect the rights which have been granted if there has been any infringement of copyright. If copyright is to have any value to its owner it must be

Writer, or the Writer and Producer jointly, any and all suits and proceedings at law or in equity, to enjoin and restrain any infringements of the rights herein granted, and hereby assigns and sets over to the Producer any and all causes of action relative to or based upon any such infringement, as well as any and all recoveries obtained thereon. The Writer will not compromise, settle or in any manner interfere with such litigation if brought; and the Producer agrees to indemnify and hold the Writer harmless from any costs, expenses, or damages which the Writer may suffer as a result of any such suit or proceeding.

9 COPYRIGHT

Regarding the copyright in and to the Work, the Writer agrees that:

(a) The Writer will prevent the Work and any arrangements, revisions, translations, novelizations, dramatizations or new versions thereof, whether published or unpublished and whether copyrighted or not copyrighted, from vesting in the public domain, and will take or cause to be taken any and all steps and proceedings required for copyright or similar protection in any and all countries in which the same may be published or offered for sale, insofar as such countries now or hereafter provide for copyright or similar protection. Any contract or agreement entered into by the Writer authorizing or permitting the publication of the Work or any arrangements, revisions, translations, novelizations, dramatizations or new versions thereof in any country will contain appropriate provisions requiring such publisher to comply with all the provisions of this clause.

capable of at least some measure of enforcement. Copyright is essentially a private legal right and it is up to the owner of the copyright to go to court to prevent a wrong from taking place or to seek compensation where a wrong has taken place. Section 96 of the Copyright, Designs and Patents Act 1988 provides that subject to the provisions of the Act, infringements of copyright are actionable by the copyright owner, and that in any action for such an infringement all relief by way of damages, injunction, accounts or otherwise shall be available to the plaintiff as is available in any proceedings in respect of infringements of other property rights. The type of remedies available are either monetary or an injunction which is an order by the court restraining a person from doing an act which is a breach of his legal duty. Actions in the court for infringement of copyright are usually initiated by serving on the defendant a writ which will contain a short statement of the nature of the complaint and the relief sought.

9 COPYRIGHT

(a) This section sets out that the Writer will not let the property fall into the public domain. This clause is essential when dealing with American writers. Some copyright materials in the United States were subject to renewals of copyright. Prior to the United States joining the Universal Convention on Copyright and the changes to US copyright law, which extended the period of copyright, there existed periods of copyright which were renewable. Therefore, producers should be wary of dealing with American copyright materials without the assistance of a US lawyer. US copyright is a minefield and professional legal advice should be sought.

With some American materials if the Writer allows the material to fall into the public domain then the Producer may have a warranty claim for damages against the Writer due to the Writer not renewing the copyright in materials that are renewable.

(b) Without limiting the generality of the foregoing, if the Work or any arrangement, revision, translation, novelization, dramatization or new version thereof is published in the United States or in any other country in which registration is required for copyright or similar protection in accordance with the laws and regulations of such country, and the Writer further agrees to affix or cause to be affixed to each copy of the Work or any arrangement, revision, translation, novelization, dramatization or new version thereof which is published or offered for sale such notice or notices as may be required for copyright or similar protection in any country in which such publication or sale occurs.

(c) At least _____ months prior to the expiration of any copyright required by this provision for the protection of the Work, the Writer will renew (or cause to be renewed) such copyright, as permitted by applicable law, and any and all rights granted to the Producer hereunder shall be deemed granted to the Producer throughout the full

(b) This is a copyright matter and this clause should be used when dealing with American literary properties. In the United States before 1 March 1989 failure to put a copyright notice on a work, if it was published, could result in loss of copyright. However the Berne Convention Implementation Act 1988 enabled the United States to establish copyright relations with various countries around the world. Notice requirements were dropped for works published after 1 March 1989. Also recording of an interest in a copyrighted work was no longer required as a pre-requisite to bringing an infringement suit. Nowadays, an American author who publishes his work and fails to attach a copyright notice is protected anyway. In the United States under current law, a copyright lasts for the lifetime of the author plus fifty years. Before 1978, the author of a work had a copyright in his work for twenty-eight years and could renew it for an additional twenty-eight years, for a total of fifty-six years of copyright protection. Works in the second term of copyright when the law changed received an extra nineteen-year extension for a total of seventy-five years. Once a copyright expires, the work goes into the public domain and anyone can use it. Another reason for this clause is that the provisions of the 1988 amendment to US copyright law are not retroactive, so that works that went into the public domain for failure to comply with notice provisions will remain in the public domain. Therefore, when dealing with American copyright works pre-1989 one should be very careful to ensure that they are not in the public domain. Recently, the US Congress passed the Copyright Term Extension Act which is a bill to extend copyright protection for an additional twenty years beyond the current law. This makes things even more confusing.

(c) This section puts an obligation on the Writer to renew copyright if it is necessary.

period of such renewed copyright, without the payment of any additional consideration, it being agreed that the consideration payable to the Writer under this agreement shall be deemed to include full consideration for the grant of such rights to the Producer throughout the period of such renewed copyright.

(d) If the Work, or any arrangement, revision, translation, novelization, dramatization or new version thereof, shall ever enter the public domain, then nothing contained in this agreement shall impair any rights or privileges that the Producer might be entitled to as a member of the public; thus, the Producer may exercise any and all such rights and privileges as though this agreement were not in existence. The rights granted herein by the Writer to the Producer, and the representations, warranties, undertakings and agreements made hereunder by the Writer, shall endure in perpetuity and shall be in addition to any rights, licences, privileges or work of the Producer referred to in this sub-clause (d).

10   CREDIT OBLIGATIONS

The Producer shall have the right to publish, advertise, announce and use in any manner or medium, the name, biography and photographs or likenesses of the Writer in connection with any exercise by the Producer of its rights hereunder, provided such use shall not constitute an endorsement of any product or service.

The Producer shall accord the Writer credit as follows:

(Set out specific credit provisions. All are subject to specific negotiations.)

Additionally, if the Producer shall exploit any other rights in and to the Work, then the Producer agrees to give appropriate source material credit to the Work, to the extent that such source material credits are customarily given in connection with the exploitation of such rights.

10 CREDIT OBLIGATIONS

The Producer will want the right to use the name and likeness of the author to promote the final form of the literary property or work whether it is a film or television programme. Some agreements may refer to the Writers Guild of Great Britain or other Writers Guild Agreement which have in their standard agreements a formula for determining who receives writing credit. (This assumes that the writer is in the Writers Guild and the production company making a film or programme is also a signatory to the same.) Sometimes the author (if different from the script writer) will want a credit whenever the script writer is mentioned. It is essential that the credit obligations are fully set out in this clause. There should also be a reference made that any casual or inadvertent failure to give credit will not constitute a breach of the agreement and if such an event does take place then this breach will be confined only to damages. The reason for this is that if a credit is not accorded and the remedy is not limited to damages

No casual or inadvertent failure to comply with any of the provisions of this clause shall be deemed a breach of this Agreement by the Producer. Writer hereby expressly acknowledges that in the event of a failure or omission constituting a breach of the provisions of this paragraph, the damage (if any) caused to the Writer thereby is not irreparable or sufficient to entitle the Writer to injunctive or other equitable relief. Consequently, the Writer's rights and remedies in the event of such breach shall be limited to the right to recover damages in an action at law. The Producer agrees to provide in its contracts with distributors of the Picture that such distributors shall honour the Producer's contractual credit commitments and agrees to inform such distributors of the credit provisions herein.

11   RIGHT OF FIRST NEGOTIATION

The term 'Right of First Negotiation' means that if, after the expiration of an applicable time limitation, the Writer desires to dispose of or exercise a particular right reserved to the Writer herein ('Reserved Right'), whether directly or indirectly, then the Writer shall notify the Producer in writing and immediately negotiate with the Producer regarding such Reserved Rights. If, after the expiration of ____ days following the receipt of such notice, no agreement has been reached, then the Writer may negotiate with third parties regarding such Reserved Right subject to Clause 12 below.

12   RIGHT OF LAST REFUSAL

The term 'Right of Last Refusal' means that if the Producer and the Writer fail to reach an agreement pursuant to the Producer's right of first negotiation, and the Writer makes and/or receives any *bona fide* offer to license, lease and/or purchase the particular Reserved Right or any interest therein ('Third-Party Offer'), and if the proposed purchase price and other material terms of a Third Party Offer are no more favourable to the Writer than the terms which were

then it is feasible that the author or script writer may have the right to stop the film being released until they receive their credit.

Producers should try and restrict any obligation to accord credit to those copies of the film or television programme that are under the control of the producer. Producers should also try and ensure that their obligation to accord credit will be subject to the usual exclusions of distributors and broadcasters in the film and/or television industries.

Writers of scripts or owners of literary property may try and negotiate the right to remove their name from the credits if they do not like the final version of the film or television programme. Producers should always refuse this request since the writer may be an important selling point of a film or television programme.

11 RIGHT OF FIRST NEGOTIATION

This clause sets out that the Writer cannot sell or dispose of any of the reserved rights unless they have first offered them to the Producer. This is usually referred to as the right of first negotiation. Producers should insist on this provision since these rights may become valuable as a result of a successful film or television programme.

12 RIGHT OF LAST REFUSAL

This clause is sometimes referred to as 'matching rights'. This clause sets out, that before selling the rights to any one else, the Writer will offer those rights to the Producer on the same terms which he was willing to sell them to another purchaser. Once again, a producer should insist on these rights for similar reasons as above.

acceptable to the Producer during the first negotiation period, the Writer shall notify the Producer, by registered mail or courier, if the Writer proposes to accept such Third-Party Offer, the name of the offerer, the proposed purchase price, and other terms of such Third-Party Offer. During the period of _____ days after the Producer's receipt of such notice, the Producer shall have the exclusive option to license, lease and/or purchase, as the case may be, the particular Reserved Right or interest referred to in such Third-Party Offer, at the same purchase price and upon the same terms and conditions as set forth in such notice. If the Producer elects to exercise thereof by registered mail or courier within such _____ day period, failing which the Writer shall be free to accept such Third-Party Offer; provided that if any such proposed licence, lease and/or sale is not consummated with a third party within days following the expiration of the aforesaid _____ day period, Producer's Right of Last Refusal shall revive and shall apply to each and every further offer or offers at any time received by Writer relating to the particular Reserved Right or any interest therein; provided, further, that the Producer's option shall continue in full force and effect, upon all of the terms and conditions of this paragraph, so long as the Writer retains any rights, title or interests in or to the particular Reserved Right. The Producer's Right of Last Refusal shall inure to the benefit of the Producer, its successors and assigns, and shall bind the Writer and the Writer's heirs, successors and assigns.

13 NO OBLIGATION TO PRODUCE

Nothing herein shall be construed to obligate the Producer to produce, distribute, release, perform or exhibit any motion picture, television, theatrical or other production, based upon, adapted from or suggested by the Work, in whole or in part, or otherwise to exercise, exploit or make any use of any rights, licences, privileges or work granted herein to the Producer.

13 NO OBLIGATION TO PRODUCE

A literary purchase agreement will also contain an explicit provision stating that the producer is under no obligation to actually produce a film or television programme. The Producer will want the right to make a film or television programme but not the obligation to do so. This will prevent the author or writer from claiming that the producer promised to produce something or that this was a condition of the contract.

14 ASSIGNMENT

The Producer may assign and transfer this Agreement or all or any part of its rights hereunder to any person, firm or corporation without limitation, and this Agreement shall be binding upon and inure to the benefit of the parties hereto and their successors, representatives and assigns forever.

15 LENDING RIGHTS

The Writer hereby assigns to the Producer all and any rental and lending rights that the Writer may leave in relation to the work and the Writer confirms that the payments set out in this Agreement include full and proper equitable remuneration in respect of any rights (including without limitation any rental and lending rights) that the Writer may have in relation to any [films] or [programming] produced.

14 ASSIGNMENT

This sets out the right to assign or license to third parties.

From the Producer's point of view it is essential that he has the ability to assign the benefit of the contract to another party. A situation may arise whereby the Producer may wish to sell the literary property to another production company or work on co-production. From the author's or writer's perspective they may not want to have their literary property sold to a company they do not want to be associated with. In general, most assignment clauses set out that the contract is assignable as long as the Producer will remain liable to the Writer for all terms and conditions under the contract.

Producers should also be aware that production financers, banks and completion guarantors that participate in the financing of a film or television programme will insist that the underlying rights are fully assignable to them as security for their loan or participation.

15 LENDING RIGHTS

This clause is in relation to European law which requires that specific individuals are given the legal right to consent to, or prohibit the originals or copies of the products of their artistic works, to be rented or lent out. This right includes authors of certain copyright work such as books, scripts and films. Although the right to consent to rental or lending can be waived by the original rights holder or even transferred to another person, the author or writer always has a right of equitable remuneration for any rental. Equitable remuneration cannot be waived. One problem is what the definition of equitable remuneration is. This will not be clear until there is specific case law on the point. This clause may not be sufficient to avoid further payments. What is clear though is that the Producer cannot require the Writer to give up his/her right to equitable remuneration.

Some say that the 'right to equitable remuneration' can be defined as meaning the author's right to be remunerated,

16 NO PUBLICITY

The Writer will not, without the Producer's prior written consent in each instance, issue or authorize the issuance or publication of any news story or publicity relating to (i) this Agreement, (ii) the subject matter or terms hereof, or to any use by the Producer, its successors, licensees and assigns, and (iii) any of the rights granted the Producer hereunder.

17 AGENT COMMISSIONS

The Producer shall not be liable for any compensation or fee to any agent of the Writer in connection with this Agreement.

18 ADDITIONAL DOCUMENTATION

The Writer agrees to execute and procure any other and further instruments necessary to transfer, convey, assign

equitably, in respect of any rental of any copies of a film or sound recording in which his work is included, taking into account the importance of his contribution to the film or sound recording. The right to equitable remuneration may be exercised by the author in respect of a film, or against the film producer to whom the author's rental right is deemed to be, or is assigned, or any successor in title to the film producer in respect of that rental right. Any remuneration offered or paid is not to be considered inequitable merely because it is to be paid or is paid: (a) by way of a single payment; (b) upon the conclusion of the assignment. In any agreement which contains provisions dealing with an author's right to equitable remuneration, the author shall not be bound by any term or condition which purports to limit the meaning to be attributed to 'equitable remuneration' by reference of actual remuneration.

16 NO PUBLICITY

Sometimes a literary purchase agreement will require the writer to refrain from engaging in any publicity activities for that project unless they are with the consent of the Producer. The eventual distributor or studio that purchases a film will want to put together their own publicity campaign without worrying about the writer giving interviews on his own or saying things that may be detrimental.

17 AGENT COMMISSIONS

This makes it clear that the Producer is not responsible for any fees payable to the Writer's agent. In some circumstances, the Writer may argue that the Producer is responsible for his agent's fees. It is better to state clearly that the Producer will not be responsible for agent commissions.

18 ADDITIONAL DOCUMENTATION

This clause puts an obligation on the Writer to sign any further documentation in relation to the project that may be necessary.

and copyright all rights in the Work granted herein by the Writer to the Producer in any country throughout the world. If it shall be necessary under the laws of any country that copyright registration be acquired in the name of the Writer, the Producer is hereby authorized by the Writer to apply for said copyright registration thereof; and, in such event, the Writer shall and does hereby assign and transfer the same unto the Producer, subject to the rights in the Work reserved hereunder by the Writer. The Writer further agrees, upon request, to duly execute, acknowledge, procure and deliver to the Producer such short form assignments as may be requested by the Producer for the purpose of copyright recordation in any country, or otherwise. If the Writer shall fail to so execute and deliver, or cause to be executed and delivered, the assignments or other instruments herein referred to, the Producer is hereby irrevocably granted the power coupled with an interest to execute such assignments and instruments in the name of the Writer and as the Writer's attorney in-fact.

19 ARBITRATION

Any controversy or claim arising out of or relating to this Agreement or any breach thereof shall be settled by arbitration in accordance with (set out specific details of type of arbitration to be used) the determination of the arbitrator in such proceeding, shall be final, binding and non-appealable.

20 NOTICES

Any notices required to be given under the provisions of this Agreement shall be in writing and shall be deemed to have been duly served if hand delivered or sent by telex or facsimile or other print out communication mechanism or within the United Kingdom by prepaid first class registered or recorded delivery post or outside the United Kingdom by prepaid registered airmail correctly addressed to the

The Producer will always ask for this to be included and it is unlikely that the Writer can avoid this. This protects the Producer if there is any problem with any documentation between the Producer and the Writer.

relevant party's address as specified in this agreement or at such other address as either party may hereafter designate from time to time in accordance with this clause with copies in the case of the Writer to [   ] of [   ] and in the case of the Producer to [   ] of [   ] and any notice so given shall be deemed to have been served:

(a) if hand delivered at the time of delivery

(b) if sent by telex or facsimile or other print out communication mechanism within eight hours of transmission during business hours at its destination or within twenty-four hours if not within business hours but subject to proof by the sender that he holds an acknowledgement from the addressee confirming receipt of the transmitted notice in readable form and

(c) if sent by prepaid post as aforesaid [when the same would have reached the addressee in the ordinary course of posting] [within forty-eight hours of posting (exclusive of the hours of Sunday) if posted to an address within the country of posting and [seven] days of posting if posted to an address outside the country of posting].

21 MISCELLANEOUS PROVISIONS

(a) Relationship: This Agreement between the parties does not constitute a joint venture or partnership of any kind.

(b) Cumulative Rights and Remedies: All rights, remedies, licenses, undertakings, obligations, covenants, privileges and other work granted herein shall be cumulative, and the Producer may exercise or use any of them separately or in conjunction with any one or more of the others.

(c) Waiver: A waiver by either party of any term, or condition of this agreement in any instance shall not be

21 MISCELLANEOUS PROVISIONS

The provisions set out in this clause are to further clarify various rights and requests.

(a) This ensures that there is no joint venture or partnership between the parties to the Agreement. This is important to clarify since some agreements can infer that a joint venture or partnership exists between the Producer and the Writer.

(c) This clause is essential since under a contract if one of the parties fails to do something which he or she has been

deemed or construed to be a waiver of such term or condition for the future, or any subsequent breach thereof.

(d) Severability: If any provision of this Agreement as applied to either party or any circumstances shall be adjudged by a court to be void and unenforceable, such shall in no way affect any other provision of this agreement, the application of such provision in any other circumstance, or the validity or enforceability of this agreement.

(e) Governing Law: This Agreement shall be construed and performed in all respects in accordance with and shall be governed by English Law and the parties irrevocably submit to the jurisdiction of the English courts [the Writer hereby irrevocably appoints [   ] of [England] to accept service of all proceedings hereunder]

(f) Clause Headings: Clause Headings are inserted for reference and convenience only and in no way define, limit or describe the scope of this agreement or intent of any provision.

(g) Entire Understanding: This Agreement contains the entire understanding of the parties relating to the subject matter, and this agreement cannot be changed except by written agreement executed by the party to be bound.

IN WITNESS WHEREOF, the parties hereto have signed this Agreement as of the day and year first above written.

SIGNED by the Writer }
in the presence of:

SIGNED by the Producer }
in the presence of:

contracted for (i.e. in the form of a term or condition) and the other party waives their rights of redress then such a waiver does not mean that the waiving party has permanently waived such a term or condition. For example, if a contract says that a writer must submit script changes every two weeks but does not and the Producer (the other contracting party) accepts script changes every four weeks the Producer may still enforce the two week provision under the contract even though the Producer waived his rights and accepted script changes every four weeks.

Exhibit B   Agreements

OPTION AGREEMENT
(Short Form for Recording at US Copyright Office)

For good and valuable consideration, receipt of which is hereby acknowledged, the undersigned hereby grants to _____ ('the Producer'), its successors and assigns, the sole and exclusive option to purchase all motion picture and certain allied rights, in the original literary and/or dramatic work (the 'Work') described as follows:

Title:
Author:
Publisher:
Date of Publication:
Copyright Registration:

The Work includes but is not limited to: (i) all contents; (ii) all present and future adaptations and versions; (iii) the title, characters and theme; and (iv) the copyright and all renewals and extensions of copyright.

This instrument is executed in accordance with and is subject to the agreement (the 'Option Agreement') between the undersigned and the Producer dated as of _____ (date) relating to the option granted to the Producer to purchase the above mentioned rights in the Work, which rights are more fully described in the Purchase Agreement, attached to the Option Agreement.

Date:_____

Signed:_____
(name of witness) (name of Writer)

EXHIBITS B & C

In some agreements a short form option and assignment will be attached to the agreement which is essentially a summary of the main agreement. The option agreement usually provides that the short form agreements will be signed at the same time as the main agreement. Once this is done then a short form agreement can be deposited at the US Copyright Office for recording and as evidence of the grant/assignment of rights.

Exhibit C (Short Form Copyright Assignment)

KNOW ALL MEN BY THESE PRESENTS that, in consideration of One Pound (£1.00) and other good and valuable consideration, receipt of which is hereby acknowledged, the undersigned _____, ('Assignor') do(es) hereby sell, grant, convey and assign unto _____ ('Assignee'), its successors, assigns and licensees forever, all right, title and interest including but not limited to the exclusive worldwide motion picture and allied rights of Assignor in and to that certain literary work to wit: that certain original screenplay written by entitled ('Literary Work'), and all drafts, revisions, arrangements, adaptations, dramatizations, translations, sequels and other versions of the Work which may heretofore have been written or which may hereafter be written with the sanction of Assignor.

Dated this day of 20___.

_____ ('Assignor')

AGREED TO:

_____ ('Assignee')

Acknowledgement

[*In the US use the following*]

STATE OF ⎫
        ⎬ ss:
COUNTY OF ⎭

On the _____ day _____ of 20__, before me personally came _____ to me known and known to be the individual described in and who executed the foregoing instrument, and he did duly acknowledge to me that he executed the same.
Notary Public

[*In the UK use the following*]

We hereby certify that this is a true copy of the original

_____

Solicitor Commissioner for Oaths (and name and address of firm).

5 Writer's agreement

The agreement between a writer and a producer is one of the cornerstones of the production process. The writer owns the copyright in what he writes and, in return for being paid, he either licenses or assigns to the producer the right to create a film or television programme and to exploit that film, television programme in any way that the producer sees fit.

The backbone of the development process is the writing of scripts and treatments. Producers will either commission a writer to write an original idea into a script or treatment or the producer may commission a writer to adapt an existing literary property such as a book. The basic writer's deals for a film or television programme are similar, however in the case of scripts commissioned for a television series there will be additional payments to be made which are known as 'residuals' or 'use fees' (see below). In agreements which are used for television, the basic fee usually only buys the right for one broadcast in the United Kingdom of the programme which is based on the script.

It is essential that users of this model contract are familiar with the present collective bargaining agreement which the Writers Guild of Great Britain (WGGB) has negotiated with the various broadcasters in the United Kingdom and members of the Producers Alliance for Cinema and Television (PACT). The following writer's agreement contains many of the essential clauses set out in the WGGB/PACT Agreement. See Appendix A for the address of PACT where a copy of the agreement can be obtained.

The WGGB/PACT Agreement sets out certain minimum fees to be paid for writing a script. Keep in mind that not all production companies or producers abide by the terms of the WGGB/PACT Agreement.

The WGGB/PACT Agreement contains provisions relating to payment for different types of productions classified as follows:

1 Feature films budgeted at two million pounds (£2,000,000) and over.
2 Feature films budgeted from two hundred and fifty thousand pound (£250,000) up to two million pounds (£2,000,000).
3 One-off television films budgeted at seven hundred and fifty thousand pounds (£750,000) and above.
4 Television series and serials with format provided by the producer.

The fees set out in the WGGB/PACT Agreement are minimum amounts and in many cases writers or their agents will require fees to be much greater than the minimum stated in the WGGB/PACT Agreement. Fees to be paid for the writing of scripts are in most cases split up into payment stages, i.e. for treatment, first draft and second draft, etc.

Under the WGGB/PACT Agreement, when payment is made for the writer's work, this is for basic exploitation of rights for the type of production for which the writer has performed services. For example, where a script has been written for a television series the fee set out in the WGGB/PACT Agreement only buys the right for one United Kingdom network transmission of the programme based on the writer's work. Any further uses will attract further payments which are known in the agreement as 'residuals' or 'use fees'. In the case of a feature film, the payments set out in the WGGB/PACT Agreement buy the right to show the film theatrically only. Other uses will also attract residuals or use fees.

In relation to copyright, the WGGB/PACT Agreement provides for copyright in each script to be transferred to the producer when each stage has been written but not until payment has been received by the writer. When dealing with American writers, if the writer is a guild member, producers may be faced with the provisions set out in the Writers Guild of America (WGA) collective bargaining agreement. The provisions of the WGA agreement can be fairly onerous and producers should try and obtain a copy of the agreement directly from the WGA in Los Angeles.

The following agreement is a writer's agreement for a screenplay in relation to a feature film. The agreement contains similar clauses which would be appropriate for other forms of exploitation of a writer's work (i.e. a television series).

Users should note that this agreement is only a guide and different circumstances will require specific clauses to reflect a Producer's agreement with a writer.

WRITER'S AGREEMENT

THIS AGREEMENT is made the   day of   200 .

BETWEEN:

(1)   [   ] of (the 'Producer' which expression shall be deemed to include its successors in title and assigns) and

(2)   [   ] of (the 'Writer' which expression shall be deemed to include the Writer's personal representatives)

The Producer wishes to engage the Writer to write a screenplay for a film and soundtrack provisionally entitled ['   '] which the Producer intends but does not undertake to produce and the Writer has agreed to do so for the consideration upon the terms and subject to the conditions hereinafter appearing.

NOW IT IS HEREBY AGREED as follows:

1   DEFINITIONS

(a) In this agreement the following words and expressions shall unless the context otherwise requires have the following meanings respectively:-
   (i)   ['the Source material'/'the Storyline']
   (ii)   'the Treatment'
   [a] [an original] treatment of approximately [   ] pages based upon   [the Source material/the Storyline]
   (iii) 'the First Draft Screenplay'
   an original first draft screenplay consisting of a continuing series of connected scenes of approximately [   ] minutes duration to be written in the English language and to be based upon [the Source Material/the Storyline/the Treatment] and provisionally entitled ['   ']

WRITER'S AGREEMENT: NOTES

PREAMBLE

The preamble should set out who the contract is between and make some reference to the name of the project which the writer is being engaged for.

1 DEFINITIONS

These definitions are for reference purposes only and should not be deemed to be exhaustive or complete. Users of this agreement should note that definitions can be anything the user would like them to be. The WGGB/PACT Agreement lists various definitions which are quite thorough and can also be utilized for this agreement. Producers should note that if a writer is not a member of the Writers Guild there is no reason to insert this definition and therefore any reference throughout the agreement should also be deleted. This also applies to the Screenwriting Credits Agreement.

(iv) 'the Second Draft Screenplay'
an original second draft of the First Draft Screenplay
if commissioned by the Producer hereunder

(v) 'Revisions'
the revisions to the First Draft Screenplay or the
Second Draft Screenplay (as the case may be) if
commissioned by the Producer hereunder

(vi) 'the Work'
[the Treatment] the First Draft Screenplay the
Second Draft Screenplay and the Revisions to the
extent commissioned by the Producer hereunder
together with all other material written or devised
by the Writer relating thereto

(vii) 'the Film'
the first class sound and colour theatrical feature
length film and soundtrack associated herewith to
be recorded originally in the English language
tentatively entitled ['   '] which the Producer
proposes but does not undertake to produce based
upon the Work

(viii) 'the Writers Guild Agreement'
the present agreement operating and made
between the Writers Guild of Great Britain (1) and
the Producers Alliance for Cinema and Television
(PACT) and any modification thereto

(ix) 'the Screenwriting Credits Agreement'
the agreement operating on and from the 1st May
1974 made between the British Film and Television
Producers Association (formerly the Film
Production Association of Great Britain) (1) and the
Writers Guild of Great Britain (2)

(x) ['Net Profits'/'Producer's Profits'
shall have the meaning ascribed thereto in
Schedule 4 to this agreement].

(b) Unless the context otherwise requires the words and
expressions used herein shall have the same meanings
as are assigned to them by the Copyright Designs and
Patents Act 1988.

2 ENGAGEMENT

The Producer hereby engages the Writer and the Writer hereby agrees to render the Writer's services upon the terms and conditions of this agreement to write [the Treatment] [the First Draft Screenplay] [and] [the Revisions thereto] and to the extent commissioned by the Producer hereunder [the First Draft Screenplay] [the Revisions thereto] [the Second Draft Screenplay] [and] [the Revisions thereto]

3 TERM OF ENGAGEMENT

(a) The Producer shall be entitled to the exclusive services of the Writer during the period for the delivery of [the Treatment][the First Draft Screenplay] [the Revisions thereto] [and] [the Second Draft Screenplay].

(b) The Producer shall be entitled to the services of the Writer on a ['first/second call'] basis during the remaining periods of delivery specified herein but so that the Writer hereby warrants that the Writer has no commitments and shall not make or accept any professional or other commitments or undertake any other activities whereby the Writer shall be prevented from providing the Writer's full services hereunder during the said remaining periods of delivery.

(c) The Producer shall also be entitled to make use of the services of the Writer upon reasonable notice if so required by the Producer (subject to the Writer's prior professional commitments notified to the Producer in advance) during the period of principal photography of the Film and during the six (6) weeks immediately prior thereto without additional remuneration in order that the Writer may make such further minor adaptations and amendments to the Work as may reasonably be required by the Producer or by the individual director or producer of the Film.

2 ENGAGEMENT

This clause sets out what the writer has been hired to do (i.e. to write a first draft screenplay or revisions to that screenplay etc.). Producers and writers must be absolutely clear as to what is expected from each other. If a writer is to write only a first draft script then that is all that should be stated, otherwise there may be a dispute regarding payments for revisions, second drafts, etc.

3 TERM OF ENGAGEMENT

In some circumstances a production company may want the exclusive services of the writer or require him/her to be available on a first or second call basis in order that the various stages of writing can be delivered. This means that the writer cannot undertake any other writing work until his/her engagement with the Producer is finished. Producers may also require that the writer be available immediately prior to the production of the film in case there are changes or re-writes of the script to be made.

Producers should insist that the writer is on an exclusive first call basis for a certain period of time prior to the start of principal photography. In some circumstances, the producer will negotiate the writer's agreement so that whenever principal photography is about to begin the writer must be available on an exclusive basis. Writers should be aware that they may have other writing work at the time of principal photography involving a previous writing job and therefore writers may want to word the contract so that their availability is subject to any prior commitments they may have. Producers should try and define what exclusive means so that the writer cannot try and find an excuse not to work on the script.

4 WRITER'S SERVICES

(a) The Writer hereby warrants to and undertakes with the Producer that the Writer shall perform the Writer's services hereunder as where and when required by the Producer diligently, willingly, conscientiously and to the best of the Writer's artistic and creative skill and technical ability and in any manner which may be required by the Producer in consultation or collaboration with such persons as the Producer shall from time to time designate and subject to the other provisions of this agreement shall:–

   (i)   attend meetings and conferences at the Producer's offices studios or elsewhere as the Producer shall reasonably require for the planning and preparation of the Film and for instruction and consultations connected therewith

   (ii)   carry out adequate research and preparation for the Work

   (iii)   make incidental and minor revisions to the Work as the Producer shall reasonably require.

(b) The Writer shall from time to time if so requested by the Producer deliver to the Producer copies of such parts of the Work as shall have been written at the time of such request and shall if so requested by the Producer or in any event upon completion of the Writer's services hereunder or upon termination of this agreement (whichever shall be earlier) deliver the Work [in triplicate] typewritten and securely bound and shall further deliver to the Producer all documents manuscripts drafts and copies thereof and all notes and other papers relating to the Work in the power, possession or control of the Writer.

5 DELIVERY

The Writer shall deliver the Work in full to the Producer in accordance with the provisions of Schedule 1 to this

4 WRITER'S SERVICES

Producers should insist that the writer attend meetings with studios and prospective financiers. Sometimes if a potential financier meets the writer and director of a proposed project, this may make the difference between passing on the project or a commitment to finance it.

5 DELIVERY

Producers will want writers to ensure that they can deliver written materials according to the dates set out in Schedule 1 of the agreement and time shall be of the essence save that the Producer at its discretion may extend the time for delivery aforesaid without prejudice to its rights hereunder whereupon time for delivery within the extended period shall become of the essence.

6 REMUNERATION

(a) Subject to the provisions of this agreement and to the due compliance by the Writer with the Writer's obligations and undertakings hereunder the Producer shall as remuneration and as full consideration for all services rendered and for all rights granted to the Producer hereunder pay or procure to be paid to the Writer the sums specified in Schedule 2 to this agreement at the times and in the manner therein provided.

(b) All payments made to the Writer in excess of any minimum fees specified in the Writers Guild Agreement shall to the extent permitted by such agreement be deemed to have been made on account of and as prepayment of use fees payable to the Writer pursuant thereto and no further sums shall be or become payable to the Writer thereunder until such time as the said prepayments shall have been fully exhausted.

(c) All payments pursuant to sub-clause (1) of this clause shall be exclusive of Value Added Tax and if and to the extent only that Value Added Tax is or becomes payable on any such payment the Writer will render to the Producer a Value Added Tax invoice in respect thereof upon receipt of which the Producer will make payment to the Writer of the amount thereby shown to be due.

(d) [The Writer hereby authorizes the Producer and the Producer hereby agrees to deduct from the contracted payment to the Writer such sum as shall equal [%] of that contracted payment and the Producer agrees to forward the same to the Writers Guild of Great Britain or its appointed agent for the credit of the Writer as a

agreement. If they cannot then they may be in breach of contract. Producers will also find that certain writers work better when there is a deadline for delivery of their work.

6 REMUNERATION

Payment is referred to in Schedule 2 of this agreement. Schedule 2 is in compliance with the WGGB/PACT Agreement and sets out how payment is to be made.

Producers and writers who are new to the film and television business should be aware that the Writers Guilds of Great Britain and America are very powerful unions and generally look after their members. In the event that a producer fails to pay a writer, the writer has several options to collect monies due. Firstly, in most circumstances the copyright from the products of the writer's work will not be assigned to the producer for non-payment of writer's fees. A producer who does not pay the writer will technically not own a script or screenplay and therefore it is unlikely that a distributor or broadcaster would ever purchase a finished programme where there is a dispute over ownership between the writer and producer.

Secondly, the relevant Writers Guild may blacklist a producer or production company which may create difficulties for the producer in having a film distributed or a programme broadcast. Most broadcasters are signatories to the various guilds and will comply with any blacklisting or sanction imposed by the union.

In the event that a writer is not a member of the Writers Guild then the writer's only recourse may be to pursue the matter in the courts.

contribution to the Writers Guild Pension Fund under the provisions of the Writers Guild Agreement].

(e) The Writer hereby authorizes the Producer to deduct and withhold from any and all compensation payable to the Writer hereunder all deductions required by any present or future law of any country wherein the Writer performs services hereunder or the country of residence of any party hereto requiring the withholding or deducting of compensation. [In the event that the Producer does not make such withholdings or deductions the Writer shall pay any and all taxes and other charges payable on account of such compensation and the Writer hereby indemnifies the Producer and agrees to keep the Producer fully and effectually indemnified from and against any liability or expense in connection therewith.]

(f) In the event that the Producer makes any payment or incurs any charge at the Writer's request for the Writer's account or the Writer incurs any charges with the Producer the Producer shall have the right and the Writer hereby authorizes the Producer to recoup any and all such payments or charges by deducting and withholding any aggregate amount thereof from any compensation then or thereafter payable to the Writer hereunder. This provision shall not be construed to limit or exclude any other rights of credit or recovery or any other remedies which the Producer may have. Nothing herein contained shall obligate the Producer to make any such payments or incur any such charge or permit the writer to incur any such charges.

7 EXPENSES AND TRANSPORTATION

(a) Whenever the Writer is required by the Producer to render services hereunder at a place outside a radius of thirty miles from the Writer's normal place of work, the Producer shall pay or reimburse the Writer the cost of transportation and all reasonable hotel and subsistence

7   EXPENSES AND TRANSPORTATION

Producers sometimes try and negotiate an all inclusive deal with writers which puts the responsibility for expenses on the writer. From a writer's point of view this is not usually acceptable and they will try and get as much as possible from the producer.

expenses wholly, exclusively and properly incurred in connection with the rendering of the Writer's services hereunder subject to the prior [written] approval of the Producer [provided that where the Writer is required by the Producer to travel by air then, subject to the Producer having prior advice of the Writer's flight, the Producer shall take out and pay for an insurance policy against the risk of personal injury or death suffered by the Writer in the course of such air travel according to the then current insurance provisions prevailing with all recognized trade unions within the industry].

OR

(a) Whenever the Writer is required by the Producer to render services hereunder at a place outside a radius of thirty miles from the Writer's normal place of work, the Producer shall pay to the Writer in respect of all living expenses of the Writer (which shall be deemed to [exclude hotel accommodation but to] include the cost of meals [bar, telephone and room service charges and all other expenses] [and hotel accommodation]) the sum of [   ]per [day/week] [payable at the option of the Producer in [pounds sterling] or [local currency] and pro rated for any part of a week].

(b) [Whenever the Writer is required by the Producer to render services hereunder at a place outside a radius of thirty miles from the Writer's normal place of work, the Producer shall at its own expense provide the Writer with [first class] [bed and breakfast] [reasonable] hotel accommodation [which shall [otherwise] be exclusive of bar, telephone and room service charges].

(c) [Whenever the Producer requires the Writer to render services hereunder at a place outside a radius of thirty miles from the Writer's normal place of work, the Producer shall at its own expense provide the writer with [first class (where available but not Concorde)/club class] return trip air transportation [for the Writer and [   ]] from to and from any place or places in

[   ] at which the Writer may be required to render the Writer's services hereunder].

(d) The Producer shall provide the Writer with [car transportation] [a car and driver for the Writer's exclusive use] to convey the Writer to and from the Writer's place of overnight residence to the studios offices or locations (as the case may be) at which and whenever the Writer is required to render the services hereunder [during the principal photography of the Film].

8 FURTHER DRAFTS AND REVISIONS

The Producer may in its sole discretion require the Writer and/or commission any other writer or writers (either alone or in collaboration with the Writer) to write:–

(a) [the First Draft Screenplay]
(b) [the Revisions to the First Draft Screenplay]
(c) [the Second Draft Screenplay]
(d) [the Revisions to the Second Draft Screenplay]

and in the event that the Writer shall be required and so provides those services to the Producer the same shall be delivered in accordance with the provisions of Schedule 1 hereto for the remuneration specified in Schedule 2 hereto.

9 CREDIT

(a) Subject to the Writer substantially rendering all the services required of the Writer hereunder and to the Film being wholly or substantially based upon the Work the Producer shall accord the Writer credit in accordance with the terms of the Screenwriting Credits Agreement:–
    (i)   on the negative and all positive copies of the Film made by or to the order of the Producer and (b) in all major paid advertising and paid publicity

8 FURTHER DRAFTS AND REVISIONS

This is an optional clause which sometimes may be difficult for a well known writer to agree upon. A well known or established writer may require that in order to proceed with a first draft no other individual may be able to work on that first draft. The first writer may insist that if a new writer is brought on, then their first draft must be completely dropped and a new first draft written.

Producers should realize that bringing on new writers can lead to disputes over credits as well as payment unless specific provisions clarify how this can be accomplished. If another writer is hired to adapt or change the first writer's work then producers may still have to pay the first writer even though very little of the first writer's work has been used. It is important that the agreement allows a reduction in payment if the first writer's work is not used in its entirety.

9 CREDIT

A writer who is engaged by a producer or production company who is a signatory to the WGGB/PACT Agreement shall be accorded such credit as he is entitled to under the terms of the Screen Writing Credits Agreement made in 1974 between the Writers Guild and the BFPA, which was the predecessor of PACT. This agreement sets out the terms in which credit is to be given and what credits a writer is entitled to in various circumstances. This clause is quite lengthy and it may be more

relating to the Film issued by or under the direct control of the Producer subject to the provisions of sub-clause (3) of this clause.

(b) In the event that the Producer shall commission another writer or writers to write the Work or any part thereof or otherwise contribute to the Film the Writer shall be accorded such credit on the negative and on all positive copies of the Film made by or to the order of the Producer as shall in the absence of agreement between the Producer and the Writer be determined by the President for the time being of the Writers Guild of Great Britain (or such person as may be nominated by him) who shall act as an expert and not as an arbitrator and whose decision shall be final and binding upon the Producer and the Writer

(c) The provisions of this clause shall not apply to exploitation or advertising falling within the following categories:–

(i) 'group' 'list' 'special' or so-called 'teaser' advertising pre-release publicity or exploitation or

(ii) any exploitation publication or fictionalization of the story screenplay or other literary or musical material upon which the Film is based or

(iii) by-products of any kind (including but not limited to sheet music and Gramophone records) or

(iv) 'trailer' or other advertising on the screen or radio or television or

(v) institutional or other advertising or publicity not relating primarily to the Film or

(vi) advertising of ten column inches or less or

(vii) advertising, or publicity material in narrative form or

(viii) special advertising publicity or exploitation of the Film relating to any member or members of the cast, the author, director, producer or other personnel concerned in its production or to academy awards or prizes or similar matters

(ix) 'roller credits' at the end of the Film

convenient to state in the writer's contract that 'credit shall be given in accordance with the Screen Writing Credits Agreement or any subsequent amendments'. Because credits can be an area for dispute it is essential that any dispute over credits will be referred immediately to the president for the time being of the Writers Guild of Great Britain or such person as may be nominated by him and whose decision will be final. Producers should closely observe credits in films which state the following:-

Written by _____,

Story by _____,

Based on a book by _____

This is a classic example of more than one writer working on a film and in many cases the final product may not be very good.

(ANY and ALL of which said items included in paragraphs to (i) inclusive may be issued without mentioning the name of the Writer therein [unless the director is mentioned therein and the Writer receives sole screen credit as the Writer of the Work under the Screenwriting Credits Agreement]).

(d) No casual or inadvertent failure by the Producer to comply with the provisions of this clause and no failure of persons other than the Producer to comply therewith or with their contracts with the Producer shall constitute a breach of this agreement by the Producer. The rights and remedies of the Writer in the event of a breach of this clause by the Producer shall be limited to the Writer's rights (if any) to recover damages in an action at law and in no event shall the Writer be entitled by reason of any such breach to enjoin or restrain the distribution, exhibition, advertising or exploitation of the Film.

(e) The Producer shall use [all reasonable/its best] endeavours to procure that the distributors of the Film accord to the Writer credit in accordance with the provisions of this clause (except as specified in sub-clause (2) of this clause) on all prints of and paid advertising for the Film issued by such distributors provided that the Producer shall not be liable for the neglect or default of any such distributor so long as the Producer shall have notified the distributors of the credit to which the Writer is entitled.

(f) [In the event of a failure by any distributor to accord credit to the Writer as aforesaid the Producer shall upon notice from the Writer use [all reasonable/its best] endeavours (short of incurring legal [or other material] expenses) to remedy such failure.]

10 RIGHTS AND CONSENTS

(a) The Writer with full title guarantee hereby assigns to the Producer by way of assignment of present and future

10 RIGHTS AND CONSENTS

(a) In an ideal world, a producer will want the writer to assign all
of his/her rights in a project which they have written. From

copyright the entire copyright and all other right, title and interest of whatsoever nature whether vested or contingent in and to the Work and in all other products of the services of the Writer hereunder including without limitation remake, sequel, serial, series, reissue, publishing, novelization and merchandising rights and all subsidiary and ancillary rights TO HOLD the same unto the Company absolutely throughout the universe (with full title guarantee) for the full period of copyright and all renewals and extensions thereof and thereafter (insofar as the Writer is able to do so) in perpetuity.

(b) The Writer hereby grants to the Producer the right at all times hereafter to use and authorize others to use:-

(i)   the Writer's name, photographs and other reproductions of the Writer's physical likeness [and recordings of the Writer's voice] and the autograph and biography of the Writer in whole or in part in connection with the advertisement, publicity, exhibition and commercial exploitation of the Film

(ii) the Writer's name and photographs of the Writer [and recordings of the Writer's voice] for the purposes of the public exhibition of the Film in association with the advertisement, publicity and commercial exploitation of any other commodities PROVIDED ALWAYS that (except with the Writer's prior written consent) the Writer's name or photograph is not directly or indirectly used to suggest that the Writer personally uses or recommends any such other commodities (but so that the Writer may be shown to recommend the Film per se).

(c) The Producer shall be entitled to use and to authorize others to use the Work or any part or parts thereof in such manner as the Producer shall in its sole discretion think fit including without limitation the right to make changes, alterations, substitutions and additions thereto and

the writer's perspective it is advisable for them to try and hold back as many rights as possible. If a writer is well known and is in a powerful position, he or she may try and only license specific rights to the producer and retain all other rights. For example, the writer may only license basic film or television rights in the script. In these circumstances the producer will try and negotiate the sharing of income from any exploitation by the writer of any of the rights which are held back. The producer can justify the sharing of incomes from further exploitation since the only reason that these rights will be able to be exploited is if the film or television series is a success. If a writer is a well known author who has produced best selling books then they will be in a position to dictate their terms to a producer.

(b) This clause is essential, especially in the United States where the mere identification of a real person whether it is deliberate or unintentional may lead to the possibility of legal action for the breach of rights of privacy and/or publicity. In the United Kingdom, the only claim that an individual would have if their voice or physical likeness has been reproduced would be if such portrayal is defamatory. Writers should always try and negotiate that their name, photograph or likeness can only be used with their prior written consent and approval.

deletions therefrom and adaptations, rearrangements and translations thereof into any and all languages.

(d) The Writer recognizing the needs of film and television production by granting the absolute and unlimited right to use the Work for all purposes granted hereunder in any manner the Producer may in its discretion think fit, hereby waives the benefits of any provision of law known as moral rights of authors or the 'droit moral' or any similar law in any country of the universe and hereby agrees not to institute, support, maintain or permit any action or lawsuit on the ground that any film and soundtrack or any other version of the Work produced and/or exploited by the Producer in any way constitutes an infringement of any moral rights or 'droit moral' of the Writer or is in any way a defamation or mutilation of the Work or contains unauthorized variations, alterations, adaptations, modifications, changes or translations.

(e) The Writer hereby irrevocably waives any right to repurchase the rights in the Work hereby assigned and granted notwithstanding the fact that the Producer shall not have commenced principal photography of the Film within two (2) years from the date of acceptance by the Producer of the First Draft Screenplay.

11   FURTHER ASSURANCE

The Writer hereby undertakes to and covenants with the Producer to do all such further acts and execute all such further documents and instruments (including without

(d) See Option and Literary Purchase Agreement, Exhibit A, Note 3 regarding moral rights.

(e) WRITERS TURNAROUND – The WGGB/PACT agreement states that the writer shall have the right to buy back the original script on payment of 50 per cent of the sums received if principal photography has not commenced within two years of delivery of the last material for which the writer had been commissioned. Where the script has not progressed beyond the first draft and/or another writer has been engaged, any subsequent writer would not benefit under the provisions of the clause set out in the agreement. In this agreement this is an optional clause whereby the writer waives any right under the WGGB/PACT Agreement to re-purchase these rights. It is always advisable for producers to include this clause since it may take more than two years to finance a project.

11 FURTHER ASSURANCE

See Option and Literary Purchase Agreement, Exhibit A Note 18.

limitation the execution of the short form assignment in the form set out in Schedule 3 to this agreement which the Producer shall have the right to forward to the United States Copyright Office for recording) as the Producer may from time to time require to vest in or further assure to the Producer the rights herein expressed to be granted and for the protection and enforcement of the same [and in the event of the Writer failing to do so within seven (7) days of receiving written notice from the Producer requesting the same the Producer shall be entitled to execute such documents and instruments in the name and on behalf of the Writer as the Writer's duly authorized attorney [in accordance with the Deed of Power of Attorney annexed hereto] and the Writer hereby agrees to execute and deliver the same to the Producer concurrently with the completion of this agreement/and this appointment shall be deemed to be a power coupled with an interest and shall be irrevocable].

12 WARRANTIES

The Writer hereby warrants to and undertakes with the Producer as follows:–

(a) that the Writer will be the first and sole author of the Work which will be wholly original to the Writer and will not be copied, adapted or reproduced from any literary, dramatic, artistic, musical or other work (except as to matters within the public domain and to any material or ideas provided by the Producer) and nothing contained in the Work nor any exercise by the Producer of any of the rights in the Work herein expressed to be assigned will infringe or violate the rights of any person, firm or Producer including without limitation any rights of copyright or trademarks or privacy or publicity or confidentiality or any other common law or statutory rights whatsoever.

(b) that the Writer will be the sole legal and beneficial owner with full title guarantee free from encumbrances

12 WARRANTIES

(a) Writers should be aware that a producer will always ask for a
warranty regarding libel and slander. In the United Kingdom
defamation is a general term which covers both libel and
slander. Libel is in relation to a defamation which is usually in
a written or recorded form and of a permanent nature.
Slander is in relation to a spoken defamation.

A producer will want to ensure that they are protected from
any defamatory statement made by the writer regarding
people written about in a film or television script. If a
defamatory statement is made regarding an individual then
that individual will have the right to take civil legal action for
an injunction or damages or both against the person making
the statement. In libel actions, not only is the person who
made the original statement exposed, but everyone who is

171

of the copyright and all like rights in the Work
throughout the universe.

(c) that the Writer has the right to enter into this
agreement and to assign and grant the rights herein
expressed to be assigned and granted and has not
previously assigned or granted or in any way
encumbered the same so as to derogate from the grant
hereunder and shall not hereafter do so.

legally responsible for making the statement can also be sued. For example, if a producer creates a programme, then not only will the writer and the producer be responsible but the broadcaster of that programme or film may also be liable.

Writers should be aware that for a statement to be defamatory, the statement must damage the reputation of the person about whom it is made in the eyes of 'right thinking people'.

Note that if a statement is true then this is a defence against any defamation claim.

A producer who has acquired the rights to a controversial book or play should consult with lawyers to help decide whether the material may be defamatory.

It is also advisable for producers to have their film or television scripts vetted by a lawyer.

Writers should be aware that the cost of defending a defamation action is immense. Writers should be aware that it is possible to be sued for defamation even where they have inadvertently referred to an event or individual who does not exist. For example, if a fictional character is created and shown in circumstances where a real person could still be identified, then this may lead to a defamation action. Writers should therefore take reasonable care to make sure that there is no unintentional defamation.

Producers should note that under an errors and omissions insurance policy they may be able to claim the cost of defending a defamation action.

Producers who create docu-dramas or movies of the week (which may be dramatizations of real events or individuals) should if at all possible try and persuade those individuals portrayed to sign a release.

Writers and producers should be aware that it is an offence to publish obscene materials. Under English law, obscenity is

(d) that the Writer is and throughout the provision of the Writer's services hereunder will remain a 'qualified person' within the meaning of the Copyright Designs and Patents Act 1988 [and a British subject ordinarily resident in the United Kingdom] [and resident in the United Kingdom although not a British subject].

(e) that copyright in the Work will subsist or may be acquired in all countries of the world whose laws provide for copyright protection and that the Writer will not at any time hereafter do or omit to do or authorize anything in relation to the Work whereby the subsistence of copyright therein or any part of such copyright may be lost destroyed or otherwise impaired or be incapable of being obtained and that the Writer will do all in the Writer's power to obtain and/or maintain the copyright in the Work in each country of the world where such rights are capable of being obtained or maintained for the full period thereof including all renewals and extensions thereof.

(f) that the Work upon delivery will not have been published in any country of the world.

(g) that [to the best of the Writer's knowledge and belief after having made all reasonable enquiries] the Work will not contain defamatory or obscene matter of any kind.

(h) that the Writer [is and shall throughout this engagement remain a member in goodstanding/will as soon as reasonably possible apply to become a Member] of the Writers Guild of Great Britain].

defined as: 'if its effect is, taken as a whole, such as to tend to deprave and corrupt the persons who are likely to read, see or hear the matter contained or embodied in it'. Writers and producers should realize that to publish obscene material is a criminal offence under the Obscene Publications Act. This Act applies to feature films and television programmes. Producers should be aware of all the above issues, since they may effect the eventual classification of a film both, in cinemas and with video distributors.

(d) Under section 154 (1) of the Copyright Designs and Patents Act 1988, a work qualifies for protection if its author is a human being who:–

   (i)   is a British citizen or enjoys one to five different categories of second class status which make him British without being a citizen; or

   (ii) lives or is domiciled in the United Kingdom.

   If the author is a body incorporated under British law, its works will also qualify for copyright protection.

   Where work is jointly authored by two or more authors, but all of whom are qualified under section 154, the work will still enjoy copyright protection.

   In some circumstances an author may not be qualified under the Act. However, this does not mean they are not protected under the Act. The answer lies in section 159 of the Act which explains that protection can still be applied to countries to which it does not extend. The effect of this is that a parliamentary order in counsel can declare that another country's authors and published works, should be treated in the United Kingdom just as if they were authors of work qualified under UK law. In this way, the UK has applied its copyright protection to most of the countries of the world. This nationality treatment is required under the two major copyright conventions which the UK is a party; The Berne Convention and The Universal Copyright Convention.

(i) that the Writer will comply with all rules and regulations for the time being in force at any studios or other places at which the Writer is required to render services hereunder.

13 GENERAL RESTRICTIONS

The Writer shall not:–
(a) order goods or incur any liability on the Producer's behalf or in any way pledge the Producer's credit or hold [himself/herself] out as being entitled to do so
(b) without the prior written consent of the Producer at any time hereafter either personally or by means of press or publicity or advertising agents or agencies make any statement or disclosure or supply any information or photographs to any person firm or corporate body (other than the Writer's agents and professional advisers) or to the public relating to any matter arising hereunder or to the general affairs of the Producer coming within the Writer's knowledge by reason of the rendering of the services of the Writer hereunder or otherwise howsoever
(c) at any time hereafter do or say anything detrimental to the Film and in the event that the Writer shall commit a breach of the provisions of this sub-clause during the term of this agreement the Producer may without prejudice to the Producer's accrued rights within 28 days after becoming aware of such conduct by written notice to the Writer determine the Writer's engagement hereunder or cancel its obligations to accord the Writer credit thereafter (as the case may be).

14 DISABILITY AND DEFAULT

(a) In the event that the Writer shall for whatever reason fail, refuse or neglect to render the Writer's services hereunder or in the event that the Writer shall fail, refuse or neglect to keep or perform any covenant or condition of this agreement after the Producer shall

13   GENERAL RESTRICTIONS

See Option and Literary Purchase Agreement, Exhibit A,
Note 16.

14   DISABILITY AND DEFAULT

have given written notice to the Writer requiring the same and such failure, refusal or neglect shall continue for a period of fourteen (14) days the Producer shall be entitled at any time during the further continuance of such failure, refusal or neglect to terminate this agreement without prejudice to such rights which shall have accrued to either party hereunder at the time of such termination and further without prejudice to any claim the Producer may have for damages arising from such failure, refusal or neglect.

(b) In the event of a termination of this agreement for whatever reason the rights hereby assigned and granted to the Producer in and to the Work and the products of the Writer's services hereunder shall remain vested in the Producer.

(c) In the event that this agreement shall be terminated hereunder by reason of the disability of the Writer to perform any covenant or condition of this agreement the Writer shall be entitled to receive such sums as shall have accrued due at the date of such payment together with such sums on account of a share of [Net Profits/Producer's Profits] as shall be due and payable to the Writer pursuant to Clause (3) of Schedule 2 to this agreement.

(d) For the purposes of this clause 'disability' shall mean any physical or mental illness, injury or other physical or mental impairment or incapacity which materially detracts from the Writer's ability to perform the Writer's services hereunder and so that the Writer undertakes that the Writer shall at the Producer's request and

(b) Producers will certainly want to have such a clause in their contracts with writers. From a writer's viewpoint the clause is fairly draconian since it protects the producer in the event that the writer is unable to perform his/her services under the contract. The reasoning for such a harsh clause is that the producer will want to utilize the products of the writer's services without any problems from the original writer. This will enable the producer to hire a new writer to continue on with an unfinished script. Writers may wish to include a proviso to this clause which enables them to repay any monies paid by the producer to the writer in order that the writer will be able to keep the work which they have produced.

expense submit to an examination by such physician as the Producer may designate in the event of any claim that such a disability exists.

15 LIABILITY EXCLUSIONS

(a) The Producer shall not be liable to the Writer or to the personal representatives of the Writer for
  (i) any loss or damage howsoever and by whomsoever caused of or to the Writer's property sustained at or whilst in transit to or from places at which the Writer shall render the Writer's services hereunder
  (ii) (to the extent permitted by law) any personal injury, ailment or death arising out of or in the course of the Writer's engagement hereunder except to such extent if at all as such injury, ailment or death is caused by the Producer's negligence and/or the Producer may be able to enforce a claim against a third party or under any policy of insurance effected by the Producer (and in this regard the Producer undertakes to effect all customary third party liability insurance).
(b) Notwithstanding and irrespective of any advertisement or announcement which may hereafter be published, nothing in this agreement contained shall be construed as to impose upon the Producer any obligation to make use of the services of the Writer or of the Work or any part or parts thereof and the Producer shall not be liable to the writer for or in respect of loss of publicity, advertisement, reputation or the like due to the Producer's failure to base the Film in whole or in part on the Work.

16 INDEMNITY

The Writer hereby indemnifies and agrees to keep the Producer fully and effectually indemnified from and against any and all losses, costs, actions, proceedings, claims,

16   INDEMNITY

Most commercial contracts provide that either one party
indemnifies the other or both parties will indemnify each other.
Parties to an agreement will require that the other party agrees to

damages, expenses (including reasonable legal costs and expenses) or liabilities suffered or incurred directly or indirectly by the Producer in consequence of any breach, non-performance or non-observance by the Writer of any of the agreements, conditions, obligations, representations, warranties and undertakings on the part of the Writer contained in this agreement. The Writer hereby expressly acknowledges that this indemnity shall survive the completion of the Writer's services hereunder [Provided that in any case in which a defence of innocent defamation is successfully established under the Defamation Act 1952 the Writer's liability to the Producer hereunder shall not exceed the Writer's remuneration paid hereunder].

17 INJUNCTIVE RELIEF

It is understood and agreed that a breach by the Writer of any of the material provisions of this agreement will or may

give an indemnity against all losses which may arise as a result of the other parties breach of contract. This means that the indemnifying party agrees that if they are in breach of contract, they will pay damages, which will cover all of the losses and damages which the injured party may suffer as a result of that breach.

Writers should realize that indemnities are an essential term for producers especially when they must agree terms with financiers or distributors. When a producer makes an agreement with a financier or distributor in relation to a film or television programme the producer will often assign the benefit of their contracts.

This means that the producer is able to transfer the benefit of the contract but cannot transfer his obligations. Although the producer can require the person to whom he has transferred the benefit to perform these obligations, the producer should still be careful, since whoever he has transferred the benefit of the contract to, does not perform certain obligations, then the producer will be liable for any unfulfilled obligations.

Producers should note, that when transferring the benefit of a contract to another party, they receive a specific warranty that the person taking the benefit of the contract will be responsible for any of their obligations. Having assigned the contract, the producer may no longer have the power to perform certain obligations under the contract. Therefore, if a breach occurs, the producer will still be liable, but may have some remedy against a third party who is ultimately responsible for such obligations.

A producer should insist that any third party taking the benefit of a contract indemnifies the producer from all losses suffered by the producer if his/her obligations to other parties are not observed.

17 INJUNCTIVE RELIEF

An injunction is a legal remedy which is made by way of a court order to prevent a defendant in a court action from stopping

cause the Producer irreparable injury and damage and the Writer expressly agrees that the Producer shall be entitled to injunctive or other equitable relief to prevent a breach of this agreement by the Writer. Resort to such equitable relief shall not be construed as a waiver of any other rights or remedies which the Producer may have for damages or otherwise.

18 NO WAIVER

No waiver by either party hereto of any breach of any of the terms or conditions of this agreement in a particular instance shall be deemed or construed to be a waiver of any preceding or succeeding breach of the same or any other terms or conditions. All rights, remedies, undertakings and obligations contained in this agreement shall be cumulative and none of them shall be in limitation of any other rights, remedies, undertakings or obligations of either party.

19 NO PARTNERSHIP

Nothing herein contained shall be construed or deemed to constitute a partnership or joint venture between the parties hereto and save as expressly herein provided no party shall hold itself out as the agent of the other.

20 PARTIAL NON-ENFORCEABILITY

If any clause or any part of this agreement or the application thereof to either party shall for any reason be

whatever it was which caused a plaintiff to sue the defendant in the first place. What is also known as injunctive relief, may be an order requiring the defendant to do something which should have been done in the first place. Injunctions are either final or interim in the form of relief that they create. The final injunction comes at the end of a court case when the court has decided that the defendant must do something which should have been done or stop doing something which should not have been done. Alternatively, the plaintiff in an action may seek an interim injunction which is usually a temporary measure aimed at reducing any potential damage which the defendant may cause at the outset of any proceedings. Writers and producers should note that obtaining an injunction is an expensive process and therefore the high cost may be a deterrent to anyone who may wish to apply for such a remedy.

18 NO WAIVER

See Option and Literary Purchase Agreement Exhibit A Note 21 (c).

adjudged by any court or other legal authority of competent jurisdiction to be invalid such judgment shall not affect the remainder of this agreement which shall continue in full force and effect.

21 NOTICES

Any notices required to be given under the provisions of this agreement shall be in writing and shall be deemed to have been duly served if hand delivered or sent by telex, facsimile or within the United Kingdom by first class registered or recorded delivery or outside the United Kingdom by registered airmail correctly addressed to the relevant party's address as specified in this agreement or at such other address as either party may hereafter designate from time to time in accordance with this clause.

22 AGENT

The Writer hereby authorizes and requests the Producer to pay all monies due to the Writer hereunder [other than expenses pursuant to Clause 7 hereof] to the Writer's duly authorized agent [of   ] whose receipt therefor shall afford the Producer a good and valid discharge for the monies so paid.

23 RIGHTS TO ASSIGN

The Producer shall be entitled to [lend the Writer's services hereunder to any third party producing the Film if other than the Producer and to] assign and charge the benefit of this agreement either in whole or in part to any third party but no such assignment shall relieve the Producer of any of its obligations to the Writer hereunder. [The Producer shall obtain an undertaking from any such assignee, to assume

23 RIGHTS TO ASSIGN

Producers and writers should be aware that under the
Screenwriting Credits Agreement which sets out credit provisions
and forms the basis of the Writers Guild of Great Britain's
Agreement, that if a producer enters into any contractual dealing
with any work for which a writer is or may become entitled to a
credit, then under the terms of the Screenwriting Credits
Agreement the producer must obtain an undertaking from the

and perform all the obligations of the Producer under the provisions of the Screenwriting Credits Agreement in relation to the production and distribution of the Film or any other film and soundtrack associated therewith based upon the Work.]

24 WRITERS GUILD

Save where varied or otherwise inconsistent with the provisions herewith the provisions of the Writers Guild Agreement and the Screenwriting Credits Agreement shall be deemed to be incorporated herein.

25 ENTIRE AGREEMENT

This agreement (including the schedules hereto which are incorporated herein by reference) replaces, supersedes and cancels all previous arrangements, understandings, representations or agreements between the parties hereto either oral or written with respect to the subject matter hereof and expresses and constitutes the entire agreement between the Producer and the Writer with reference to the terms and conditions of the engagement of the Writer in connection with the Work and no variation of any of the terms or conditions hereof may be made unless such variation is agreed in writing and signed by both of the parties hereto.

26 GOVERNING LAW

This agreement shall be construed and performed in all respects in accordance with and shall be governed by English Law and the parties irrevocably submit to the jurisdiction of the English Courts [The Writer hereby irrevocably appoints [of   England] to accept service of all proceedings hereunder].

other contracting party or parties to assume and perform all the obligations of the producer in relation to the production and/or distribution of any film or television programme based on the writer's work. A copy of the Screenwriting Credits Agreement can be obtained from The Writers Guild of Great Britain.

24 WRITERS GUILD

Producers should note that a writer's agreement does not necessarily have to make reference to the Writers' Guild or other Union agreements. It is possible to have a non-union agreement with a non-union writer, however, by not conforming with specific collective bargaining agreements, this could affect a sale of the film or programme to a broadcaster or distributor.

27 CLAUSE HEADINGS

The clause headings in this agreement are for the convenience of the parties only and shall not limit govern or otherwise affect its interpretation in any way.

AS WITNESS the hands of the Writer and of a duly authorized representative of the Producer the day, month and year first above written

SIGNED by the Writer
in the presence of:

SIGNED by
(a duly authorized representative)
for and on behalf of
the Producer in the presence of:

SCHEDULE 1 – DELIVERY OF THE WORK

(1) The Work shall be delivered to the Producer at the
address mentioned in this agreement or any such other
address as may be notified to the Writer at the following
times:
  (a) [the Treatment as soon as reasonably practicable
      and in any event not later than (   )]
  (b) [the First Draft Screenplay as soon as reasonably
      practicable and in any event [not later than
      (   )]/[not later than (   )] days after notice
      requiring the same has been given to the Writer
      such notice to be given if at all and at the Producer's
      sole discretion within [(   )] days of delivery of the
      Treatment]
  (c) [the Revisions to the First Draft Screenplay as soon
      as reasonably practicable and in any event [not later
      than (   )]/[not later than (   ) days] [after notice
      requiring the same has been given to the Writer
      such notice to be given if at all and at the Producer's
      sole discretion within [(   )] days of delivery of the
      First Draft Screenplay]/[after the Producer shall
      have notified the Writer of its comments on the First
      Draft Screenplay]]
  (d) [the Second Draft Screenplay as soon as reasonably
      practicable and in any event [not later than (   )]/[not
      later than (   )] days [after notice requiring the same
      has been given to the Writer such notice to be given if
      at all and at the Producer's sole discretion within (   )
      days of delivery of the First Draft Screenplay or the
      Revisions thereto as the case may be]/[after the
      Producer shall have notified the Writer of its
      comments on the First Draft Screenplay or the
      Revisions thereto as the case may be]]
  (e) [the Revisions to the Second Draft Screenplay as
      soon as reasonably practicable and in any event [not
      later than (   )]/[not later than (   )] days [after
      notice requiring the same has been given to the

SCHEDULE 1 – DELIVERY OF THE WORK

It is always practical to set out exactly when a writer should deliver various treatments, drafts and revisions. It is practical for the producer to have the ability to request postponement of the delivery of the revisions, the second draft and any subsequent revisions. Writers should ensure that they can deliver according to the agreed schedule.

Producers should be aware that this schedule of delivery is only a guide and that for individual projects any delivery schedule can be agreed between the producer and the writer. This delivery schedule is set out in accordance with the provisions of the collective bargaining agreement of the Writers Guild of Great Britain.

Writer such notice to be given if at all and at the Producer's sole discretion within (   ) days of delivery of the Second Draft Screenplay] [after the Producer shall have notified the Writer of its comments on the Second Draft Screenplay]]

(2) In the event that the Writer shall deliver the Treatment pursuant to the provisions of this agreement and the Producer shall not serve notice upon the Writer within [(   )] days of receipt thereof extending the Writer's engagement hereunder to the writing of the First Draft Screenplay the copyright therein granted to the Producer by the Writer hereunder shall revert to the Writer [unless the Producer shall within the aforesaid period pay to the Writer a further [(   )] and the Producer shall at the Writer's expense execute all such deeds, documents and instruments as the Writer shall reasonably require to give effect to this clause].

(3) [If the Producer shall have requested the postponement of the delivery of the [Revisions to the First Draft Screenplay] the Second Draft Screenplay or the Revisions to the Second Draft Screenplay or shall not have given to the Writer its comments on the First Draft Screenplay or the Revisions thereto or the Second Draft Screenplay within the periods above mentioned the Producer shall not forfeit its rights to require the Writer to write the said material but the Writer's obligation with respect thereto shall be subject to the Writer's prior professional commitments].

SCHEDULE 2 – REMUNERATION

The following compensation for the Writer's services hereunder shall be payable

(1) Subject as provided in Clause (5) of this Schedule 2 upon the following dates:–
   (a) upon the date hereof the sum of   (receipt whereof the Writer hereby acknowledges)
   (b) upon delivery to the Producer of [the Treatment] the sum of
   (c) upon commencement of the First Draft Screenplay the sum of
   (d) upon delivery of the First Draft Screenplay the sum of
   (e) [upon commencement of the Revisions to the First Draft Screenplay the sum of (   )]
   (f) [upon delivery of the Revisions to the First Draft Screenplay the sum of (   )]
   (g) [upon commencement of the Second Draft Screenplay the sum of (   )]
   (h) [upon delivery of the Second Draft Screenplay the sum of (   )]
   (i) [upon commencement of the Revisions to the Second Draft Screenplay the sum of (   )]
   (j) [upon delivery of the Revisions to the Second Draft Screenplay the sum of (   )].
(2) In the event that the Producer produces the Film or causes the Film to be produced [based wholly or substantially on the Work]/[and the Writer receives sole screen credit as the writer of the Work pursuant to the Screenwriting Credits Agreement] upon the first day of principal photography of the Film the sum of [(   )] less the aggregate of the sum or sums paid to the Writer under sub-clauses (a) to (j) inclusive of Clause (1) of this Schedule 2 [Provided that if the Writer's entitlement to sole screen credit shall be the subject of an arbitration pursuant to the Screenwriting Credits Agreement the

SCHEDULE 2 – REMUNERATION

Producers should clearly set out when payment is due in the contract. This payment schedule is in accordance with the WGGB/PACT Agreements.

Producers should be aware that in Clause 8 of the agreement there exists an option clause which enables other writers to be brought on for further drafts and revisions. Producers should ensure that the first writer agrees to this (See note 8 above).

This clause clearly states that the writer must receive sole screen credit as the writer in order to receive remuneration set out in Clause I of Schedule 2. Writers should be aware that if they do not receive sole screen credit then they will not be paid in full. From a writer's perspective they should try and negotiate a less onerous clause.

This schedule is only a guide and does not have to be adhered to in all circumstances. Producers should be aware that payment schedules can be freely negotiated and therefore producers must take into consideration issues such as their ability to cashflow the development of a project.

In some circumstances remuneration may be linked to the award of development funding from a government or public sector funding agency.

sum payable to the Writer under this Clause (2) shall be paid within fourteen (14) days of the determination as to the Writer's entitlement to sole credit pursuant to such arbitration].

(3) In the event that the Producer produces the Film or causes the Film to be produced and the Writer receives sole screen credit as the writer of the Work pursuant to the Screenwriting Credits Agreement such sums as from time to time equal [per cent (%)] of the [Net Profits/Producer's Profits] (as defined and payable in accordance with the provisions of Schedule 4 to this agreement).

(4) In the event that the Producer produces the Film or causes the Film to be produced and the Writer receives a screen credit other than sole screen credit pursuant to the Screenwriting Credits Agreement no further payment shall be made by the Producer to the Writer hereunder other than

(a) those sums paid pursuant to Clause (1) of this Schedule 2 in respect of the drafts of and revisions to the Work actually written and delivered by the Writer

(b) [if the writer shall receive a shared main writing credit the sums payable pursuant to Clause (2) (and the share of [Net Profits/Producer's Profits] referred to in Clause (3)] of this Schedule 2) reduced pro rata in proportion to the number of main writing credits accorded on the Film.]

OR

(b) [such sums as from time to time equal a reasonable proportion of [the sums payable under Clause (2) of this Schedule 2][and of][the share of [Net Profits/Producer's Profits] referred to in Clause (2) of this Schedule 2] having regard to the manner in which the screen credit shall have been shared such proportion to be determined in the absence of agreement by arbitration pursuant to the provisions

of clause 9(2) of the agreement of which this schedule forms part].

(5) If the Writer shall not deliver any part of the Work or if the Producer shall not commission the Writer to deliver further parts thereof no compensation shall be payable in respect of the undelivered part or said further parts of the Work not so commissioned.

(6) All payments made to the Writer hereunder shall be inclusive of any payment to the Writer for the Producer's right to use the Work wholly or partly in any book, journal or other publication.

(7) [Notwithstanding the Writer's contribution of the layout or format for the Film the Writer shall not have any interest in any merchandising therein or derived therefrom and all payments made to the Writer hereunder shall be inclusive of any payment to the Writer in respect thereof].

SCHEDULE 3 – SHORT FORM ASSIGNMENT

KNOW ALL MEN BY THESE PRESENTS: that for good and valuable consideration receipt of which is hereby acknowledged the undersigned [   ] ('Assignor') hereby grants and assigns to ('Assignee') the following rights:-

The entire unencumbered copyright and all other right, title and interest including but without limitation all the motion picture, television and videogram rights and all allied rights (as such expressions are commonly understood in the motion picture and television industries) and as more particularly described in the agreement made between the Assignor and the Assignee dated   200 ('the Main Agreement')

in and to the following literary and dramatic work:–

Title:
Written by:
Copyright Registration:
Effective Date of
Copyright Registration:

This Assignment is executed in accordance with and subject to the provisions of the Main Agreement

IN WITNESS whereof the undersigned has executed this Assignment on   200

....
[   ](Assignor)

SCHEDULE 3 – SHORT FORM ASSIGNMENT

This enables the producer to send a copy to the US Copyright Office for registration purposes.

Producers should be aware that registration of a copyright work at the US Copyright Office was at one time a pre-requisite of copyright protection in the United States. Although this is no longer necessary, producers who wish to exploit a copyright work in the United States should try and register their work.

SCHEDULE 4 – NET PROFITS/PRODUCER'S PROFITS

SCHEDULE 4 – NET PROFITS/PRODUCER'S PROFITS

In order to avoid disputes at a later date these definitions should clearly set out how net profits or producer's profits are to be recouped and paid. Producers who negotiate producer's or net profits agreements should always consult a lawyer for advice on how to structure these payments. In many circumstances litigation is a result of improper producer or net profits definitions.

See Appendix B.

DEED OF POWER OF ATTORNEY

BY THIS POWER OF ATTORNEY given on the   day of 200] of

[('the Appointor') HEREBY APPOINTS of [ ] ('the Attorney') to be the Appointor's lawful Attorney in the Appointor's name and on the Appointor's behalf to execute all deeds documents and instruments which the Attorney shall be entitled to execute pursuant to and subject strictly to the terms of Clause 11 of the agreement made between the Attorney and the Appointor and dated the day of 200[ ] to which a copy of this Deed of Power of Attorney is annexed AND the Appointor hereby declares that all and everything which shall be done by the Attorney for the aforesaid purpose shall be as good, valid and effectual to all intents and purposes whatsoever as if the same had been executed by the Appointor

AND the Appointor hereby undertakes from time to time and at all times to ratify and confirm whatsoever the Attorney shall lawfully cause to be done by virtue of this Power of Attorney

AND the Appointor hereby declares that this Power of Attorney is coupled with an interest and shall be irrevocable.

IN WITNESS whereof the Appointor has signed this instrument as a **DEED** in the presence of the person mentioned below the day month and year first above written

SIGNED AND DELIVERED AS A DEED
by THE APPOINTOR
in the presence of:

Writer's agreement: Notes

ACKNOWLEDGEMENT

[In the US use the following]

State of

County of

On this day of   200 before me, the undersigned, a
Notary Public in and for the said County and State,
personally appeared [known to me to be the person who
executed the within written instrument]

WITNESS my hand and official seal

....
Notary Public in and for said
County and State

[In the UK use the following]

We hereby certify that this is a true copy of the original.

....
Solicitor's name and address

6 Co-production agreement

The majority of co-productions are initiated in order to finance film and television productions through raising finance from more than one source. In Europe, co-productions are actively supported by various funding programmes created by the Council of Europe and the European Union.

For European producers there are some financial advantages in entering into a co-production. Producers can take advantage not only of the various pan European funding schemes but also of state, regional and local subsidies which exist in many European countries.

Aside from the obvious financial advantages of co-production, it has been said by some that co-production provides a unique opportunity to enrich the quality of programming through cross-fertilization of creative talents and ideas across different European nations. From a practical perspective, co-production enables independent production companies to create their own programme libraries by turning down straight commissions from broadcasters and allowing them to have greater control both creatively and in terms of ownership.

The term co-production describes any type of production where more than one party is involved. A co-production could be defined as a production where two or more producers play an active role in the physical production of a programme by supplying the services of individuals on the production, jointly contributing to the financing of it, and jointly, proportionate to their relative contributions, owning rights in the completed production.

Producers must differentiate between a co-production agreement and a co-financing agreement. A co-financing agreement is where a participant's involvement is purely financial. In a co-financing agreement, the participants' interest in a completed programme will be purely financial and be based on the return on investment from the various international sales of the programme.

One important factor to be considered in a co-production agreement is which party will be contracting with whom. In some circumstances one producer will contract individually with each of the other parties involved in the production. In this case the lead producer has generated a programme idea and will most likely want to retain final creative control of the project. However, the expectations of each party to a co-production agreement on such key matters as editorial control, ownership of rights, share of profits will vary greatly depending on the actual structure of the deal. Note that broadcasters and private and public funding bodies may apply certain standard criteria to the terms and structure of a co-production deal. Producers should realize that all deals are negotiable and because of the variable nature of film and television production there are no specific rules to apply to the final outcome of negotiations.

Co-production check list

1 Before entering into a co-production agreement producers should determine whether they are compatible as co-producers and whether or not they will achieve a satisfactory working relationship.
2 Producers should identify, comment on and resolve potential problem areas before any pre-production begins. Co-producers must ensure that the eventual final form co-production agreement will meet their particular creative and commercial requirements.
3 Producers must realize that finalizing contracts for co-productions can be a lengthy process particularly when more than two parties are involved. It is strongly advised that contracts are finalized before production

starts. Various contractual matters can create a deadlock situation through irreconcilable differences between the parties to an agreement. When approaching or approached by a potential co-production partner it is important before starting negotiations to obtain background information on potential partners. It is essential that a company search is undertaken, and that background information is sought on the directors of a company, shareholding structure, whether accounts have been filed, if there are any charges on the companies' assets and if annual returns have been made. Previous production credits are also a relevant gauge whether or not a potential co-producer is worth doing business with. Asking a producer or production company for a reference or recommendation is quite common.

Producers should be aware that when they enter into a co-production with other partners a completion guarantee will in most circumstances be a requirement of the financing.

Completion guarantees are a form of insurance whereby the completion guarantor guarantees to take over and complete production if it becomes apparent that the production cannot be completed within the approved total budget.

Before undertaking to guarantee a production, the completion guarantor will require approval of all key production elements such as the producer, director, script, principal cast and of course the production budget. If the guarantor considers that any one of these represents an unacceptable risk, then changes will be required as a condition of the guarantee. The budget for the production must contain a general contingency equivalent to 10 per cent of the cost of production. The completion guarantors' fee is negotiable but is usually in the region of 3 to 6 per cent of the budget. In some circumstances it is possible to negotiate a rebate on a portion of this fee if the film is completed on time and on budget.

The following agreement takes into account some of the basic provisions that should be included in a co-production between two or three producers. Users of this agreement should be aware that this is only a guide and that most co-productions are very complex and therefore legal advice from an experienced lawyer must be obtained.

Co-production agreement

CO-PRODUCTION AGREEMENT

A DATE

This agreement is made the   day of   200 .

B PARTIES TO THE CONTRACT

Between:

(1) [company name] of [address] a company incorporated in [country] (hereinafter referred to as 'A' or the Managing Producer)
(2) [company name] of [address] a company incorporated in [country] (hereinafter referred to as 'B')
(3) [a company name] of [address] a company incorporated in [country] (hereinafter referred to as 'C') (collectively referred to as 'the Co-Producers')

C PREAMBLE

WHEREAS:

(A) The Co-Producers wish to produce a [television film] provisionally entitled ['   '] ('the Film') based upon the following source material ('the Underlying Works'): [original literary work] entitled [   ] written by [author] first published by [publisher] in [country] in [year] [published]/[unpublished] screenplay [based upon the above-mentioned literary work] entitled ('title') written by [author] dated [date] ('the Screenplay')

The Co-Producers agree as follows:

1 BUDGET

The Film shall be produced in accordance with the Budget for the Film which is set out as Appendix A ('the Budget'). Any change to the Budget shall require the written approval of all Co-Producers.

CO-PRODUCTION AGREEMENT: NOTES

A DATE

The date should be inserted until all co-producers have agreed and signed a final version of the co-production contract.

B PARTIES TO THE CONTRACT

The full name, legal description, address, official registration number of the company and the country of each co-production company shall be indicated. Each party to the co-production contract should be given an identifiable shortened name which will be a defined term. Note that this example refers to three co-producers. In the case of a bilateral co-production only two names will be used.

C PREAMBLE

Not only does the preamble state what the parties intend to co-produce, it may also set out which party originated the project, which party initially owned, or acquired, the underlying rights, which party made the initial approaches for co-production interest and which party secured production funding and from which source. If a co-production proposes to apply for pan-European funding such as that provided by Eurimage then this should also be stated in the preamble. If a co-production is to be set up as an official co-production via the various treaties which exist between countries, then this should also be stated in the preamble.

1 BUDGET

The contract must set out what the budget is and in most cases the budget itself is attached as an appendix to the agreement. As a general rule the contract must provide that any increases in the budget require the prior written approval of all co-production parties.

2 UNDERLYING WORKS

(a) ['A'] hereby licenses to the Co-Producers the certain rights in the Underlying Works and the period of the licence shall commence on the date on which the amounts for such rights are reimbursed in full to ['A'] or, in the case of amounts not yet paid by ['A'] are paid to the relevant third party, in each case out of the Budget. The period of the licence shall end on the expiry of ['A's'] interest in the underlying works or

(b) ['A'] shall be responsible for arranging any copyright registration to record the interest of the Co-Producers (to the extent of such interest) in the Underlying Works and the Co-Producers shall execute any documents required for this purpose.

(c) ['A'] shall renew or exercise any option acquired by ['A'] in respect of any Underlying Works, provided that all the Co-Producers agree in writing that such options shall be renewed or exercised.

3 ROLE OF EACH CO-PRODUCER/CO-PRODUCTION CONTROL

(a) The Co-Producers agree to produce the Film in accordance with the terms of this Agreement.

(b) Any decisions relating to production and delivery of the Film shall if possible be made by the Co-Producers jointly and in the event that within a 24-hour period during principal photography or within a 72-hour period outside of principal photography, the Co-Producers are unable to reach a joint decision on any particular matter, then the matter shall be decided by ['A'] provided that ['A'] shall not make any decision which increases the production costs of the Film above the Budget unless ['A'] provides or procures the additional finance required to cover such

2 UNDERLYING WORKS

Parties to the agreement should ensure that any pre-existing contracts for underlying rights materials are in order, or that the originating co-producer has acquired rights in copyright materials prior to entering into the co-production contract. Once the co-production contract is drafted the co-producer will either assign these rights to the actual co-production entity or licence rights to each specific co-producer with the managing producer holding the actual copyright. This is usually done so that any bank lending money for the production can take security over the copyright. Producers should note that terms for any assignment or licence of rights will be governed by the terms and conditions of the contract under which any underlying rights were acquired from the original copyright owners (i.e. if the underlying rights were to a book for children the rights acquired may be restricted to a limited licence for television rights only). The co-producer who acquired the rights will usually be reimbursed for the cost of acquiring those rights. There are an unlimited number of possibilities for structuring ownership of underlying rights. Therefore, this is a key question which should always be considered very carefully and where specialised legal advice should be taken.

3 ROLE OF EACH CO-PRODUCER/CO-PRODUCTION CONTROL

The detailed responsibilities of each co-producer must be clearly set out within the contract. Their respective roles, responsibilities and entitlements must be stated. It is also preferred that one individual is nominated the managing producer, who will have overall responsibility for various aspects of the production including editorial, creative, administrative, financial and legal control. The designation of the managing producer is a pre-requisite for a co-production agreement. In some cases, the managing producer will be the producer who has contributed or procured the largest share of production finance.

In some co-productions, various producers will have the responsibility for preparing separate segments of a programme.

increase, subject to the rights of any financiers and
completion guarantor (if any).

4 OVERSPEND

Subject to the approval of the Managing Producer and
completion guarantor (if any), no expenditure on
production and delivery of the Film above the amount of
the Budget shall be incurred unless the Co-Producers agree
in writing setting out between them the responsibility for
providing or procuring the additional finance required to
cover such overcost.

5 UNDERSPEND

(a) In the event that the Budget exceeds the total costs
    actually incurred by the Co-Producers on the items in
    the Budget and the amount of any fee payable on the
    calling of the completion guarantee (if any) but not paid
    because the completion guarantee was not called shall
    be provided between the Co-Producers in the same
    proportions as the respective contributions to the
    Budget.
(b) The amount of any underspend on any particular item
    in the Budget may be utilized for other items in the
    Budget, subject to the requirements of the completion
    guarantor (if any).

6 FINANCIAL CONTRIBUTION OF EACH CO-PRODUCER

(a) The financial contribution of each Co-Producer for the
    Film is equal to the amount of the Budget and is
    annexed as Appendix B ('The Financing Plan'). Any
    change to the Financing Plan shall require the approval
    of all Co-Producers.
(b) 'A' agrees to provide or procure finance or other
    contributions of a total value equal to [   ] percentage
    of the Budget, according to that part of the Financing

In these circumstances detailed specifications of what is required from each co-producer must be stated.

4 OVERSPEND

A procedure should set out that any increases in the budget require the prior approval of all the co-production parties. If an overspend is unavoidable then there must be some agreement between the co-producers by which an increase in costs can be met by savings in other budget areas. If increased costs cannot be met from the budget and there is no completion guarantee then the co-producers must agree a strategy for finding additional finance.

5 UNDERSPEND

This clause should be drafted in order to provide a formula whereby any underspend on any particular item in the budget which is not utilized in another area of the budget should be divided between the co-producers in an equitable manner. Usually this is done in the same proportions as each producer's respective financial contribution.

6 FINANCIAL CONTRIBUTION OF EACH CO-PRODUCER

The amount of finance provided or procured by each co-producer should be stated as a percentage of the budget. This should be reflected in a financing plan which should be attached as an appendix to the main agreement. The co-producers' prospective percentages must add up to 100 per cent of the budget.

Producers should be aware that when entering into a co-production each party to the co-production will be responsible

Plan which has been allocated to 'A'. 'B' agrees to provide or procure finance or other contributions of a total value equal to [   ] per cent of the Budget according to that part of the Financing Plan allocated to 'B'. 'C' agrees to provide or procure finance or other contributions of a total value equal to [   ] per cent of the Budget according to that part of the financing plan allocated to 'C'.

7 EUROPEAN FUNDING BODIES/CO-PRODUCTION TREATIES

(a) 'A' shall apply to [name of funding body] for funding and/or co-production support in accordance with the requirements set out in the Budget.
(b) 'B' shall apply to [name of funding body] for funding and/or co-production support in accordance with the requirements set out in the Budget.
(c) 'C' shall apply to [name of funding body] for funding and/or co-production support in accordance with the requirements set out in the Budget.

8 CASH FLOW

(a) The Co-Producers agree to negotiate in good faith and agree a cash flow schedule drawn up in the relevant currency or currencies of expenditure for the Budget no later than [ ] days before the start of principal photography.
(b) The Co-Producers agree to provide or procure advances in the relevant currency or currencies in accordance

for a specific amount of the overall budget. Sometimes a co-producer may include in his financing, monies awarded to that particular producer from a regional or national funding agency (i.e. a German producer may receive money from the North Rhine Westfalia Film Fund or other German regional funding agency). Therefore, the other co-producers must be clear as to whether their co-producing partners' funding includes or excludes agency funding.

Sometimes if a co-production involves three co-producers from three different European countries (except the United Kingdom) they may be eligible for Eurimages funding which is the Pan-European Fund of the Council of Europe for the support of the co-production of feature films and creative documentaries.

7 EUROPEAN FUNDING BODIES/CO-PRODUCTION TREATIES

If the parties to the co-production wish to obtain co-production status based on a bilateral or multi-lateral co-production treaty or if they wish a European funding body to contribute to the co-production then this should be set out in the contract. Details of the relevant treaties and national film authorities should be inserted. If an application is being made to Eurimage then one of the co-producers must act as the designated producer. Parties to the co-production agreement should also set out whether support by one of the various agencies is a condition precedent to the co-production agreement. If funding by one of these bodies is not a condition precedent to the agreement then this should be clearly stated in the agreement.

8 CASH FLOW

This clause should set out and identify which of the co-producers is responsible for providing or procuring their specific part of the cash flow for the film. In some agreements, the cash flow should be set out in a schedule to the main agreement and should specify the timing for remittance of funds to the production by the various co-producers or their respective financiers.

with that part of the cashflow schedule which is allocated to each individual Co-Producer.

(c) The Managing Producer shall arrange for a Production Account to be set up at [name of bank] in the name of [either each individual co-producer or in the Managing Producer's name] any monies deposited in such account shall be co-owned by the Co-Producers in the same proportions as the Co-Producers' respective contributions to the Budget and such money and any interest accruing thereon shall be applied exclusively towards production and delivery of the Film.

9 SCRIPT/SCREENPLAY

(a) The final shooting script for the Film shall be based upon the screenplay and for this purpose the Co-Producers shall agree in writing an approved screenplay ('the Approved Screenplay') no later than [60 days] before the start of principal photography.

(b) In the event that any changes to the approved screenplay are required then such changes shall be minor and shall not increase the production costs of the Film without prior written approval of all Co-Producers.

10 PRODUCTION SPECIFICATIONS

The Film shall conform to the specification set out in Appendix (C) ('the Specifications'). Any changes to the

With co-productions there are often logistical difficulties in ensuring that funds are remitted from the production financiers in accordance with the cash flow requirements of the production. There is also the concern of protecting the co-producers against fluctuations in currency rates between the time of entering into an agreement and the time when the funds are required. One way of avoiding risk of currency fluctuations is for each co-producer to purchase sufficient foreign currency at the outset and place it in an appropriate foreign currency account to await expenditure. Any costs or charges associated with this should be dealt with in the budget.

The co-producers should mutually agree and record in the contract a designated production account or accounts. A provision should be inserted that all of the co-producers are entitled to receive copies of bank statements in relation to a production account. Provision should also be made for accounting reports, so that each co-producer will receive at weekly intervals, throughout the production period, a statement of account.

9 SCRIPT/SCREENPLAY

This clause should provide that no substantive changes should be made without the agreement of all co-producers to the agreed script during the course of production. It should be stated that the managing producer will have final approval in the event that all the co-producers are unable to agree on creative issues.

10 PRODUCTION SPECIFICATIONS

It is essential that provisions are made in this clause setting out the mutually agreed specifications of all the key elements of the

Specifications shall require the written approval of all the Co-Producers subject to the Managing Producer's final decision.

production. This will enable the co-producers to ensure that all known elements of the co-production are thoroughly explored between the parties before commencement of production. The following list contains items to be included in the specifications although not all may be applicable in certain circumstances. Certain specifications may be required to qualify for subsidy funding or specific requirements of financiers. Producers should try and ensure that none of the specifications are considered essential elements of the production. If an essential element exists then the producer may have to arrange and purchase essential element insurance which can be very expensive. Also an essential element may affect the ability to completion bond a production. A sample list is as follows:

1 Title
2 Number of programmes
3 Running time
4 Source materials
5 Script/screenplay
6 Principal contributors:

Managing Producer	Co-Producers
Executive Producers	Designer
Director	Assistant Director
Writer	Associate Producer
Production Manager	Principal Cast
Music: Composer/Performer	Editor
Lighting Cameraman	Production Accountant

7 Budget
8 Production Schedule
9 Locations
10 Studios
11 Production materials (film, video tape, stereo)
12 Delivery medium
13 Delivery requirements
14 Facilities house (post production)
15 Production bank account
16 The agreed script/agreed treatment
17 Production schedule.

11   CONTRACTS WITH THIRD PARTIES/INDIVIDUAL PRODUCTION CONTRACTS

(a) The benefit of all contracts concluded by a Co-Producer in relation to the Film (except the underlying rights agreements) shall be held by that Co-Producer for itself and the other Co-Producers.

(b) All contracts for production of the Film shall be in a form usual to the film and television industry and shall be consistent with this Agreement and with the requirements of any completion guarantor and financiers. Such contracts shall contain a grant of rights to permit the widest legally permissible exploitation of the Film. Such grant of rights shall specifically include the unrestricted authorization of exploitation of the Film by means of rental and lending rights and the contract shall include an acknowledgement that the payment provided in the contracts includes an element representing equitable remuneration for the authorization of rental and lending. Further, any such contracts shall include a waiver of moral rights, to the extent if any that such waiver is legally permissible.

(c) [   ] shall be responsible for obtaining music clearances in relation to music used for the Film.

12   INSURANCE

(a) The Managing Producer shall procure that the usual production insurances in relation to feature film production shall be effected and maintained and that each policy for such insurances shall have each of the Co-Producers named as insured in relation to their respective interests.

(b) Each Co-Producer shall notify the others on the happening of any event which may give rise to a claim under any insurances.

11 CONTRACTS WITH THIRD PARTIES/INDIVIDUAL PRODUCTION CONTRACTS

See Chapter 4, Option and Literary Purchase Agreement, for notes on rental and lending rights and moral rights.

Producers should be aware that further fees may be payable in relation to additional transmissions of a television programme. Care should be taken to ensure that any obligations to make additional payments for wider or additional uses than those set out in the contract fee are either passed on to those responsible for the distribution of the programme or an additional amount is included in the budget for buyouts.

Use of music should also be properly cleared by obtaining the proper licences for exploitation.

12 INSURANCE

The agreement should specify that production insurance is required. Producers should be aware that the usual forms of insurance that are required include:

1 Liability to third parties during production of the film.
2 Insurance against damage or loss of the negative and other property used in the production of the film.
3 Insurance against the risk of accident, illness or death of the director, principal cast and crew and any other person who

(c) Each Co-Producer agrees that it will not do or permit to be done anything which may cause any such insurance policy to lapse or become wholly or partially void or voidable by the insurers.

(d) Any sums paid out by insurers for claims against such insurance policies shall be applied towards unpaid production costs or subject to the requirements of any completion guarantor.

13 PRODUCTION

(a) Principal photography of the Film is to commence no later than [   ] or such later start as may be agreed in writing by all the Co-Producers ('the Start Date').

(b) The Co-Producers agree to negotiate in good faith and agree a shooting schedule for the film no later than 30 days before the start date.

(c) In the event that principal photography has not commenced by the start date then the Co-Producers shall negotiate in good faith a new start date.

14 DELIVERY

The Co-Producers agree to negotiate in good faith and agree a Delivery Schedule ('the Delivery Schedule') no later than 30 days before the start date. Failing such agreement the Delivery Schedule shall be the Delivery Schedule annexed as Appendix (D). Thereafter, the Delivery Schedule shall not be changed without written approval of all the Co-Producers.

may be an essential element and such insurance should include the risk of abandonment of the film resulting from any accident, illness or death.

4 Employee liability insurance for the duration of the production.
5 Errors and omissions insurance ('E&O insurance').
6 Insurance against moral rights claims and claims for equitable remuneration for rental or lending.
7 Any other insurance which may be required by law before the production takes place.

13 PRODUCTION

It is essential that the co-producers agree a shooting schedule for the film or programme. This will be a requirement of the financiers and the completion bond.

Producers should also set out provisions in case principal photography has not commenced by a certain date. Without a specific date, then it is possible that one of the co-producers will drop out of the production. Producers should be aware that it is quite common for co-producers not to start principal photography as set out in their original agreement.

14 DELIVERY

The delivery date should be indicated in this clause. This will be a requirement of the financier and completion bonders. It should also be decided which of the co-producers is responsible for actual delivery of the film. It is advisable to put the name of the country in which the laboratory for processing will be situated. The co-producers may wish to agree in greater detail the terms of their access to the materials (i.e. in the form of a laboratory access letter). Co-producers will usually be required by the financiers and completion bonders to attach an agreed minimum schedule of delivery items in an appendix to the agreement.

15 OWNERSHIP OF RIGHTS

(a) [The Co-Producers shall be the joint authors of the Film.]

(b) All copyright and all other rights which are owned or acquired by the Co-Producers in the Film shall be owned [by the Managing Co-Producer and licensed to the other Co-Producers in respect of each Co-Producer's individual territory] [by them jointly] [as Tenants in Common] [in the same proportions as their respective contributions to the Budget.]

16 EXPLOITATION OF RIGHTS IN THE PRODUCTION/DISTRIBUTION

(a) The Managing Producer hereby licenses to [   ] to exploit the Film for the duration of copyright in the Film in the [   ] language in all media in the following territories:–

[   ]

(b)   The Managing Producer authorizes [   ] to negotiate and conclude all agreements with third parties relating to the exploitation of the Film in the territory of [   ]. [The terms of such agreement shall be subject to the prior written approval of all the Co-Producers.]

17 CREDIT

The Co-Producers shall receive on screen credit as follows: [see notes for guidance].

15   OWNERSHIP OF RIGHTS

The contract should address the question of physical ownership of the master negative and unused footage. Most importantly, there should be a clear statement of who owns the copyright in the production. It is essential that this clause determines the ownership as between the co-producers of the types of rights which they may own in the production. Whatever the arrangements to be made for the ownership of copyright are, the contract should record the copyright notice which is to appear on the production, and if the copyright is to be divided on a territorial basis between different co-producers then provisions for these variations should be made in this clause.

The contract should also specify which co-producer will be responsible for registering the copyright at the US Copyright Registry and for other copyright registrations as may be required under the laws of the countries of the co-producers.

16   EXPLOITATION OF RIGHTS IN THE PRODUCTION/DISTRIBUTION

The duration of each co-producer's exploitation rights are also subject to negotiation. The co-producer may own and control the rights in his territory for the full period of copyright and be entitled to retain all revenues from any licences concluded in that territory. However, in some circumstances a co-producer's ownership and control of rights and entitlement to revenues may end after a certain period of time.

17   CREDIT

The co-producers need to agree the wording, size and placing of the credits for their companies, their individual credits and also the credits of creative talent such as the director, writer and actors. There may also be requirements by the financiers to

18   RECOUPMENT AND PROFIT PARTICIPATION

Recoupment and profit participation shall take place in accordance with a recoupment schedule ('the Recoupment Schedule') consistent with the requirements of the financiers which the Co-Producers agree to negotiate in good faith and agree no later than 30 days before the Start Date. The recoupment schedule once agreed shall not be changed without the written approval of all Co-Producers.

19   COLLECTIONS

Any receipts from the exploitation of the Film shall be paid into a collection account in the name of [   ] which will be administered by [   ] who shall be designated as the Official Collection Agent.

receive credits. In some circumstances, the credits appearing in each co-producer's territory may be arranged differently (i.e. in Germany, the German co-producer's name will appear first, followed by the other co-producers, whereas in the UK the UK producer's name is positioned first).

18   RECOUPMENT AND PROFIT PARTICIPATION

There are many possible arrangements for recoupment. Ownership and control of rights as well as recoupment in the completed production will ultimately be governed by any agreements with financiers. The contract should set out the treatment of the rights in a production which have not been sold off for the purposes of raising production finance. If applicable, the contract should specify each co-producer's accounting responsibilities to the other co-producers for their share of revenue from his or her territory; the contract should also specify the agreed levels of distribution commissions and costs which may be charged by the co-producers.

The co-producers may agree to appoint a distributor to handle sales of the production outside their own territories. The selection and contractual terms for a third party distributor to handle sales from which co-producers will jointly share any revenues should be subject to the approval of all the parties. The contract should specify which parties are to contract with a third party distributor. It may be the co-producers jointly, or one co-producer may enter into the contract to hold it for his benefit and for the benefit of the others. There should also be detailed definitions of net profits, producer's profits and net receipts. See Appendix B for sample definition of net/producers profits.

19   COLLECTIONS

This clause sets out the mechanism for collection of revenues (if any) realized by the sale of the completed production. It is necessary to insert details of the name of the account, the name of the bank and the address of the bank branch of any collection accounts used.

20   REPRESENTATIONS, WARRANTIES AND INDEMNITIES

Author's Note: Because of the highly complex nature of co-production agreements this section of the contract must be drafted depending on the specific circumstances of the deal. Legal advice is highly recommended.

See notes and other agreements in this book for guidance.

21   TERMINATION

(a) In the event that any Co-Producer commits a material breach of its obligations under this agreement and the other Co-Producers jointly give written notice to the defaulting Co-Producer specifying the breach and stating whether or not it is capable of being remedied and such breach is still not remedied fourteen days after the date of the notice then the Co-Producers giving the notice shall be entitled to terminate this Agreement by written notice as against such defaulting Co-Producer.

As an alternative to separate collection accounts, the co-producers may agree between themselves to collect and recoup through a single collection account operated by an independent agency that handles these types of transactions. If a bank is financing production and cashflowing against pre-sales then the bank will usually require the co-producers to instruct distributors to pay any advances direct to the bank for its own account usually on delivery.

20 REPRESENTATIONS, WARRANTIES AND INDEMNITIES

The contract will require customary legal warranties and indemnities in respect of the following matters:

1 Performance of the contract
2 Financial responsibilities
3 Infringement of copyright
4 Obligation to third parties
5 Exclusion of libellous, obscene or defamatory material

These clauses should be drafted according to the specific transaction and circumstances. This is an area where specialist legal advice is highly recommended.

21 TERMINATION

The contract must specify the grounds for termination, which are generally breach of contract or insolvency.

(a) Breach of contract – provisions should be made for the co-producers jointly (if more than two) to give written notice to a co-producer of any breach of the agreement, specifying the breach and if the breach is capable of remedy, giving the party in breach a period of 14 days (fewer days during production) in which to remedy it. If the breach is not remedied or is not capable of remedy, the co-producers must have the right to terminate the contact with the defaulting party, and on termination, the defaulting co-producer's entire right and interest in the co-production together with any

(b) In the event that any Co-Producer becomes insolvent or makes an arrangement with their creditors then, as against that Co-Producer, the other Co-Producers shall be entitled to terminate this Agreement by notice in writing.

(c) Upon termination in accordance with this clause the defaulting Co-Producer's interest in the Film and any physical materials, money in production accounts or collection accounts relating to the Film shall, so far as legally permissible, automatically terminate and shall be transferred to the other Co-Producers. For this purpose the defaulting Co-Producer shall execute all documents reasonably required by the other Co-Producers to effect such transfer.

22 MISCELLANEOUS PROVISIONS

See notes for guidance.

production funding held by the co-producer must so far as possible be transferred to the other co-production partner(s) who should be entitled to take over the defaulting co-producer's role in respect of production and proceed to completion.

(b) Insolvency – one of the most difficult problems to deal with in a co-production agreement is when one of the co-production partners becomes insolvent. The contract should provide a legal mechanism by which the co-production itself or the other co-producers can be protected against claims by creditors of the co-producer who has become insolvent. This will vary greatly depending on the co-producer's country of residence. This is a matter on which co-producers must seek specialist legal advice in relation to the laws of their respective countries in order to determine the best method of providing such a mechanism.

(c) Substitution of a co-production partner – a provision should be inserted entitling the remaining co-producers to appoint a substitute co-producer in a situation where the contract of one of the co-production partners has been terminated.

22 MISCELLANEOUS PROVISIONS

(a) Dispute procedures. The co-producers should agree on a mechanism for arbitration in the event of a dispute. Arbitration can be a relatively quick and simple method of dispute resolution instead of pursuing a court action. Note that if co-producers are in such fundamental disagreement then it is unlikely that a good working relationship can be maintained.

(b) Variations to the agreement. The contract should specify that any variations to the agreement must be confirmed in writing and signed by all parties.

23 ASSIGNMENT

This Agreement cannot be assigned except without the prior written consent of the other Co-Producers and such written consent shall not be unreasonably withheld.

24 GOVERNING LAW/JURISDICTION

The Co-Producers hereby agree to submit to the jurisdiction of the following Court:

[   ]

(c) No partnership. The co-producers should try and set out that the terms of the co-production do not constitute a partnership. Note that under the laws of certain countries a co-production contract would constitute a partnership between the producers.

(d) Notices. The contract should specify condition which notices under the contract are to be given.

(e) Registration of the contract. In certain European countries it is necessary for the contracts to be registered. The contracts should specify which co-producer is responsible for making such registration.

(f) Duty of confidentiality. It is recommended that the co-producer should be bound by a duty of confidentiality regarding the co-production agreement and the co-producer's business in general.

23   ASSIGNMENT

A co-production agreement in most circumstances is personal to the parties and is not capable of assignment without the express prior consent in writing of all other parties.

24   GOVERNING LAW/JURISDICTION

The contract must specify the country under whose laws it is to be governed. Note that if a dispute arises between the parties and the governing law (or jurisdiction) has not been specified then this alone may create complex legal questions. Usually the governing laws are determined by either the co-producer who contributes the greatest amount of funding or by the managing co-producer. The contract should also stipulate in which court any dispute between the parties will be heard.

25 SIGNATURES

Signed by
duly authorized on behalf
of [   ]

in the presence of
[   ]

26 SCHEDULES   [A] [B] [C] [D] [E] [F]

[Insert schedules as required]

25 SIGNATURES

The full name of each company should be specified. The individual proposing to sign the agreement for a company should be the individual who can commit the company and is authorized to do so. It is advisable that signatures should be witnessed by an independent witness for purposes of giving evidence if it were later disputed whether the contract had been properly signed.

26 SCHEDULES [A] [B] [C] [D] [E] [F]

Any schedules should be attached at the end of the agreement.

7 Distribution agreement

The primary goal of a producer is to finance their film or television production. Independently produced projects are often dependent on distribution deals (selling off various domestic and foreign distribution rights) to finance their production.

The distribution of films and television programmes is a specialized and complex industry where distributors either acquire rights which are already owned by a producer or alternatively put up money at an early stage in order to acquire rights for a limited licence period or for the full period of copyright. Although the process of film and television distribution are somewhat different, there are elements common to both. This agreement will focus on theatrical feature films.

A distributor is usually based in the territory of the producer. Once the distributor has acquired the rights from the producer it will negotiate the release of the film through various cinemas, organize the making of the necessary prints, and will plan the advertising and publicity campaign for the film. In addition to the theatrical/cinema rights, a distributor may also acquire from the producer ancillary rights which it will license according to the requirements of each specific territory. The number of rights a distributor acquires is a matter for negotiation between the producer and the distributor. When granting a distributor the right to handle the distribution rights of a film or television programme the producer should try and negotiate either a substantial advance (money) against distribution revenues or alternatively a guarantee from the distributor that certain revenues will be achieved with the distributor having to pay the producer the guaranteed amount if the producer has not raised certain funds for himself within a certain period.

The distributor will expect to deduct standard distribution commissions and direct costs and expenses from first sales revenue and will then retain all the revenue until the sum of the advance (possibly with interest) has been recouped. After this the distributor will continue to sell the film or programme. Then, after deduction of commissions and expenses the revenue will be paid to the producer in the form of profit participation. If the advance has been substantial then the distributor may be entitled to receive a profit share of sales after recoupment of the advance and the deduction of commissions. The level of the advance usually depends on the number of territories and markets for which distribution rights are being acquired.

The type of rights which are granted to distributors can either be primary or secondary rights. Primary rights are usually the audio visual exhibition and transmission rights in a film or television production whereas secondary rights, which are also known as ancillary rights, give the right to sell merchandise, publish novelizations of the screenplay, etc.

Producers should be careful when choosing distributors since large distributors may handle almost anything and everything whereas other distributors have a particular speciality and will only acquire certain films or programmes in a specific subject area. Sometimes producers should choose a small distributor who will work closely with the producer and give the producer more individual attention. This may ensure that the film or programme will not be lost within the catalogue of a large distributor. A large distributor may have more contacts and will have the ability to pay larger distribution advances and create higher quality sales and promotional material.

The following agreement is in relation to a theatrical feature film in a specific territory. The agreement contains most of the clauses which will be found in distribution agreements. The agreement does not make any reference to distribution commissions that may be charged by the distributor. This is an issue which should be negotiated directly between the producer and the distributor. Producers are strongly advised to seek legal advice in relation to any distribution agreement they are about to sign.

Distribution agreement

DISTRIBUTION AGREEMENT

This Agreement is dated the [   ]
BETWEEN
[   ] ('the Producer')
of [   ]
and
[   ] ('the Distributor')
of [   ]

1 THE FILM

The term 'Film' refers to the Feature Film set forth in
Schedule A hereof.

2 TERRITORY AND TERM

(a) Territory: The territory covered hereby ('the Territory') is
set forth in Schedule A.
(b) Distribution Term: The term of this Agreement and the
rights granted the Distributor hereunder for each
country or place of the Territory shall be the period of
time specified in Schedule A ('the Distribution Term').
The term of this Agreement shall commence on the date
hereof and expire upon the expiration of the
Distribution Term unless terminated as provided
herein.

3 REMUNERATION

(a) The Distributor undertakes to pay to the Producer the
advance at the times and in the manner specified in
Schedule A [on account of and recoupable by the
Distributor from the royalty (which shall mean the
percentage of gross receipts) set out in Schedule A].

DISTRIBUTION AGREEMENT: NOTES

PREAMBLE

Producers should ensure that when contracting with the distribution company they use the proper company which owns the rights in the film. Producers usually set up a separate company to produce a film and therefore it is essential that the proper owner of the copyright in the film contracts directly with the distributor.

1 THE FILM

The title of the film can either be inserted directly into the contract or attached in a schedule to the agreement. It is always easier to put all the various details in a schedule for quick and easy reference.

2 TERRITORY AND TERM

The agreement must reflect that the producer is assigning or licensing specific rights for a specific period of time and in a specific territory. These details can either be inserted directly into the contract or attached into a schedule. If a producer is licensing or assigning his/her rights in a film to the distributor for more than one territory then it is always easier to list those territories in the schedule to the agreement.

3 REMUNERATION

Distribution agreements usually refer to payment as an advance which is recoupable against money generated from either the theatrical release and/or sales of the film.

There are various types of deals which can be negotiated between the producer and the distributor. Usually the first sums earned by a film are from box office receipts.

Gross Receipts shall mean one hundred per cent (100%) of all gross monies and income including without limitation any awards, subsidies or government allowances received or receivable by the Distributor, its sub-distributors directly or indirectly from the exercise of the rights in the Territory during the Term together with all other sums arising whether or not by way of judgement, settlement or compromise for infringement or interference with any other rights that have been granted.

(b) The amount of the Advance which the Distributor is permitted to recoup from each medium of exploitation of the Film is listed in Schedule [   ].

(c) All distribution expenses incurred by the Distributor in connection with the exploitation of the rights pursuant to this Agreement shall be borne by the Distributor from the portion of Gross Receipts which the Distributor shall be entitled to retain provided that the distribution expenses incurred by the Distributor in connection with the exploitations by the Distributor of the rights granted shall be recouped by the Distributor in accordance with the provisions of Clause 3(d).

(d) The Distributor warrants and undertakes that the Gross Receipts in respect of the Film shall be retained by the Distributor until the amount retained equals the amount of the Advance in respect of the Film plus the amount of distribution expenses actually expended by the Distributor directly in connection with the exploitations of the rights in the Film in the Territory and after the Distributor shall have recouped such sums that percentage of the Gross Receipts as set out in Schedule A under the heading 'Royalty' shall be paid to the Producer in accordance with the provisions of this agreement.

The distributor and exhibitor of the film will enter into an agreement which makes reference to the 'Exhibitor's Gross' which means 100 per cent of all the sums received at the box office less any VAT. From the Exhibitor's Gross there will then be a deduction which is the 'Exhibitor's Percentage' which is usually an amount subject to negotiation between the exhibitor and the distributor. Usually the exhibitor retains between 30 and 60 per cent of the Exhibitor's Gross. Sometimes the agreement between the distributor and exhibitor will incorporate a sliding scale, with the percentage going to the distributor increasing with higher earnings. The exhibitor will also seek to retain a guaranteed amount before the division in order to cover the cinema's overheads which is sometimes called the 'house nut'. The sum which is then paid by the exhibitor to the distributor will be the 'Distributor's Gross'. The eventual division of the Distributor's Gross between the distributor and the producer will then depend on the nature of the deal between the distributor and the producer.

In relation to feature films, there are two types of agreements, gross deals and net deals. Producers should note that there can be variations which include a mixture of both, however in both cases the distributor will take some form of a commission for their services.

In a gross deal, the distributor deducts a commission based on the Distributor's Gross out of which the distributor will also deduct all of its expenses. Usually these expenses include the following:

a) The cost of negatives, soundtracks, release prints, etc.
b) The cost of press-books, artwork, advertising and stills.
c) Carriage and freight involved in the movement and shipping of prints.
d) Charges for registration, censorship and insurance.

A gross deal guarantees a flow of income from the first receipts but the percentage due back to the producer will be correspondingly low.

4 RIGHTS GRANTED

(a) Grant: Producer hereby grants to the Distributor throughout the Territory the exercise of all rights of [theatrical] [television] [(free pay and syndication)] and [home video (cassette, disc and DVD)] exhibition and distribution with respect to the Film and trailers thereof and excerpts and clips therefrom in any and all languages and versions including dubbed, sub-titled and narrated versions. The rights granted herein shall include without limit the sole and exclusive right:

    (i)   To use the title or titles by which the Film is or may be known or identified.

    (ii)   To use and perform any and all music, lyrics and musical composition contained in the Film and/or recorded in the soundtrack thereof in connection

In a net deal, the distributor will deduct its expenses from the Distributor's Gross and split the rest 50:50 with the producer. Sometimes the distributor will deduct (for example) a 30 per cent distribution commission based on the Distributor's Gross and deducts expenses from the producer's share of the Distributor's Gross before sending the balance to the producer. If the distributor's expenses represent 40 per cent of the Distributor's Gross then both types of deal will return the same amount to the producer.

In other cases it may be worthwhile to do an outright sale where a producer is unsure whether a distributor will see any income from the territory in question. Usually the film will be sold for a fixed period somewhere between three and twenty-five years.

Producers should be aware that this agreement is only a guide and that different scenarios require different definitions of gross and net receipts. This is an area where specialized legal advice should always be obtained.

4 RIGHTS GRANTED

(a) Producers should be aware that depending on the nature of the financing arrangements a producer may only have certain rights to sell. For example if a UK broadcaster has contributed finance to a production for all free television rights then the producer will be unable to grant free television rights to a distributor.

Generally rights which can be sold are sold according to the different distribution patterns set out below:

Theatrical rights usually defined as 'the exhibition of a film in 35mm or 16mm in cinemas or other places of public viewing to which the general public is admitted and for which an admission fee is made or rental is paid for the hire of the film'.

with the distributions, exhibition, advertising, publicizing and exploiting of the Film.

(iii) To make such dubbed and titled versions of the Film and the trailers thereof including without limitation cut-in, synchronized and superimposed versions in any and all languages for use in such parts of the Territory as the Distributor may deem advisable.

(iv) To make such changes, alterations, cuts, additions, interpolations, deletions and eliminations into and from the Film and trailer [subject to prior written approval of Producer and Director] as the Distributor may deem necessary or desirable, for the effective marketing distribution, exploitation or other use of the Film.

(v) To publicize, advertise and exploit the Film throughout the Territory during the Distribution Term including without limitation the exclusive right in the Territory for the purpose of advertising, publicizing and exploiting the Film including but not limited to the right:

to publish and to license and authorize others to publish in any language and in such forms as the Distributor may deem advisable synopses, summaries, adaptions, novelizations and stories of and excerpts from the Film and from any literary or dramatic material included in the Film or upon which the Film is based in book form and in newspapers, magazines, trade periodicals, booklets, press books and any other periodicals and in all older media of advertising and publicity whatsoever not exceeding 7,500 words in length taken from the original material;

to broadcast by radio and television for advertising purposes and to license and authorize others to so broadcast in any language or any parts or portions of the Film not exceeding five minutes in length and any literary

Non-theatrical rights usually mean the right to exhibit the film and/or authorize others to do so before an audience by persons institutions or organizations not primarily engaged in the business of exhibiting motion pictures to the public, including educational, social and religious institutions, churches, businesses, industrial and civic organizations, hospitals, libraries, prisons, convents, orphanages, marine and military installations, hotels, motels and similar establishments.

Free television rights usually mean the right to exploit a film by free television which is television using any format without a charge being made to the viewer for the privilege of viewing.

Pay television rights usually mean any broadcast for the reception of which a decoding decrypting or similar device has to be used and a fee or subscription is payable by the viewer whether on a 'once only' or on a 'pay per view' or 'pay per channel' or 'video on demand' or 'near video on demand' or other periodic basis.

Satellite television rights usually mean any broadcast transmitted from the territory granted to a satellite for retransmissions to and reception in the territory including without limitation by means of so-called 'direct broadcast by satellite', 'direct to home' and 'satellite master antenna television'.

Videogram rights usually mean any video cassette, video disc, compact disc or other electronic, magnetic or other device by means of which visual images with or without sound derived from the film may be received, reproduced or otherwise communicated directly or with the aid of any machine or device. (This definition is sometimes split into videogram rental rights and videogram sale rights and now digital video disc ('DVD') sale and rental rights.)

(i) Producers should ensure that they have the right to change the title of the film. Distributors may wish to change the title for marketing purposes

or dramatic material included in the Film or upon which the Film was based alone or in conjunction with other literary dramatic or musical material;
and to use, license and authorize others to use the name, physical likeness and voice (and any simulation or reproduction of any thereof) of any party rendering services in connection with the Film for the purpose of advertising, publicizing or exploiting the Film or Distribution including commercial tie-ins.

(vi) To use the Distributor's name and trade mark or the name and trade mark of any of the Distributor's licensees on the positive prints of the Film and in trailers thereof and in all advertising and publicity relating thereto in such a manner, position, form and substance as the Distributor or its licensees may elect.

(vii) to permit commercial messages to be exhibited during and after the exhibition of the Film.

(viii) to cause trailers of the Film and prints thereof and of the Film to be manufactured, exhibited and distributed by every means, medium, process, method and device now or hereafter known.

(b) Grant of Other Rights: Producer hereby grants to the Distributor throughout the Territory the sole and exclusive right, license and privilege to exercise [all literary publishing rights] [live televisions rights] [merchandising rights] [music publishing rights] [soundtrack recording rights] [radio rights] [additional motion Film rights] subject to the terms and conditions of the agreements pursuant to which Producer acquired the foregoing rights with respect to the literary dramatic and/or musical material used by Producer in connection with the Film Producer agrees that, at the request of the Distributor, Producer will execute and deliver to the Distributor for recordation purposes a separate document pursuant to which Producer

(ii)(iii)(iv)(v) Producers should be aware that the distributor will ask for the right to dub and sub-title the film as well as make specific changes and cuts to the film. Producers should ensure that there are no restrictions by the director against cutting the film. This could bring up a moral rights issue since the distributor is manipulating the director's original work.

The distributor may require editing or changing the final cut of the film in order to comply with censorship requirements when the film is released for home video. This also applies when the distributor wishes to sell the film to a broadcaster so that the broadcaster can insert advertisements at regular intervals.

(b) This clause deals with ancillary rights. Producers should be aware that these rights can be very valuable and therefore should not necessarily be granted outright to a distributor. The producer may wish to license these ancillary rights to other distribution companies that specialize in the manufacture of toys, merchandising etc. Producers should also be aware that the music or soundtrack rights may be very valuable.

confirms the transfer and assignment of the Distributor of said rights.

(c) Rights Free and Clear: The above-stated rights are granted by Producer to the Distributor without qualifications and free and clear from any and all restrictions, claims, encumbrances or defects of any nature and Producer agrees that it will not commit or omit to perform any act by which any of these rights, licences, privileges and interests could or will be encumbered, diminished or impaired and that Producer will pay or discharge and will hold the Distributor harmless from any and all claims that additional payments are due to anyone by reason of the distribution, exhibition, telecasting or re-running of the Film or the receipt of its proceeds. Producer further agrees that during the Distribution Term, Producer shall neither exercise itself nor grant to any third party the rights granted to the Distributor pursuant to the terms hereof.

(d) [Producer's Reservation of Rights: Producer reserves for its use non-theatrical distribution.]

(e) Credits: The statements of credits required to be given pursuant to Exhibit [   ] shall conform to the Distributor's standard credit provisions for comparable talent including without limitation the Distributor's standard art work title provisions as set out in Exhibit [   ] attached thereto.

(c) Distributors will usually ask for a warranty from the producer that there are no restrictions, claims or defects in any legal ownership of the film. Producers must ensure that there are no liabilities against the film otherwise this clause puts a responsibility on the producer to pay for or rectify any problems.

(d) Producers should always try and reserve certain rights for themselves. Sometimes the producer will be able to hold back certain non-theatrical rights in a feature film. This really depends on the type of deal between the producer and distributor. Depending on how much a distributor pays the producer the distributor will usually try and include these rights. Producers should also be aware that airline rights have become a valuable means of revenue and therefore the producer should try and carve out airline rights from theatrical rights.

(e) The producer should be aware that a distributor will ask for a list of all the credits which are required to be given in the film. This will include the obligations to accord credit to actors, director, producer, etc. This is usually attached to the agreement as an exhibit. The distributor will usually ask that their standard credit provision will be shown on all copies of the film and therefore the distributor will attach as an exhibit to the agreement their standard credit provisions.

5 PRODUCER'S WARRANTIES AND REPRESENTATIONS

Producer represents and warrants to the Distributor, its successors, licensees and assigns as follows:

(a) Quality: The Film is completely finished, fully edited and titled and fully synchronized with language dialogue, sound and music and in all respects ready and of a first class quality suitable for theatrical [television and videogram] release and commercial exhibition [and will conform to the final script and budget approved by the Distributor].

(b) Content: The Film consists of a continuous and connected series of scenes, telling or presenting a story, free from any obscene material and suitable for exhibition to the general public.

(c) Unrestricted Right to Grant: Producer is the sole and absolute owner of the Film, the copyright therein and all rights associated with or relating to the distribution, including the absolute right to grant to and vest in the Distributor all the rights, licences and privileges granted to the Distributor under this Agreement, and Producer has not sold, assigned, licensed, granted, encumbered or utilized the Film or any of the literary or musical properties used therein in any way that may effect or impair the rights, licences and privileges granted to the Distributor hereunder and Producer will not sell, assign, license, grant or encumber or utilize the rights, licences and privileges granted to the Distributor hereunder.

(d) Discharge of Obligations: All the following have been fully paid or discharged or will be fully paid and discharged by Producer or by persons other than the Distributor:

    (i)   All claims and rights of owners of copyright in literary, dramatic and musical rights and other property or rights in or to all stories, plays, scripts, scenarios, themes, incidents, plots, characters, dialogue, music, words, and other material, used or recorded in the Film;

5 PRODUCER'S WARRANTIES AND REPRESENTATIONS

Producers should be aware that these are standard warranties and representations that distributors ask for and in most cases cannot be substantially altered.

(a) A distributor will ask for certain delivery requirements which sometimes include a completely finished film ready for exhibition. Usually the agreement will have a list of delivery materials attached.

(b) If a producer delivers a film which substantially deviates from the original script then a distributor may not pay for the finished film if they were involved in the financing of the film.

(c) Producers must ensure that there are no adverse charges, claims or further payments in relation to the film (i.e. all actors and writers must have been paid for the work which was undertaken for the film).

(d) The distributor will ask for a warranty that the producer has acquired all rights free and clear in the underlying materials which the film is based upon. Distributors will also want to ensure that they are not responsible for any further payments with regards to the music used in the film.

(ii)   All claims and rights of owners of inventions and patent rights with respect to the recording of any and all dialogue, music and other sound effects recorded in the Film are with respect to the use of all equipment, apparatus, appliances and other materials used in the photographing, recording or otherwise in the manufacture of the Film;

(iii)   All claims and rights with respect to the use, distribution, exhibition, performance and exploitation of the Film and any music contained therein throughout the Territory.

(e) No Infringement: To the best of Producer's knowledge and belief neither the Film nor any part thereof, nor any materials contained therein or synchronized therewith, nor the title thereof, nor the exercise of any right, licence or privilege herein granted, violates or will violate or infringe or will infringe any trademark, trade name, contract, agreement, copyright (whether common law or statutory), patent, any literary, artistic, dramatic, personal, private, civil or property right or right of privacy or 'moral rights of authors' or any other right whatsoever of or slanders or libels any person, firm, corporation or association whatsoever. In connection therewith, the Producer shall supply the Distributor with a script clearance in a form acceptable to the Distributor.

(f) No Advertising Matter: The Film does not contain any advertising matter for which compensation, direct or indirect, has been or will be received by Producer or to its knowledge by any other person, firm, corporation or association.

(g) No Impairment of Rights Granted: There are no agreements, commitments or arrangements with any person, firm, corporation or association that may in any manner or to any extent affect the Distributor's rights hereunder or the Distributor's share of the proceeds of

(e) If a bank is involved in the financing of the film then they will require that a solicitor or another qualified individual give a full title report in relation to the copyright and underlying rights which the project was based on.

(f) Some broadcasters have a code of practice against product placement or advertising in relation to films or television programmes. A distributor may ask for a film that does not contain any advertising if that distributor's sole purpose is to sell the film to broadcasters such as the BBC which prohibit advertising. There are now agencies which can provide funds to producers who utilize products in their film.

(g)(h)(i)(j) Distributors always ensure that the film which is delivered to them is free and clear of any other obligations. Producers should realize that once they have sold or licensed their film to a distributor any contract which the producer has previously entered into and has not been fully satisfied, then

the Film. The Producer has not and will not exercise any right or take any action which might tend to derogate from impair or compete with, the rights, licences and privileges herein granted to the Distributor.

(h) Contracts: All contracts with artists and other personnel for purchases, licenses and all other obligations and undertakings of whatsoever kind connected with the production of the Film have been made and entered into by the Producer and by no other party and no obligation shall be imposed upon the Distributor thereunder and the Producer shall indemnify and hold the Distributor harmless from any expense and liability thereunder. All such contracts are in the form customarily in use in the film industry and are consistent with the provisions of this Agreement particularly with reference to the warranties made by the Producer and the rights acquired by the Distributor hereunder. The above mentioned contracts shall not without the Distributor's prior written consent be terminated, cancelled, modified or rescinded in any manner which would adversely affect the Distributor rights hereunder.

(i) All Considerations Paid: All considerations provided to be paid under each and all the agreements, licences or other documents relating to the production of the Film have been paid in full or otherwise discharged in full and there is no existing outstanding obligations whatsoever either present or future under any of the said contracts, agreements, assignments or other documents.

(j) Full Performance: All terms, covenants and conditions required to be kept or performed by the Producer under each and all of the contracts, licences or other documents relating to the production of the Film have been kept and performed and will hereafter be kept and performed by the Producer and there is no existing breach or other act of delay by the Producer under any such agreement, licence or other document nor will there by any such breach or default during the term hereof.

the producer will still be liable for any obligations under that contract.

(k) No release/No Banning: Neither the Film nor any part thereof has been released, distributed or exhibited in any media whatsoever in the Territory nor has it been banned by censors or refused import permits for any portion of the Territory.

(l) Valid Copyright: The copyright in the Film and the literary, dramatic and musical material upon which it is based or which is contained in the Film will be valid and subsisting during the Distribution Term with respect to each country or place of the Territory and no part of any thereof is in the public domain.

(m) Peaceful Enjoyment: The Distributor will quietly and peacefully enjoy and possess each and all of the rights, licences and privileges herein granted or purported to be granted to the Distributor throughout the Distribution Term for each country or place of the Territory without interference by any third party.

(n) Guild/Union/Performing Rights Society/Participation Payments: Any payments required to be made to any performing rights society or to any body or group representing authors, composers, musicians, artists, any other participants in the production of the Film, publishers or other persons having legal or contractual rights of any kind to participate in the receipts of the Film or to payments of any kind as a result of the distribution or exhibition of the Film and any taxes thereon will be made by the Producer or by the exhibitors and need not be paid by the Distributor.

(o) Music Performing Rights: The performing rights to all musical compositions contained in the Film are: (i) controlled by the American Society of Composers, Authors and Publishers (ASCAP), Broadcast Music, Inc., (BMI) or similar organizations in other countries such as the Japanese Society of Rights of Authors and Composers (JASEAC), the Performing Rights Society Ltd (PRS), the Society of European Stage Authors and Composers (SESAC), the Société des Auteurs Compositeurs et Editeurs de Musique (SACEM),

(n)(o)   Producers should be aware of music licensing. Whenever music is incorporated into a film or television production, it becomes the producer's responsibility to obtain the necessary permissions and clearances for each and every item of music required. Without the necessary licences, the producer will infringe copyright. In some cases a programme or film can be injuncted which may prevent its broadcast or distribution. Certain rights in songs and other musical compositions are administered on behalf of composers and publishers by a network of music rights organizations throughout the world. In the UK, the relevant bodies are the Performing Rights Society and The Mechanical Copyright Protections Society. Some of the other organizations listed in the agreement are in respect of other countries.

Gesellschaft fur Musikalische Auffuhrungs und Mechanische Vervielfaltigunsrechte (GEMA) or their affiliates, or (ii) in the public domain in the Territory or, (iii) controlled by the Producer to the extent required for the purposes of this Agreement and the Producer similarly controls or has licences for any necessary synchronization and recording rights.

(p) Television Restriction: The Film will not be exhibited in or telecast or cablecast in or into the Territory during the Distribution Term for each country or place of the Territory by anyone other than the Distributor or its licensees.

(q) Authority Relative to this Agreement: The Producer has taken all action necessary to duly and validly authorize its signature and performance of this Agreement and the grant of the rights, licences and privileges herein granted and agreed to be granted.

(r) Litigation: To the Producer's knowledge there is no litigation proceedings or claims against the Producer which may adversely affect the Producer's exclusive rights in and to the Film, the copyright pertaining thereto or the rights, licences and privileges granted to the Distributor hereunder.

6 INDEMNITY

The Producer shall at all times indemnify and hold harmless the Distributor, its sub-Distributors and licensees, their officers, directors and employees and their exhibitors, licensees and assignees, from any and all charges, claims, damages, costs, judgements, decrees, losses, expenses (including reasonable legal fees), penalties, demands liabilities and causes of action, of any kind or stature based upon, relating to, or arising out of a breach or claimed breach or failure of any of the convents, agreements, representations or warranties of Producer hereunder or by reason of any claims, actions or proceedings relating to or arising out of any breach or failure or conduct or activity resulting in a breach or

6 INDEMNITY

See earlier chapters for notes on indemnities.

claim of breach. All rights and remedies hereunder shall be cumulative and shall not interfere with or prevent the exercise of any other right or remedy which may be available to the Distributor. Upon notice from the Distributor of any such claim, demand or action being commenced, the Producer agrees to adjust, settle or defend the same at the sole cost of the Producer. If the Producer shall fail to do so, the Distributor shall have the right and is fully authorized and empowered by the Producer to appear in any such claim, demand or action, to adjust, settle, compromise, litigate, contest, satisfy judgements and take any other action necessary or desirable for the disposition of such claim, demand or action. In any such case, the Producer within 20 days after demand by the Distributor, shall fully reimburse the Distributor for all such payments and expenses, including reasonable attorneys' fees. If the Producer shall fail to reimburse the Distributor, then, without waiving its right to otherwise enforce such reimbursement, the Distributor shall have the right to deduct the said amount of such payments and expenses or any part thereof, from any sums accruing under this Agreement or any other agreement to or for the account of the Producer. Also, in the event of any matter to which the foregoing indemnity relates, the Distributor shall have the right to withhold from disbursements to or for the account of the Producer a sum which in the Distributor's opinion may be reasonably necessary to satisfy any liability or settlement in connection with such matter, plus a reasonable amount to cover the expenses of defending such claim and shall have the further right to apply the amount withheld to the satisfaction of such liability or settlement and to the reimbursement of such expenses.

7 COPYRIGHT

(a) Ownership: The Producer warrants that the Producer has not transferred its ownership in and to all copyrights pertaining to the Film throughout the world, including without limitation the rights to secure

7 COPYRIGHT

Distributors will always ask that the producer is the proper copyright owner of all materials pertaining to the film. Distributors will either ask for a licence or an assignment of the copyright in order that they can exploit the film on the producer's behalf.

copyright registration anywhere in the world with respect to all copyrights in the Film and to secure any renewals and extensions thereof wherever and whenever permitted. Producer warrants that upon delivery of the Film to the Distributor, the Producer will own all copyrights in the Film throughout the world for the full period of copyright and all extensions and renewals.

(b) Defence of Copyright: The Distributor hereby agrees to take all reasonable steps to protect such copyrights from infringement by unauthorized parties and in particular, at the request of the Producer, to take such action and proceedings as may be reasonable to prevent any unauthorized use, reproduction, performance, exhibition or exploitation by third Parties of the Film or any part thereof or the material on which it is based which may be in contravention of the exclusive rights granted to the Distributor in respect to the Film.

For the purpose of permitting the Distributor to defend and enforce all rights and remedies granted to the Distributor hereunder, and to prevent any unauthorized use, reproduction, performance, exhibition or exploitation of the Film or any part thereof or the material on which it is based, the Producer hereby irrevocably appoints the Distributor its sole and exclusive attorney-in-fact, to act in the Producer's name or otherwise. The Distributor agrees, in its own name or in the name of the Producer, to take all reasonable steps to enforce and protect the rights, licences and privileges herein granted, under any law and under any and all copyrights, renewals and extensions thereof, and to prevent the infringement thereof, and to bring, prosecute, defend and appear in suits, actions and proceedings of any nature under or concerning all copyrights in the Film and to settle claims and collect and receive all damages arising from any infringement of or interference with any and all such rights, and in the sole judgement of the Distributor exercised in good faith to join the Producer as a party, plaintiff or

Many distributors wish to take an assignment of copyright so that they can fight against any copyright infringement. In some countries, if someone does not own the copyright outright then they will be unable to sue for infringement in their own name. The distributor will often ask for the right to undertake legal action on the producer's behalf against any party infringing the copyright of the film.

Producers should be aware that in some circumstances any legal fees incurred by the distributor may be passed on as a distribution expense to the producer.

defendant in such suit, action or proceeding. The Producer hereby irrevocably appoints the Distributor as its sole and exclusive attorney in-fact during the term of this Agreement, with full and irrevocable power and authority to secure, register, renew and extend all copyrights in the Film and all related properties upon each thereof becoming eligible for copyright, registration, renewal and extension.

(c) Limitation of Liability: The Distributor shall not be liable, responsible or accountable in damages or otherwise to the Producer for any action or failure to act on behalf of the Producer within the scope of authority conferred on the Distributor under this Clause, unless such action or omission was performed or omitted fraudulently or in bad faith or constituted wanton and wilful misconduct or gross negligence.

8 ERRORS AND OMISSIONS INSURANCE

The Distributor shall obtain and maintain or cause to be obtained and maintained throughout the Distribution Term Errors and Omissions Insurance in a form acceptable to the Producer, from a qualified insurance company acceptable to the Producer naming the Distributor and the Producer and each and all the parties indemnified herein as additional named insureds. The amount and coverage shall be for a minimum of $1,000,000/$3,000,000 with respect to any one or more claims relating to the Film or if the Distributor pays an advance, the amount of the advance, whichever shall be greater. The policy shall provide for a deductible no greater than $10,000 and thirty (30) days' notice to the Producer before any modification, cancellation or termination.

9 INSTRUMENTS OF FURTHER ASSURANCE

The Producer shall execute and deliver to the Distributor, promptly upon the request of the Distributor, any other

8 ERRORS AND OMISSIONS INSURANCE

Producers should be aware that it is very easy to name a distributor as one of the insured on an E&O policy. Usually this is done at no extra cost. Sometimes a distributor will ask for E&O insurance to run from the period of delivery of the film and therefore producers should ensure that their E&O policy runs for the correct period of time. E&O insurance is usually taken out on the first day of principal photography and therefore the policy may run out prior to the period asked for in the distribution agreement.

instruments or documents considered by the Distributor to be necessary or desirable to evidence, effectuate or confirm this Agreement, or any of its terms and conditions.

10 NO DISTRIBUTOR REPRESENTATIONS AND WARRANTIES

The Producer acknowledges and agrees that the Distributor makes no express or implied representation, warranty, guarantee or agreement as to the Gross Receipts to be derived from the Film or the distribution, exhibition or exploitation thereof, nor does the Distributor guarantee the performance by any sub-Distributor, licensee or exhibitor of any contract for the distribution, exhibition or exploitation of the Film, nor does the Distributor make any representation, warranty, guarantee or agreement as to any minimum amount of monies to be expended for the distribution, advertising, publicizing and exploitation of the Film. The Producer recognizes and acknowledges that the amount of gross receipts which may be realized from the distribution, exhibition and exploitation of the Film is speculative, and agrees that the reasonable business judgement exercised in good faith of the Distributor and its sub-distributors and licensees regarding any matter affecting the distribution, exhibition and exploitation of the Film shall be binding and conclusive upon the Producer.

11 DISTRIBUTION AND EXPLOITATION OF THE FILM

The Distributor shall have the complete, exclusive and unqualified control of the distribution, exhibition, exploitation and other disposition of the Film (directly or by any sub-distributor or licensee) in the media granted to the Distributor hereunder throughout the Territory during the Distribution Term with respect to each country or place, in accordance with such sales methods, plans, patterns, programmes, policies, terms and conditions as the Distributor in its reasonable business judgement may

10 NO DISTRIBUTOR REPRESENTATIONS AND WARRANTIES

Sometimes a distributor will insist that a clause is inserted which expressly states that the distributor may not sell the film or realize a minimum amount of revenue from the distribution of the film. Producers should be aware that even though they have entered into a distribution agreement the film may do poorly at the box office and the distributor may have problems selling the film to other territories.

11 DISTRIBUTION AND EXPLOITATION OF THE FILM

Producers should note that this clause is only a guide and that in many circumstances a distributor will work very closely with the producer in making sales to other territories. In some cases, a producer will have substantial input in the sales and marketing of the film prior to its theatrical release. This clause is heavily weighted in the distributor's favour.

determine proper or expedient. The following rights of distribution and exploitation shall in no way limit the generality or effect of the foregoing:

(a) Terms: The Distributor may determine the manner and terms upon which the Film shall be marketed, distributed, licensed, exhibited, exploited or otherwise disposed of and all matters pertaining thereto and the decision of the Distributor on all such matters shall be final and conclusive. The Producer shall have no control whatsoever in or over (i) the manner or extent to which the Distributor or its sub-distributors or licensees shall exploit the Film (ii) the terms and provisions of any licences granted by the Distributor to third parties or (iii) to the sufficiency or insufficiency of proceeds from the Film.

(b) Refrain from Distribution, Exhibition or Exploitation: The Distributor may refrain from the release, distribution, re-issue or exhibition of the Film at any time in any country, place or location of the Territory in any media or in any form. The Producer acknowledges that there is no obligation to exploit the soundtrack, recording rights or music publishing rights or merchandising rights or literary publishing rights and it is agreed that the Distributor may elect to exercise any or all of the said rights as the Distributor may determine.

(c) 'Outright Sales': The Distributor may make outright sales of the Film as the Distributor may determine.

(a)(b)   Distribution contracts usually set out that there is no obligation on the distributor to exploit a film or programme. Therefore producers should ensure that any advance that they receive from the distributor is reasonable and that it is large enough to ensure that the distributor will seek out sales for the film or programme in order to recoup monies invested by them.

(c) Distributors work on the basis of charging a commission usually on gross revenues received. This means the actual sums paid by all buyers of the film or programme. Distributors always charge commissions but depending on the specific deal these rates are negotiable. Certain markets and territories which the distributor has the right to sell in may be negotiated at a lower percentage. Commissions generally range from 25 to 35 per cent. Sometimes these commissions are lower. Producers should also be aware that distributors use sub-agents in certain parts of the world and therefore commissions may be higher than what is stated above. Usually producers negotiate a higher commission if a

(d) Contracts and Settlements: The Distributor may distribute the Film under existing or further franchise or license contracts which contracts may relate to the Film separately or to the Film and one or more other Films distributed by or through the Distributor. The Distributor may in the exercise of its reasonable business judgement exercised in good faith make, alter or cancel contracts with exhibitors, sub-distributors and other licensees and adjust and settle disputes, make allowances and adjustments and give credits with respect thereto.

(e) Means of Release: The Distributor may exhibit or cause the Film to be exhibited in theatres or other places owned, controlled, leased or managed by the Distributor. The Distributor may enter into any agreement or arrangement with any other major Distributor for the distribution by such other major distributor of all or a substantial portion of the Distributor's theatrical films. The Distributor may also enter into any agreement or arrangement with any other major distributor or any other party for the handling of the shipping and inspection activities of the Distributor's exchanges or the handling of other facilities in connection with the distribution of films.

(f) Time of Release: The initial release of the Film in any part of the Territory shall commence on such date or dates as the Distributor or its sub-distributors or licensees in their respective sole judgement and discretion may determine. Such releases shall be subject to the requirements of censorship boards or other governmental authorities, the availability of playing time in key cities, the securing of the requisite number of film copies and delays caused by reason of events of force majeure or by reason of any cause beyond the control of the Distributor or its sub-distributors or licensees. If any claim or action is

sub-agent is engaged. (i.e. 5 per cent over and above the commission earned by the distributor).

(e)(f)(g)   In some distribution deals a producer negotiates a specific release date so that the distributor does not shelve the film for an indefinite period of time.

made or instituted against the Distributor or any of its sub-distributors or licensees as to the Film, the Distributor or such sub-distributors or licensees shall have the right to postpone the release of the Film (if it has not been released) or to suspend further distribution thereof (if it has been released) until such time as such claim or action shall have been settled or disposed of to the satisfaction of the Distributor or such sub-distributors or licensees.

(g) Duration of Release: Distribution of the Film shall be continued in the Territory or any part thereof in which it is released by the Distributor or its licensees only for [ ] years. The distributor shall not be obligated to reissue the Film at any time in the Territory but shall have the right to do so from time to time as it may deem desirable.

(h) Withdrawal of the Film: Should the Distributor or its sub-distributors or licensees deem it inadvisable or unprofitable to distribute, exhibit or exploit the Film in the Territory or any part thereof the Distributor or its sub-distributors or licensees shall have the right to withhold or withdraw the Film from such Territory or any part thereof.

(i) Banning of Release: If by reason of any law, embargo, decree, regulation or other restriction of any agency or governmental body the number or type of films that the Distributor is permitted to distribute in the Territory or any part thereof is limited then the Distributor may in its absolute discretion determine which films then distributed by Distributor will be distributed in the Territory or any part thereof and the Distributor shall not be liable to the Producer in any manner or to any extent if the Film is not distributed in the Territory or any part thereof by reason of any such determination.

(j) Collections: The Distributor shall in good faith every six months audit, check or verify the computation of any payments and press for the collection of any monies which, if collected, would constitute gross receipts.

There shall be no responsibility or liability to the Producer for failure to audit, check, verify or to collect any monies payable.

(k) Advertising: The Distributor agrees to commit a minimum of $[   ] with respect to the advertising and publicity of the Film.

(l) Expenses: The Distributor may incur any expenses which the Distributor, in the good faith exercise of its reasonable business judgement, deems appropriate with respect to the Film or the exercise of any of the Distributor's rights hereunder. Alternatively, [the Distributor may incur expenses as set out in Schedule [   ]].

(k) Although there is no direct correlation between the amount of money spent on advertising and publicity of a film and the film's box office success, in some cases when the distributor spends more money on the advertising or publicity of the film then that film will usually gross more revenue in the cinemas. However in some cases the distributor will spend substantial sums on the theatrical release of a film and that film will not succeed at the box office.

Producers should insist that the distributor spends a specific amount on the advertising and publicity of the film otherwise the distributor may not release the film theatrically and release it straight to video.

(l) Producers should ensure that there is a limit on the expenses that the distributor spends on the film. It is always best to set out in a separate schedule what expenses the distributor may spend money on. (This is known as recouping only direct costs incurred in making a sale.) (Producers should try and cap expenses at 10 per cent of gross sales.) Producers should be aware that the distributor may often be selling the film in conjunction with other films at a major market or festival and therefore the producer should try and set out some basis for sharing or apportioning the distributor's expenses in relation to the producer's film. If this is not agreed then there is nothing to stop the distributor from deducting his entire expenditure for a market or festival against any income realized from the sale of a specific film.

The producer should also be aware of the term 'cross collateralization'. Producers should try and prohibit cross collateralization of the expenses from the selling of one film against income from the sale of another film. Producers should try and ensure that the distributor keep separate accounts for each film as well establishing a mechanism for apportioning expenses when a distributor attempts to sell two or more films on the same occasion (such as a festival or market).

12 PRINTS OF THE FILM

The Distributor shall be entitled to obtains such prints, negatives and master prints of the Film which the Distributor shall deem advisable for distribution of the Film in the Territory. All such prints shall remain the property of the Distributor.

13 CENSORSHIP/FORCE MAJEURE

(a) Adjustment of Advance: If the Distributor is required to pay or advance to the Producer any fixed or other sum before it is collected from the distribution of the Film, and the Distributor is unable to distribute the Film in any country or area of the Territory for any reasons, including without limitation, censorship, import restriction, force majeure or failure to secure permits, the fixed payment or advance shall be reduced by the amount reasonably allocated to such country or area. The amount allocated to such country or area shall be the amount indicated in Schedule [ ] or in the absence of such indication in Schedule [ ] or if the country or area where distribution is prevented is one to which no allocation is made or which is part of a country or area for which an overall allocation is made or which is part of a country or area for which an overall allocation is made then a reasonable allocation shall be made by the Distributor for such country or area in which distribution is prevented. If the Film is classified as unsuitable for children under 18 years of age or suitable for adults only in any country or area the fixed payment or advance payment for such country or area shall be reduced by [ ] per cent.

(b) Adjustment of Distribution Expenses: If the Distributor is for any reason unable to distribute the Film in any country or area in the Territory and the Distributor has incurred any Distribution Expenses in connection with the distribution of the Film in such country or area the

12 PRINTS OF THE FILM

Distributors will ask for the right to obtain prints either directly in the agreement or through a laboratory access letter which is attached as an exhibit in a schedule to the agreement. Producers should ensure that any prints are obtained by the distributor at the distributor's own cost.

13 CENSORSHIP/FORCE MAJEURE

Producers should be aware that sometimes a distributor will advance funds to the producer in order to complete production. Therefore the distributor will ask that in the event that the film is not completed as a result of an event of force majeure or that the film does not comply with the censorship requirements of the specific territory, the producer will have to refund a part or all of the advance which is made.

Producer will on demand reimburse the Distributor or at the Distributor's election Distributor shall be repaid by the Producer from any sum thereafter due from the Distributor to the Producer.

14 DISTRIBUTOR'S DEFAULT

The Producer shall not be entitled to bring any actions or proceedings of any nature against the Distributor or its sub-distributors or licensees whether at law or in equity or otherwise based upon or arising in whole or in part any claim that the Distributor or its sub-distributors or licensees has in any way violated this Agreement unless the action is brought within one (1) year from the date of the Producer's discovery of such alleged violations. It is agreed that if the Distributor breaches this Agreement and fails to remedy such breach within a period of thirty (30) days after receipt by the Distributor of written notice from the Producer specifying the alleged breach and fails to cure such breach within sixty (60) days thereafter, or if after delivery of the Film the Distributor shall fail to make any payments at the time and in the manner provided and the Producer has given the Distributor ten (10) days' written notice to that effect, then in either of such events the Producer shall have the right to proceed against the Distributor for monies due to the Producer in accordance with any and all remedies available to the Producer both at law and in equity. In no event however shall the Producer have any right to terminate or rescind this Agreement nor shall the rights acquired by the Distributor under this Agreement be subject to revocation, termination, diminution because of any failure or breach of any kind on the part of the Distributor or its sub-distributors or licensees. In no event shall the Producer be entitled to an injunction to restrain any alleged breach by the Distributor or its sub-distributors or licensees of any provision of this Agreement.

14   DISTRIBUTOR'S DEFAULT

Producers should be aware that this clause is one-sided in favour of the distributor. Producers should try and water down the strength of this clause so that if a distributor cannot remedy a breach within a certain period of time then the producer can terminate the agreement.

15 ARBITRATION

[Any controversy or claim arising out of or relating to this agreement or any breach thereof shall be settled by arbitration in accordance with [   ].

The prevailing party shall be entitled to reimbursement for costs and reasonable legal fees. The determination of the arbitrator in such proceeding shall be final, binding and non-appealable.]

16 WAIVER

No waiver of any breach of any provision of this Agreement shall constitute a waiver of any other breach of the same or any other provision hereof and no waiver shall be effective unless made in writing.

17 RELATIONSHIP OF PARTIES

Nothing herein contained shall be construed to create a joint venture or partnership between the parties hereto.

18 ASSIGNMENT

The Distributor may assign this Agreement to and/or may distribute the Film through any of its subsidiaries, parents or affiliated corporations or any agent or other means determined by the Distributor provided that the Distributor shall not be relieved of its obligations hereunder. The Producer may assign the right to receive payment hereunder to any third party provided that the Producer shall not be permitted to assign any of its obligations hereunder.

15   ARBITRATION

See earlier notes on arbitration.

16   WAIVER

See earlier notes on waiver.

18   ASSIGNMENT

Producers should ensure that they have the right to assign their right to receive payment to any third party. This is in order that the producer has the ability to raise production finance from a bank or lender who will lend money and take security against various distribution contracts which a producer may enter into.

19 NOTICES

All notices from the Producer or the Distributor to the other with respect to this Agreement shall be given in writing by post or facsimile and addressed to the Distributor or the Producer as appropriate at the address set forth in the preamble hereof. A courtesy copy of any notice to the Producer shall be sent to [   ] and a courtesy copy of any notice to the Distributor shall be sent to [   ].

20 GOVERNING LAW

This Agreement shall be governed by the laws of [   ].

21 CAPTIONS

The captions of the various paragraphs and sections of the Agreement are intended to be used solely for convenience of reference and are not intended and shall not be deemed for any purpose whatsoever to modify or to be used as an aid in the construction of any provisions.

22 AMENDMENTS IN WRITING

This Agreement cannot be amended, modified or changed in any way whatsoever, except by a written instrument duly signed by authorized officers of the Producer and the Distributor.

23 ENTIRE AGREEMENT

This Agreement, which is comprised of the general terms above ('Main Agreement') and the attached Schedule and Exhibits, represents the entire agreement between the

19 NOTICES

See earlier notes on notices.

20 GOVERNING LAW

Producers should try and restrict the governing law to their own jurisdiction. This may be difficult if a foreign distributor is involved.

parties with respect to the subject matter hereof and supersedes all previous representations, understandings or agreements, oral or written, between the parties regarding the subject matter hereof.

By signing in the spaces provided below, the parties accept and agree to all the terms and conditions of this Agreement as of the date first above written.

Signed by the Producer
in the presence of: } _____

Signed by the Distributor
in the presence of: } _____

SCHEDULE A

Territory: [   ]

Term: [   ]

Advance payable
as follows: [   ]

                      [   ]

Royalty: [% of Gross Receipts]

SCHEDULE A

Producers should try and include specific information of the agreement in Schedule A. This is for quick reference to the various essential terms and conditions of the contract.

8 Finder/executive producer agreement

The increase in international co-productions and co-financing has resulted in many film and television producers utilizing the services of individuals to help fill deficits in their production budgets. Finders, or executive producers are usually ex-distribution or broadcasting executives who are well connected in the film and television industry.

Producers will pay the finder a fee which is negotiable but is usually between 5 and 10 per cent of the money raised by the finder. In addition, the finder will require an executive producer or other similar credit. The following agreement is only a guide and should be drafted to suit the particular needs of the producer and the specific circumstances of the transaction.

Finder/executive producer agreement

FINDER/EXECUTIVE PRODUCER AGREEMENT

THIS AGREEMENT is made the   day of   [year]

BETWEEN:

('the Producer') whose registered office is at [   ] and Finder of [   ] ('the Finder')

Whereas the Producer owns, controls or otherwise has the exclusive right to produce a [feature film] [television film] [television series] provisionally entitled [   ] (hereafter referred to as 'the Film') based upon a screenplay written by [   ]

Whereas the Finder is engaged in financing and seeking finance in the film and television industry.

Whereas the parties to this agreement wish to enter into an agreement whereby the Finder will introduce the Producer to third parties who may be interested in lending for, investing in, or in any other way financing all or a portion of the [development] [production] [distribution] [exploitation] of the Film and who hereinafter shall collectively be referred to as 'the Financier' or 'Financiers'.

The parties hereby agree as follows:

1 TERM AND SERVICES

(a) Commencing on the date hereof and continuing until terminated by either party as provided in this agreement, the Finder shall use its best efforts on an [exclusive basis] in [territory] on a [non-exclusive basis] in [territory] to introduce the Financiers who may be interested in co-producing, financing, investing or lending money (either their own or that of third parties) to the Producer in connection with the Film. The term of this agreement shall continue for a period of [   ] automatically renewable for a further period of [   ] unless one party notifies the other in writing of their

FINDER/EXECUTIVE PRODUCER AGREEMENT: NOTES

PREAMBLE

Producers should clearly set out the type of project which the finder will be working on. The producer should state whether the finder will introduce them to third parties who will either lend money, invest money or provide facilities to the production. Producers should be aware that some individuals will invest in a production by lending their post-production facilities in return for a stake in the production. Therefore, it is essential that this is clarified in the preamble of the agreement.

1   TERM AND SERVICES

Producers should state whether the finder's services are on an exclusive or non-exclusive basis and whether the finder's efforts are restricted to a specific territory. For example, if an English film producer wishes to enter into a three-country co-production and already has a French partner then it does not make any sense to engage a finder who wishes to bring French money into the production.

The actual term of the agreement should be quite specific. Most producers tend to set up the agreement for periods of three to six months. Even though the term of the agreement ends, if the

election to terminate this agreement by giving no less than thirty (30) days' written notice of that fact, but in any event the term shall automatically terminate on the [date].

2 CONSULTATION

(a) During the term of this agreement the Finder and Producer shall consult with each other in respect of the creative elements of the Film for the purposes of maximizing the opportunity of the Finder to interest Financiers in the Film.

(b) The Finder shall keep the Producer fully informed of all parties contacted and all negotiations carried out with any and all Financiers and the Finder shall in no event enter into any agreements that in any way binds the Producer or do or refrain from doing any act without the prior written consent of the Producer.

(c) The Producer shall keep the Finder fully informed of all parties contacted by the Producer and/or any third parties acting on its behalf together with all relevant terms of negotiations made by them in connection with the financing of the Film.

3 REMUNERATION

(a) If at any time during the term of this agreement or at any time thereafter the Producer enters into any agreement with any Financier or Financiers introduced by the Finder [to invest in], [lend for] or [finance the development], [production] [distribution] or [exploitation] of the Film, the Finder shall be entitled to remuneration in the amount equal to [five per cent (5%)] of the total amount committed to the Film by such Financier or Financiers.

(b) In the event that any of the contributions made by any Financier is of a technical nature or is provided as production services to the Film, the Finder shall be entitled to remuneration in the amount equivalent to

producer enters into an agreement with one of the finder's contacts, the producer will still be liable for commission or payments to the finder.

2 CONSULTATION

Both the producer and the finder should ensure that a free-flow of information regarding potential contacts, meetings, be disclosed to each other. It can be embarrassing if the producer takes a project to a potential financier only to discover that the finder has already taken the project to that individual on the producer's behalf.

3 REMUNERATION

(a) Although payments are usually negotiable, it is the industry's standard to pay a finder 5 per cent of the total amount committed and collected by the producer as a result of the finder's efforts.

(b) See above note regarding payment for production/post-production facilities. Sometimes, a finder will bring products and services such as transport or flights to a production and may require some form of payment in return.

[two per cent (2%)] of the total cash value committed to the Film in the above mentioned form.

(c) The Producer hereby agrees that the Finder's compensation shall be paid [no later than five (5) working days following the receipt of any and all sums by the Producer]. [On the first day of principal photography of the Film.]

4 EXPENSES

The Finder hereby acknowledges that the services being provided to the Producer are on a contingency basis and the Finder shall not be entitled to any expenses for these services unless such expenses are agreed between the Producer and Finder in writing.

5 CREDIT

In the event that the Finder obtains [per cent (%) or more of the total financing needed to produce the Film] [agreed amount or presale] the Finder shall receive an [Executive, determine type of credit] and the size, position and design of such credit shall be at the Producer's sole discretion.

6 CONFIDENTIALITY

The Producer hereby agrees and undertakes to maintain the confidentiality of any Financier or Financiers introduced by the Finder in respect of the Film and the Finder agrees in good faith to maintain the confidentiality of any information acquired from the Producer in relation to the Film and by virtue of this agreement.

(c) Producers should be aware that from the finder's point of view, the finder will usually set out exactly how and when he/she is to be paid. Sometimes, the finder will even set out his bank's sort code and account number for payment.

4 EXPENSES

Producers should clearly set out whether the finder will be paid expenses. Sometimes, the producer will agree to pay for the finder's flights and accommodation, if they travel to see one of their contacts. There is no industry standard and this should be subject to negotiations between the producer and finder. One should not agree to pay the finder any expenses unless agreed in advance.

5 CREDIT

Credits can sometimes be a contentious issue and therefore must be agreed prior to commencement of any of the finder's services. Forms of credit such as executive producer, co-executive producer, co-production executive, and associate producer are quite common when engaging a finder. Sometimes, other financiers already involved with the production will not accept another credit for a finder. Producers should be aware of this and ensure that the existing financial partners consent before agreeing to an additional credit.

6 CONFIDENTIALITY

Finders may wish to protect their contacts and therefore will ask for a confidentiality clause. From a producer's perspective, they should also ask for a confidentiality clause, since the finder may discover certain aspects about the producer's business and the producer will not want these disclosed.

7 NO OBLIGATION

(a) Nothing in this agreement shall oblige the Finder to obtain any Financier or Financiers nor shall anything in this agreement oblige the Producer to enter into an agreement or agreements with any Financier or Financiers introduced by the Finder.

(b) The Finder hereby agrees not to sell or offer to sell any form of securities relating to and vesting in the development, production and/or exploitation of the Film.

8 WARRANTIES AND REPRESENTATIONS

(a) The Producer hereby represents and warrants that it is the sole and exclusive owner of the rights in the Film and are fully authorized to enter into this agreement and will remain so for the full term of this agreement.

(b) The Finder hereby warrants and represents that it is entitled to enter into this agreement.

9 INDEMNITIES

Each party to this agreement hereby indemnifies and agrees to keep the other party fully and effectually indemnified from and against any and all losses, costs, actions, proceedings, claims, damages, expenses (including reasonable legal costs and expenses) or liabilities suffered or incurred directly or indirectly by each party in consequence of any breach, non-performance or non-observance by the other of any of the agreements, conditions, obligations, representations, warranties and undertakings on the part of each party contained in this agreement.

7   NO OBLIGATION

Producers should set out in the agreement that they will not necessarily enter into an agreement with any financier or source of finance which the finder has introduced them to. In most agreements, the finder will also state that they are not obliged to find a financier for the producer. The producer should ensure that the finder does not have the right to sell securities such as shares on an investment market in relation to the film. It is possible that a producer could engage a finder and that finder could set up some scheme on a stock exchange to raise funds for the producer. Raising funds on a public market can be very expensive and there are specific disclosure requirements that must be complied with.

8   WARRANTIES AND REPRESENTATIONS

This is an area where specific legal advice may be necessary. Most warranties and representations are fairly standard (see earlier chapters).

9   INDEMNITIES

Producers should be aware that when utilizing finders, there is always a danger of the finder entering into some unauthorized transaction in the name of the producer without the producer's consent. Therefore, it is essential that the producer obtain an indemnity from the finder.

10 RELATIONSHIP BETWEEN THE PARTIES

(a) The Finder is an independent contractor and shall not act as an employee, agent or joint venturer of the Producer and nothing in this agreement is intended to or shall be deemed to constitute a partnership between the parties.

(b) The Finder is authorized by the Producer to represent the Producer in respect of the Film in negotiations with third parties subject to the final decision of the Producer.

(c) The parties to this agreement shall each be entitled to develop other projects and engage in other activities within the Film and television industries separate and apart from the Film.

11 ASSIGNMENT

This agreement is personal to the Producer and Finder and shall not be assigned in whole or in part without the prior written consent of each party.

12 ADDITIONAL DOCUMENTS

Each of the parties to this agreement agrees to execute any additional documents which may be required to fully effectuate the purposes and intents of this agreement or to carry out the obligations of the parties hereunder provided that they are consistent with the provisions of this agreement.

13 ENTIRE AGREEMENT

This agreement constitutes the entire agreement between the parties and may only be varied by written instrument signed by either party to this agreement.

10   RELATIONSHIP BETWEEN THE PARTIES

A statement to the effect that the finder is an independent contractor is essential in this agreement. Producers should also restrict the agreement to a particular project and not to other projects which the producer may have in development.

12   ADDITIONAL DOCUMENTS

Producers should be aware that from the finder's perspective that this clause is a necessity. The finder will want to ensure that the producer signs further agreements in order that the finder will be paid.

14 NOTICES

All notices required or desired to be given under the provisions of this agreement shall be in writing and shall be deemed to have been duly served if hand delivered or sent by facsimile or pre-paid first class post addressed to the relevant parties addressed herein as stated or as otherwise advised frown time to time.

15 GOVERNING LAW

This agreement shall be read and construed in all aspects in accordance with and shall be governed by the Laws of [England] and the parties hereby submit to the exclusive jurisdiction of the [English] Courts.

16 GENERAL PROVISIONS

(a) The parties hereby agree that they shall not incur any debts or obligations in respect of the other and nothing in this agreement is intended or should be construed so as to give any right or benefit to any third party as against either or both the Finder and/or the Producer.

(b) The clause headings in this agreement are for convenience only and do not form part of this agreement.

(c) Each party to this agreement hereby acknowledges that no representation or warranty not expressly set forth in this agreement has been made to the other party and this agreement constitutes the entire agreement of the parties regarding the subject matter hereof and supersedes all prior agreements either oral or written.

IN WITNESS WHEREOF the parties have executed this agreement on the date set forth above

SIGNED by
for and on behalf of
the Producer
in the presence of:

SIGNED by
for and on behalf of
the Finder
in the presence of:

9 Confidentiality/non-disclosure agreement

The following non-disclosure agreement provides that the recipient will keep certain information such as a story, script, or treatment, confidential.

Although ideas cannot be copyrighted, a treatment or screenplay can be. Writers should note that writing an idea down in a treatment or outline form, will be classified as recording that idea in a material form which is a vital prerequisite for copyright protection. Writers should express all aspects of their idea in as much detail as possible including a full description of the characters, a statement of the plot and other information which will set out the originality and distinctiveness of the actual idea. The name of the writer or the person who owns the copyright should be in a prominent position and there should be a copyright notice which consists of the symbol ©, followed by the owner's name, and the year which the idea was first put into a material form.

The following agreement is to be used when a writer is concerned that there is a real chance of an idea in material form being taken by a producer. In most circumstances, a producer will not sign a non-disclosure agreement. However, when a producer actually wants to see certain materials then the writer is in a strong position to have the producer sign a non-disclosure agreement.

CONFIDENTIALITY/NON-DISCLOSURE AGREEMENT

THIS AGREEMENT made this _____ day of ____ [year]

BETWEEN: _____ ('the Writer')

and _____ ('the Producer'),

WHEREAS the Writer has written a [script] [treatment] [storyline] ('Submission') for a possible future [feature film production] [television production].

WHEREAS the Writer wishes the Producer to evaluate the 'Submission' for the sole purpose of determining whether the Submission may be further developed into a [feature film] [television production] ('Project')

NOW THEREAFTER in consideration of the premises and mutual covenants herein contained, the parties agree as follows:

1 All information disclosed by the Writer to the Producer, in writing, whether or not such information is also disclosed orally, that relates or refers, directly or indirectly, to the Submission, including the Submission itself, shall be deemed confidential and shall constitute 'Confidential Information', and shall include (i) all documents generated by the Producer which contain, comment upon, or relate in any way to any Confidential Information received from the Writer, and (ii) any written samples of the Submission received from the Writer together with any information derived by the Producer therefrom.

CONFIDENTIALITY/NON-DISCLOSURE AGREEMENT: NOTES

1 Most producers will be reluctant to sign such an agreement unless they are desperate to see the writer's work. If the writer can convince the producer to sign the agreement then this clause attempts to clarify exactly what should be kept confidential if there is an eventual breach of confidence.

If the producer does sign a confidentiality or non-disclosure agreement it will still be necessary to prove exactly what it was that should have been confidential and in certain cases when the idea was created. When signing non-disclosure agreements there should be an exclusion that says that the producer is not liable if they have already seen or developed a similar project. Sometimes it may be prudent for a producer to write the following words in a letter in addition to signing the non-disclosure agreement:

'This Company [or name of producer] receives a very large number of proposals, many of which are similar to each other.

2 Confidential Information shall not include any information that:
  (i)   the Producer can show by documentary evidence was known to the Producer or prior to the date of its disclosure to the Producer by the Writer; or
  (ii) becomes publicly known, by publication or otherwise, not due to any unauthorized act or omission of the Producer or any other party having an obligations to the Writer; or
  (iii) is subsequently disclosed by the Writer to any person, firm or corporation on a non-confidential basis; or
  (iv) the Producer can conclusively show by documentary evidence that such information was developed independent of any access to the Confidential Information.

3 The Writer will disclose the Confidential Information to the Producer solely for the purpose of allowing the Producer to evaluate the Submission to determine, in its sole discretion, whether the Submission may be further developed into a Project.

4 The Producer agrees to accept disclosure of the Confidential Information and to exercise the same degree of care to maintain the Confidential Information secret and confidential as is employed by the Producer to preserve and safeguard its own materials and confidential information.

5 The Confidential Information shall remain the property of the Writer and shall not be disclosed or revealed by the Producer or to anyone else, except employees of the

For this reason, I am sure that you will appreciate that even if in the future we produce or commission a programme or film which you believe is the same or similar to your suggestion, but which has come coincidentally from another source, we cannot compensate you'.

This paragraph is used by many broadcasters in the UK as added protection against legal action.

2 This clause sets out certain factors which may make it impossible to enforce confidentiality. Information in the public domain or a similar project which was developed by another writer may absolve the producer from any liability.

Other factors which may make it impossible to enforce confidentiality or a non-disclosure agreement may be that it is not in the public interest to keep the submitted material secret. The producer should also realize that if the material which they are reading is widely known to the public as a whole it may be impossible to enforce confidentiality.

From a writer's perspective they should try and register their script or treatments with a solicitor or send a copy to themselves at their home address by registered or recorded post. By doing this the writer can attempt to prove when the specific project was initially written.

3/4/5 Note that some employees of a production company may not have a secrecy or confidentiality agreement with their employer. Therefore it is possible that an employee may decide to pass on a writer's idea to someone else. Writers should be aware that this could happen.

Producer who have 'a need to know' in connection with the Producer's evaluation of the Submission, and who have entered into a secrecy or confidentiality agreement with the Producer under which such employees are required to keep confidential the Confidential Information of the Writer, and such employees shall be advised by the Producer of the confidential nature of the information and that the information shall be treated accordingly. The Producer shall be liable for any improper disclosure of the Confidential Information by its employees.

6 (i)   If the Producer shall notify the Writer of any decision with respect to the further development of the Submission, then the Producer shall not directly or indirectly disclose any Confidential Information to any third party, without the consent of the Writer.

(ii)   If the Producer determines that the Submission cannot be further developed into a Project, within [_____] months of the receipt of the Submission, the Producer shall within five (5) business days after such decision is made return any and all Confidential Information to the Writer, along with all copies or derivatives thereof and all writing generated by the Producer in connection with the Producer's evaluation of the Submission or the Confidential Information.

7 If the Producer determines that the Submission is suitable for further development into a Project, the Producer and the Writer will agree on a schedule for development, and compensation to the Writer for the Submission.

8 Other than as specifically provided herein, the Producer will not use the Confidential Information for any purpose whatsoever other than for the sole purpose permitted in paragraph 3 hereof, unless and until a further executed agreement is first made between the parties setting forth the terms and conditions under

6 There should always be a requirement to return a script or treatment within a certain time frame. Producers can further protect themselves by including a provision in a non-disclosure agreement that they will notify the writer that they have a similar project which they are either developing or producing. This should be done at least six months prior to producing a similar project.

7 From the writer's perspective the writer may wish to set out in further detail a schedule for development and a range of compensation which the writer will receive if the submission is accepted by the producer.

which rights to the Submission and the Confidential Information are to be licensed to, or acquired by, the Producer.

9 The Writer agrees that it will not contact any party or parties other than the Producer concerning the Confidential Information without prior written authorization from the Producer during the term of this agreement.

10 The Producer's obligations under paragraphs 3, 4 and 8 of this agreement shall extend from the date of this agreement and shall survive the expiration or termination of this agreement, provided, however, that the Producer's obligations under paragraphs 3 and 4 of this agreement shall terminate immediately in the event that the Writer shall purposefully disclose the Confidential Information to any other person, firm or corporation on a non-confidential basis, during the term of this Agreement.

11 The Writer hereby expressly warrants that it has the full right and authority to disclose the Confidential Information to the Producer, and that no prior disclosure of the Confidential Information has been made by the Writer nor, to the best of Writer's knowledge, by any other party.

12 Nothing in this agreement shall be deemed a sale or offer for sale of the Submission, and nothing contained herein shall in any way obligate the Writer to grant the Producer a licence or any other rights, directly or indirectly to the Confidential Information or the Submission.

13 Subject to paragraph 10 above, this agreement shall terminate _____ [years] [months] from the date of this agreement, unless extended by mutual agreement of the parties. This agreement may be terminated prior to the expiration of _____ from the date of this agreement by either the Writer or the Producer upon thirty (30) days' written notice to the other parties of an intention to terminate.

13 A date of termination of the agreement should always be set
   out in order that the confidentiality period does not run
   forever.

14 This agreement sets forth the entire agreement between the parties and may not be amended or modified except by writing and signed by all of the parties.
15 This agreement shall be governed by the laws of [   ] and the parties irrevocably submit to the jurisdiction of [   ].
16 This agreement may be executed in counterparts.

IN WITNESS WHEREOF the parties have executed this agreement as of the day and year first above written.

WRITER   **PRODUCER**

By: ....   By: ....

Name: ....   Name: ....

                               Title:

Date: ....   Date: ....

10 Director's agreement

Director's employment agreements share many of the same provisions that writer's agreements provide for. In many cases, a director's deal may be structured as a direct employment or through a loan out arrangement. A loan out arrangement is where self-employed individuals set up a specific company for more efficient regulation of their tax affairs. In the case of directors, the director's company will agree with the producer's company that they are entitled to the director's exclusive services. Producers wishing to use the services of a director will have to contract with the director's company. The contract will be similar with the director's company as it would be with the director as an individual. However, if the contract is with the director's company, the producer cannot sue the director if there is a breach. Even worse, is that most directors' companies are just shells with no assets and therefore any claim against it would probably be worthless.

To avoid this, a producer should contract with not only the director's company but ensure that the director (personally) signs an 'inducement letter' which is a direct contract between the director and the production company. The inducement letter sets out that the director will perform all of the requirements under the contract with the director's company. If the director's company does not perform all of its requirements, then the producer can sue the director personally for any non-performance or breach.

Readers should note that loan out arrangements also apply to other freelance personnel such as writers (see Appendix C for a sample inducement letter).

Like other behind-the-camera personnel, directors belong to unions and these unions have agreements with broadcasters and producers. The Producers Alliance for Cinema and Television ('PACT') have model contracts in the form of a director's Letter of Engagement as well as a Director's Loan Out Agreement. These agreements are based on the PACT conditions of engagement for directors which can be obtained from PACT. The precedent found in this chapter incorporates many of those terms and conditions found in the PACT agreement.

These agreements are straightforward. The major issues which should be dealt with are issues such as assignment of copyright, moral rights, rental and lending rights, credit and final cut.

Directors must assign the copyright in the products of their services and moral rights should be dealt with at the same time by asking the director to waive moral rights.

Recently, the Directors Guild of Great Britain has created its own standard terms of engagement which provide for more extensive rights to be given to directors as part of their minimum contractual entitlement. This includes residual payments and an attempt to limit the moral rights waiver.

When dealing with American directors who are members of the Directors Guild of America (DGA), producers should be aware that they may be subject to the rules and regulations of the DGA collective bargaining agreement. Although many of the clauses found in the following agreement are similar, other clauses specifically found in the DGA contract are not present. Producers who engage DGA members should consult the DGA agreement or receive legal advice from an American lawyer.

Possible problems on the horizon are the European Union directives which are proposing to harmonize the copyright laws of member states. Under the directive on rental and lending rights, the 'author' of a film has the right to authorize or prohibit rental or lending of the original or copies of a film. The directive states that 'the principal director' shall be considered as the author or one of the authors of a film. If directors acquire the ability to share in the proceeds of exploitation of a film or television programme as a result of the directive, then the issue of 'equitable remuneration' may have important consequences in contractual negotiations. See earlier chapters for notes on 'equitable remuneration'.

Depending on how well known a director is, he/she may or may not have the right of 'final cut', which is the power to determine the composition and the final edited version of a film or television programme. In some circumstances, a director may be required to produce two versions of a film, one for theatrical release and another for television broadcast. In some circumstances, a director may have the right to select key personnel such as the director of photography, production manager and editor. A veteran director with clout will have the power to hire certain cast and crew members without anyone else's approval.

This precedent can be utilized for either a feature film, television programme or television series. However, it makes reference to a feature film throughout.

DIRECTOR'S AGREEMENT

DATE:

PARTIES:

(1) [   ] of [   ] ('the Company' which expression shall be deemed to include its successors in title and assigns) and;

(2) [   ] of [   ] ('the Director' which expression shall include the Director's personal representatives).

The Company wishes to engage the Director to direct the [cinematograph film and soundtrack] [television programme] [television series] provisionally entitled ['   '] which the Company intends but does not undertake to produce and the Director has agreed to do so for the consideration upon the terms and subject to the conditions hereinafter appearing.

NOW IT IS HEREBY AGREED as follows:

1 DEFINITIONS

(1) In this agreement the following words and expressions shall unless the context otherwise requires have the following meanings respectively:

(a) ['the Film'] ['Television Programme'] ['Television Series']
the first class sound and colour [theatrical feature length] [cinematograph film and soundtrack][Television Programme] [Television Series] associated therewith to be recorded originally in the English language tentatively entitled ['   '] and based upon [   ] which the Company intends but does not undertake to produce

(b) 'the Start Date'
a date commencing on or about [   ]

324

DIRECTOR'S AGREEMENT: NOTES

1 DEFINITIONS

(a) This definition should be tailored for the type of product being made (i.e. film, television programme, television series, etc.)

(c) 'the Term'
the period from the Start Date until completion of the Film and delivery to the Company of the [first married] answer print thereof conforming in all respects with the Company's specifications therefor

(d) 'the Director's Cut' shall mean a fine cut of the Film with rough assembly or sound

(e) [(e) ['Deferment'] [and] ['Net Profits'/'Producer's Profits']
shall have the meaning[s] ascribed thereto in Schedule 2 to this agreement].

(2) Unless the context otherwise requires words and expressions used herein shall have the same meanings as are assigned to them by the Copyright, Designs and Patents Act 1988.

(c) Producers should be aware that the definitions of 'delivery' and 'completion' must adhere to those definitions in any distribution agreements otherwise the producers may find themselves in breach of contract with distributor and director.

(d) The term 'Director's Cut' must conform with other contracts especially delivery requirements set out in any distribution agreements. Also see note in (c) above.

(e) A deferment must be explained in depth to avoid confusion at a later date. If a director is to be paid a deferment then the actual definition should include when and how the director is to be paid.

A deferment generally means that a certain portion of an individual's remuneration will be deferred until a film or television programme recoups certain costs. Sometimes a deferment is recouped from any monies that are received from the producer (i.e. from sales to unsold territories). Producers should note that deferments can be structured in various ways and are sometimes tied in closely with net or producer's profits. See Appendix B for sample definition of producer/net profits.

Producer's profits or producer's net profits are sometimes defined as all the proceeds of exploitation of the film or television programme after deductions such as distribution expenses, sales agency commissions, the cost of production, repayment of any deferments and the repayment of any share of net profits payable to a third party investor which are not retainable by the producer for its own benefit.

Net profits are in certain circumstances defined as all proceeds of exploitation of a film or television programme after deduction of distribution commissions, distribution expenses, sales agency commissions, the cost of production and any deferments. Note that net profits are in most circumstances recouped before producer's profits/producer's net profits.

2   ENGAGEMENT

The Company hereby engages the Director and the Director hereby agrees to render the Director's services as the individual director of the Film upon the terms and subject to the conditions of this agreement.

3   TERM OF ENGAGEMENT

(1) The Company shall be entitled to the exclusive services of the Director from [the Start Date] [a period of [   ] weeks prior to the scheduled first day of principal photography] until [the expiry of the Term] [the delivery of the Director's Cut].

(2) The Company shall also be entitled to the services of the Director on [an exclusive/a non-exclusive but first/second call basis] [from the Start Date until a period of [   ] weeks prior to the scheduled first day of principal photography] [and] [from delivery of the Director's Cut until the expiry of the Term] [but so that the Director shall not undertake any activities which would prejudice or delay the completion of the Film].

(3) The Company shall also be entitled to make use of the services of the Director subject to the Director's prior professional commitments notified to the Company prior to and/or after the Term in connection with publicity of the Film including the giving of press and publicity interviews and the making of personal appearances [in the major territories of the Film's release] with regard thereto.

(4) The Company shall further be entitled to the services of the Director before and after the Term for the performance and completion of any of the matters contemplated in Clause 4 hereof and such services shall be exclusive to the Company insofar as this is necessary for the performance of the Director's obligations hereunder [but this shall not prevent the Director from performing other non-conflicting obligations to third parties during such period outside the Term].

2 ENGAGEMENT

If this contract is modified for a television series then producers should make reference to the fact that other directors may be engaged on the series.

3 TERM OF ENGAGEMENT

Producers should ensure that the director does not have any conflicting engagements which will affect the shooting schedule of the production.

4 DIRECTOR'S SERVICES

The Director hereby warrants to and undertakes with the Company that the Director shall perform the Director's services hereunder as where and when required by the Company diligently, willingly, conscientiously and to the best of the Director's artistic and creative skill and technical ability and in any manner which may be required by the Company in collaboration with such persons as the Company shall designate and subject to the other provisions of this agreement shall:

(1) consult with and advise the persons responsible for the writing of treatments, screenplays and other story material upon which the Film is based and procure the carrying out of all customary revisions thereto;

(2) forthwith upon the completion of the final shooting script of the Film and its approval by the Company do all things, supply all information at the Director's disposal and co-operate wholeheartedly with the Company to enable the Company to prepare a proper comprehensive and detailed budget and shooting schedule for the production of the Film;

(3) assist in the casting of the Film and in all necessary preparations for the shooting thereof in accordance with the approved budget and shooting schedule therefor including without limitation selection of designs for the sets and costumes, scouting and selection of locations, attendances at casting conferences, selection of cast and crew, selection of materials and equipment, attendances at screen and recording tests, readings and rehearsals, consultations and discussions with studios and in relation to publicity stills, interviews and all such other supervisory work required of a first class director during the pre-production of the Film;

(4) advise the Company and keep the Company informed of all matters material to the production, delivery and exploitation of the Film of which the Director shall become aware;

4 DIRECTOR'S SERVICES

Although this clause is fairly straightforward, from a director's point of view he/she may not want to give such wide ranging warranties and undertakings. This section puts a strong responsibility on the director to conform with all matters relevant to the production of a film or television programme. Directors may wish to shorten this section by setting out that the director will use his/her best efforts to perform his/her services as a first class director in relation to the film or television programme.

Producers should insist that most of these clauses are included for the reason that the director is such a key individual in the production process.

(5) direct the photography and recordings of the Film in the manner of a first class film director [of international repute] as efficiently and economically as possible and unless otherwise specified by the Company in accordance with the final shooting script budget and shooting schedule prepared and approved by the Company;

(6) do all things that may reasonably be required by the Company to ensure that the photography and recordings of the Film shall be of the highest quality and consistent with the budget approved by the Company;

(7) both during and after the completion of the principal photography and recording of the Film assist in and supervise the cutting, editing, post-synchronizing, scoring, dubbing, special and optical effects and titling and direct any retakes, added or substituted scenes of the Film as may be required by the Company in order to make due and proper delivery of the Film to the Company's distributors in a first class condition and suitable for exploitation to the public in first class theatres;

(8) from time to time to select for exhibition to a representative or representatives of the Company and its nominees daily rushes and assemblages thereof;

(9) render all those services usually rendered by a first class director of first class feature length sound and colour cinematograph films and soundtracks during the continuance of the Director's engagement hereunder.

5 REMUNERATION

(1) Subject to the provisions of this agreement relating to suspension and termination and to the due compliance by the Director with the Director's obligations and undertakings hereunder the Company shall as remuneration and as full consideration for all services rendered and for all rights granted to the Company

5   REMUNERATION

(1) There are no specific rules regarding how payment can be made for a director's services. This is only a guide.

hereunder pay or procure to be paid to the Director the following sums:

(a) [the sum of [( )] payable upon or before signature hereof (receipt whereof the Director hereby acknowledges)];

(b) [the sum of [( )] payable by [( )] equal consecutive [monthly/weekly] instalments the first of which shall be paid on [   ]];

(c) [the sum of [( )] payable upon the first day of principal photography];

(d) [the sum of [( )] payable by [( )] equal consecutive weekly instalments the first of which shall be paid at the end of the first completed week of principal photography];

(e) [the sum of [( )] payable by equal consecutive [monthly/weekly] instalments the first of which shall be paid one [month/week] following completion of principal photography [and upon delivery of the Director's Cut such sum (if any) as will bring the total payments under this paragraph (e) up to [(   )]]];

(f) [the sum of [( )] payable upon delivery of the Director's Cut];

(g) [the sum of [( )] payable upon completion and delivery of the [first married] answer print of the Film];

(h) [the sum of [( )] payable as a Deferment (as defined and payable in accordance with the provisions of Schedule 2 to this agreement)];

(i) [such sums as shall from time to time equal [per cent (%)] of the [Net Profits/Producer's Profits] (as defined and payable in accordance with the provisions of Schedule 2 to this agreement)].

(2) All payments made to the Director in excess of any minimum daily and/or weekly salary (as the case may be) specified in any union, guild or craft agreement which shall apply to the engagement of the Director's services hereunder shall to the extent permitted by such agreement be deemed to have been made on

(2) The contract does not necessarily have to make reference to any union, guild or craft agreement. Many feature films are non-union productions. However, any television company who may purchase a film or programme will want a warranty that any outstanding obligations to any union or guild such as payments are satisfied.

account of and as prepayment of use fees payable to the Director pursuant thereto and no such further sums shall be or become payable to the Director thereunder until such time as the said prepayments shall have been fully exhausted.

(3) All payments pursuant to paragraphs [(b) (d) and (e)] of sub-clause (1) of this clause shall be made at the end of the [week] [or] [month] in which they arise [as the case may be].

(4) All payments pursuant to subclause (1) of this clause shall be exclusive of Value Added Tax and if and to the extent only that Value Added Tax is or becomes payable on any such payment the Director will render to the Company a Value Added Tax invoice in respect thereof upon receipt of which the Company will make payment to the Director of the amount thereby shown to be due.

6 EXPENSES AND TRANSPORTATION

(1) Whenever the Director is required by the Company to render services hereunder at a place outside a radius of [thirty miles from Charing Cross in London] the Company shall pay to the Director in respect of all living expenses of the Director (which shall be deemed to [exclude hotel accommodation but to] include the cost of meals [bar, telephone and room charges and all other expenses] [and hotel accommodation]) the sum of [( )] per [day/week] [payable at the option of the Company in [pounds sterling or local currency] and pro-rated for any part of a week].

(2) [Whenever the Director is required by the Company to render services hereunder at a place outside a radius of [thirty miles from Charing Cross in London] the Company shall at its own expense provide the Director with [first class] [bed and breakfast] hotel accommodation [which shall [otherwise] be exclusive of bar, telephone and room service charges].]

336

6 EXPENSES AND TRANSPORTATION

Expenses and transportation provisions are always negotiable. However from the director's perspective, he/she will try and negotiate as much as possible out of the producer in order to increase his/her remunerations. This can be in the form of expenses including all meals as well as a daily cash allowance (i.e. £100) for each day that the director is engaged on a film or television programme. Directors may also want the producer to pay for airline travel for his/herself and his/her partner during the shoot as well as transportation to and from premieres of a film in major distribution markets.

From a producer's perspective, in order to keep costs down, the producer may wish to pay the director a fee which includes all expenses including meals, accommodation and transportation.

These are matters which should be negotiated prior to the commencement of principal photography of a film or television programme in order to avoid any misunderstandings at a later date.

(3) [The Company shall further pay to the Director's Secretary [('the Secretary') a salary [payable at the option of the Company in [pounds sterling] or local currency] at the rate of [   ] per week pro-rated for any part of a week that the Secretary renders services as the Director's Secretary during any period of principal photography of the Film that the Secretary is required in connection with the Film to remain overnight more than thirty miles from the Secretary's normal residence and shall reimburse to the Secretary all the Secretary's reasonable living expenses properly and necessarily thereby incurred [but not exceeding [( )] per week]].]

(4) Whenever the Company requires the Director to render services hereunder at a place outside a radius of [thirty miles from Charing Cross in London] the Company shall at its own expense provide the Director with [first class (where available but not Concorde)] [club class] return trip air transportation [for the Director and [   ] from [   ] to and from any place or places in [   ] at which the Director may be required to render the Director's services hereunder [and shall farther provide the Director's Secretary with return trip air transportation to like destinations [save where the Director uses the car referred to in subclause (5) below which the Director shall be entitled to do for such journeys as the Company shall approve and which the Director shall use for such journeys as the Company may specify] [and in such cases the Secretary shall travel with the Director]].

(5) The Company shall provide the Director with [car transportation] [a car and driver for the Director's exclusive use] to convey the Director to and from the Director's place of overnight residence to the studios, offices, locations or otherwise (as the case may be) at which and whenever the Director is required to render services hereunder [during principal photography of the Film].

7 CREDIT

(1) Subject to the Director substantially rendering all of the services required of the Director hereunder the Company shall accord the Director
   (a) on the negative and all positive copies of the Film made by or to the order of the Company
      (i) a presentation credit in the form of 'A [   ] Film' or [['s] Film of   ] or such other words as may be agreed between the Director and the Company and still be consistent with the underlying agreements with the author of the original screenplay upon which the Film is based. Such presentation credit shall appear above the title of the Film on a single card in a size of lettering equal to [%] of the title of the Film or [%] of the most prominent credit accorded to the major star artist(s) (whichever is the larger). [No other presentation credits shall be accorded other than [to the producer [(and the presentation credit accorded to the producer shall be [below the title] and in words similar to 'A [   ] Production' [and such producer's presentation credit shall not be in a larger or more prominent size of the lettering than that used to announce the presentation credit of the Director)]];]
      (ii) credit as the director of the Film in a size of lettering equal to that used for the title of the Film [or of the most prominent credit accorded to the major star artist(s) (whichever is the larger)] and on a separate card immediately prior to the fade in of the Film.
   (b) [The presentation credit and] credit as the director of the Film in all major paid advertising issued by or under the direct control of the Company subject to the provisions of sub-clause (3) below [save that the Director's presentation credit shall be in a size of lettering equal to [%] of the title of the Film].

7 CREDIT

(1) Producers should always set out exactly how the director's credit will be presented. This clause can be shortened to reflect that credit will be given in accordance with industry standards. However this may lead to a dispute later on. Since directors are a crucial factor in the production process, the director will usually be quite specific as to position of his credits as well as size and how it is presented in relation to other key actors and personnel of the film. Positions and size of credits includes placement on the negative and all copies of the film or television programme as well as on all advertising materials in relation to the film. Credit size is usually based on percentage of the size of the title. Producers should ensure that all credit provisions fit within the parameters of the production (i.e. make sure that lead actors are not given credit provisions that offend those credits set out in the Director's Agreement).

Producers should be aware that a well known director will ask for his credit before the title of the film, as well as before any of the lead actors in relation to advertising and publicity materials (i.e. a film poster).

In relation to on screen credits, the director's name is usually the last credit before start of the film; however, the opening title may say 'A *(name of director)* Film'.

(2) [In according credit in paid advertising if the title of the Film or the title or name(s) of any individual(s) is used more than once in such paid advertising, i.e. a so called 'regular' use and a so called 'artwork' use (such as for example the weaving of the title and/or the name(s) of any individual(s) as part of the background of the advertisement or a display use or a fanciful use), the reference herein to the title of the Film shall be to the 'regular' use of the title or the name(s) of any individual(s) as distinguished from the 'artwork' use of the title or the name(s) of any individual(s) [provided however in no event shall the size of type accorded to Director be less than the greater of:

(a) [per cent (%)] of the size of the regular title; or

(b) [per cent (%)] of the size of the artwork title].]

(3) The provisions of sub-clause (1) of this clause shall not apply to:

(a) 'group', 'list', 'special' or so-called 'teaser' advertising pre-release publicity of exploitation; or

(b) any exploitation, publication or fictionalization of the story, screenplay or other literary or musical material upon which the Film is based; or

(c) by-products of any kind (including but not limited to sheet music and gramophone records) or

(d) 'trailer' or other advertising on the screen or radio or television; or

(e) institutional or other advertising or publicity not relating primarily to the Film; or

(f) advertising of ten column inches or less; or

(g) advertising or publicity material in narrative form; or

(h) 24 sheets and 6 sheets;

(i) special advertising, publicity or exploitation of the Film relating to any member or members of the cast the author, producer or other personnel concerned in its production or to academy awards or prizes or similar matters;

(ANY and ALL of which said items included in paragraphs (a) to (i) inclusive may be issued without

mentioning the name of the Director therein) or
(j) 'roller credits' at the end of the Film.

(4) No casual or inadvertent failure by the Company to
comply with the provisions of this clause and no failure
of persons other than the Company to comply therewith
or with their contracts with the Company shall
constitute a breach of this agreement by the Company.
The rights and remedies of the Director in the event of a
breach of this clause by the Company shall be limited to
the Director's rights (if any) to recover damages in an
action at law and in no event shall the Director be
entitled by reason of any such breach to enjoin or
restrain the distribution, exhibition, advertising or
exploitation of the Film.

(5) The Company shall use [all reasonable/its best]
endeavours to procure that the distributors of the Film
accord to the Director credit in accordance with the
provisions of this clause (except as specified in
sub-clause (3) of this clause) on all prints of and paid
advertising for the Film issued by such distributors
provided that the Company shall not be liable for the
neglect or default of any such distributor so long as the
Company shall have notified the distributors of the
credit to which the Director is entitled.

(6) In the event of a failure by any distributor to accord
credit to the Director as aforesaid, the Company shall
upon notice from the Director use its [all
reasonable][best endeavours] (short of incurring legal [or
other material] expenses) to remedy such failure.

8   RIGHTS AND CONSENTS

(1) The Director hereby acknowledges that the Company as
the maker of the Film shall be the sole owner of the
entire copyright therein with the full unfettered right to
make such use of the Film as it shall think fit and
insofar as the Director may be vested with the same by

(4)/(5)/(6) These clauses protect the producer in the event that the director's credit has not been set out properly or a distributor has failed to accord credit to the director. If these clauses were not present, then a litigious director could try and stop the distribution or exhibition of a film.

A producer or his/her production company should try and substitute a specific obligation with a best or reasonable endeavours clause. This is done to protect the producer, since the producer cannot absolutely guarantee that a distributor or third party will accord the director the proper credit. Producers should note that the obligation set out under best endeavours is very high. Best endeavours places a strong burden on a producer to try and achieve a certain result if something can actually be done. Reasonable endeavours places a lower standard of obligation on someone. For example, reasonable endeavours may mean that the person may only undertake corrective measures that are commercially feasible. Users of these contracts should use a 'best' or 'reasonable' endeavours clause when an individual or company cannot absolutely guarantee that an obligation will be fulfilled.

(4) This clause is for protecting the production company in the event that a third party fails to comply with any aspect of the credit provision. Because of the importance of credit, without this clause the director may have the ability to injunct the film or stop the film from being exploited.

8 RIGHTS AND CONSENTS

(1) A production company will always ask that the director assign all of his rights in the product of his services in order that the company may exploit the film or television programme to the fullest extent possible throughout the world.

way of assignment of present and future copyright the Director with full title guarantee hereby assigns to the Company all such copyright as aforesaid and all other right, title and interest of whatsoever nature whether vested or contingent in and to all the products of the Director's services hereunder including, but not limited to, all literary, dramatic, musical and artistic material contributed by the Director (including contributions to the shooting script of the Film) TO HOLD the same unto the Company absolutely throughout the universe for the full period of copyright and all renewals and extensions thereof and thereafter (insofar as the Director is able to do so) in perpetuity.

(2) The Director, recognizing the needs of Film and Television production, shall grant to the Company the absolute and unlimited right to use the Film for all purposes granted hereunder in any manner the Company may in its discretion think fit and the Director hereby waives the benefits of any provision of law known as moral rights of authors or the 'droit moral' or any similar law in any country of the universe and hereby agrees not to institute, support, maintain or permit any action or lawsuit on the ground that any Film and soundtrack or any other version of the Film produced and/or exploited by the Company in any way constitutes an infringement of any moral rights or 'droit moral' of the Director or is in any way a defamation or mutilation of the Film or contains unauthorized variations, alterations, adaptations, modifications, changes or translations.

(3) The Director hereby assigns to the Company all and any rental and lending rights that the Director may have in relation to the Film and the Director confirms that the remuneration set out in this agreement includes full and proper equitable remuneration in respect of any rights (including without limitation any rental and lending rights) that the Director may have in relation to the Film.

(2) See Moral Rights notes in Chapter 4.

(3) See Rental and Lending Rights notes in Chapter 4.

(4) The Director hereby grants to the Company the right at all times hereafter to use and authorize others to use the Director's name, photographs and other reproductions of the Director's physical likeness and recordings of the Director's voice taken or made hereunder and the autograph and biography of the Director in whole or in part

(a) in connection with the advertisement, publicity, exhibition and commercial exploitation of the Film and any music records and book publications derived therefrom; and

(b) for the purposes of the public exhibition of the Film in association with the advertisement, publicity and commercial exploitation of any other commodities PROVIDED ALWAYS that (except with the Director's prior written consent) the Director's name or photograph is not directly or indirectly used to suggest that the Director personally uses or recommends any such other commodities (but so that the Director may be shown to recommend the Film per se).

(5) The Director shall do all such acts and execute all such documents as the Company may require to vest in or further assure to the Company the said copyright and all other rights herein expressed to be granted.

9   CUTTING RIGHTS

(1) The Director shall complete and deliver the Director's Cut for showing to the Company within [days][weeks] following completion of principal photography of the Film, it being hereby acknowledged and understood that the Director's Cut may not at that stage be a dubbed version of the Film. In the event that the Director does not do so, the Company may itself (without prejudice to the Company's rights in this regard) take such steps to cut, edit and in every respect complete the Film in order that delivery of the Film may take place no later than

(4) Producers should note that directors may wish to limit a producer or production company's right to use the director's name, photograph or biography. The director may wish to negotiate that any of the above can only be used with the director's prior permission. Directors may ask for approvals regarding the use of their photographs and publicity materials.

9   CUTTING RIGHTS

Producers and production companies should try and negotiate a specific date of delivery for a rough cut of a film or television programme as well as a date for the final cut.

Producers should keep in mind that a financier or broadcaster of a film or television programme will insist that a film or television programme is delivered by a certain date (usually known as 'the Delivery Date'). Therefore it is essential that not only is a date set out when the director's cut is delivered, but also a date must be determined when the final cut of a film or programme is to be

[( )] months following completion of principal photography thereof.

(2) After completion of the Director's Cut which cut shall not be performed on the original negative of the Film the Director shall [immediately inform the Company of such completion and the Company shall make arrangements to view the Film as soon as possible thereafter. The Company shall have the right to make such additional cuts, alterations, changes and re-editing in and to the Film as it shall in its absolute discretion determine [subject to consultation with the Director with regard thereto] and thereafter the Director shall] proceed to complete all dubbing of music and effects and the post-synchronization of all dialogue within a further period of not more than [( ) days/weeks] from the date of the showing of the Director's Cut to the Company.

(3) [Upon completion of all dubbing of music and effects and post-synchronization as aforesaid the Director shall immediately inform the Company of such completion and the Company shall make arrangements to view the Film as soon as possible thereafter. [Following the delivery of the Director's Cut complete and fully dubbed in accordance with the foregoing the Company shall have the right to make such additional cuts, alterations, changes and re-editing in and to the Film as it shall in its absolute discretion determine [subject to consultation with the Director with regard thereto].] If after such viewing the Company requires the Director to make any cuts, additions, changes, amendments, alterations or other editing to the Film which the Director is unwilling to make then the Company shall forthwith arrange a public preview of the Film at which audience reaction shall be canvassed and tested. The Company shall have the right to select the city and the theatre(s) for such preview. If the Company shall not have required any cuts, changes, alterations or further editing of the Film after completion of the first complete

delivered. In director's agreements it is essential that the term 'Director's Cut' is defined and even more important if the director does not have final cut that the term 'Final Cut' is also defined.

Producers should also be aware that broadcasters and financiers will not pay for a film or programme that substantially deviates from the original script. Sometimes the broadcaster or financier will want approval over any substantial changes to the script. Therefore it may be advantageous for the producer to retain final cut of a programme in the event that the director radically cuts the programme from the original script.

Sometimes, a director may insist that he/she has final cut of the film. However, when dealing with major US studios, unless the director is very powerful, then the studio may insist that it has final cut.

Cutting rights is an optional clause but it is advised that in order to avoid any dispute over the final version of the programme or film there must be some reference to who has final cut.

fully dubbed cut by the Director, then it shall be deemed to have accepted the Film for theatrical exhibition in the form delivered by the Director at that stage.]

(4) [Immediately following such preview and evaluation of audience reaction, the Director shall have the right to make a second cut of the Film having regard to the results of such audience sampling, such cut to be completed within thirty (30) days of the completion of the evaluation of such audience reaction.]

(5) [If the Company does require changes and such public preview takes place, then following the delivery of the Director's second cut in accordance with the foregoing the Company shall have the right to make such additional cuts, changes, alterations and re-editing in and to the Film as it shall in its absolute discretion determine.]

(6) [Whilst no remuneration additional to that payable under Clause 5 hereof shall be payable to the Director in connection with any services rendered by the Director in connection with the editing of the Film pursuant to this clause, the Company shall nonetheless be obliged to pay and provide to the Director expenses and transportation in accordance with the provisions of Clause 6 hereof.]

10 NOTICES

Any notices required to be given under the provisions of this agreement shall be in writing and shall be deemed to have been duly served if hand delivered or sent by telex or within the United Kingdom by first class registered or recorded delivery or outside the United Kingdom by registered airmail correctly addressed to the relevant party's address as specified in this agreement or at such other address as either party may hereafter designate from time to time in accordance with this clause.

10 NOTICES

See notes in Chapter 4.

11 AGENT

The Director hereby authorizes and requests the Company to pay all monies other than expenses pursuant to Clause 6 hereof due to the Director hereunder to the Director's duly authorized agent [of whose receipt therefor shall afford the Company a good and valid discharge for the monies so paid].

12 RIGHT TO ASSIGN

The Company shall be entitled to [lend the Director's services hereunder to any third party producing the Film if other than the Company and to] assign and charge the benefit of this agreement either in whole or in part to any third party but no such assignment shall relieve the Company of any of its obligations to the Director hereunder.

13 ENTIRE AGREEMENT

This agreement (including the Schedule[s] hereto which [are/is] incorporated herein by reference) replaces, supersedes and cancels all previous arrangements, understandings, representations or agreements between the parties hereto either oral or written with respect to the subject matter hereof and expresses and constitutes the entire agreement between the Company and the Director with reference to the terms and conditions of the engagement of the Director in connection with the Film and no variation of any of the terms or conditions hereof may be made unless such variation is agreed in writing and signed by both of the parties hereto.

14 GOVERNING LAW

This agreement shall be construed and performed in all respects in accordance with and governed by English Law and the parties irrevocably submit to the jurisdiction of the English Courts.

11 AGENT

See notes in Chapter 4.

12 RIGHT TO ASSIGN

See notes in Chapter 4.

13 ENTIRE AGREEMENT

See notes in Chapter 4.

14 GOVERNING LAW

See notes in Chapter 4.

15   CLAUSE HEADINGS

The clause headings in this agreement are for the convenience of the parties only and shall not limit govern or otherwise affect its interpretation in any way.

AS WITNESS the hands of a duly authorized representative of the Company and the Director the day month and year first above written.

SIGNED by
a duly authorized representative
for and on behalf of THE
COMPANY in the presence of:

SIGNED by THE DIRECTOR in
the presence of:

15 CLAUSE HEADINGS

See notes in Chapter 4.

SCHEDULE 1: Standard Terms and Conditions of Engagement

1 GENERAL OBLIGATIONS

The Director shall:
(1) promptly and faithfully comply with all the Company's reasonable directions, requests, rules and regulations from time to time;
(2) not make additions to or deletions from the final shooting script or final shooting schedule of the Film without the prior written approval of the Company other than minor so called 'on the floor' revisions customarily made during principal photography or recording;
(3) obtain knowledge of and comply with all the rules and regulations for the time being in force at such places at which the Director is required to render the Director's services hereunder and observe all orders given by the Company or its representatives from time to time;
(4) cause the Film to be produced in compliance with the terms of any applicable union guild or craft agreements relating thereto;
(5) keep the Company informed of the Director's whereabouts and telephone number (if any) at all times throughout the term of this engagement and not absent [himself/herself] without first obtaining the Company's consent; and
(6) deliver to the Company upon request all manuscripts, documents and papers in the Director's possession relating to the Film or copies thereof.

2 RESTRICTIONS

The Director shall not:
(1) without the written consent of the Company order goods or incur any liability on the Company's behalf or in any way pledge the Company's credit or hold [himself/herself] out as being entitled to do so or pay or

SCHEDULE 1: STANDARD TERMS AND CONDITIONS OF ENGAGEMENT

1 GENERAL OBLIGATIONS

These are standard terms and conditions of engagement that can either be included in the main body of the contract or set out as shown in a schedule. These are standard commercial terms and conditions that either create obligations or restrictions on the director.

2 RESTRICTIONS

These are general restrictions which are usually set out in many employment and commercial agreements. Some employment agreements have much wider and detailed restrictions.

agree to pay any bonus to any person engaged for or in connection with the production of the Film;

(2) without the prior written consent of the Company at any time hereafter either personally or by means of press or publicity or advertising agents or agencies make any statement or disclosure or supply any information or photographs to any person firm or corporate body.

(3) the Director will at all reasonable times when so required attend and submit to such medical examination as the Company or its medical advisers shall desire or deem necessary for insurance purposes (in the presence of the Director's own doctor at the Director's expense if the Director shall so require provided that such doctor shall be available upon reasonable notice when the Company shall so require) and will make true and accurate replies and statements and will sign all necessary forms and documents for the purpose of any such insurance.

3   LABOUR PERMITS AND UNION MEMBERSHIP

The Director shall [at the Director's sole cost and expense] apply for or assist the Company in applying for and do all such things as may be required in support of any application for the Director's membership of a properly designated labour organization or for any foreign entry permits, visas, passports, licences, permissions, consents or other matters necessary or desirable to enable the Company to make use of the Director's services in such territory or territories of the world where the Film may be made and insofar as the Director shall be required to become a member of any union, guild or labour organization the Director shall after becoming a member remain a member in good standing throughout the term of this engagement. If as a result of any such application being refused, revoked or cancelled the Company is unable to make use of all or any part of the Director's services in

3   LABOUR PERMITS AND UNION MEMBERSHIP

In certain countries, it is essential that the director is a member of that country's labour union or guild. Depending on the circumstances, the director or the producer's company may be responsible for becoming a member of that specific union or guild.

Producers shooting in a foreign jurisdiction should ensure that necessary payments are made.

the Film the Company shall be entitled by written notice to the Director to terminate this agreement and the Director's engagement hereunder.

4 COMPENSATION

(1) The compensation payable to the Director pursuant to Clause 5 of this agreement shall be deemed to accrue on a daily basis pro rata to the payment to be made in respect of the period in which the days occur (except during periods of suspension) and all compensation under Clause 5 of this agreement shall constitute payment in full for all of the Director's services in connection with the Film and no increased or additional compensation shall accrue or be payable to the Director by reason of any additional services rendered by the Director hereunder. No increased or additional compensation shall accrue or be payable to the Director by reason of any of the Director's services being rendered at night or on Sundays or holidays or on a distant location or after the expiration of any particular number of hours of service in any period. Demand upon the Company for payment of any compensation due to the Director under any provision of this agreement must express the amount claimed to be due and must be in writing.

(2) [Except as otherwise provided to the contrary] the Director authorizes the Company to deduct and withhold from any and all compensation payable to the Director hereunder all deductions required by any present or future law of any country wherein the Director performs services hereunder or the country of residence of any party hereto requiring the withholding or deducting of compensation. [In the event that the Company does not make such withholdings or deductions the Director shall pay any and all taxes and other charges payable on account of such compensation and the Director hereby indemnifies the Company and

4 COMPENSATION

Directors and producers should both be clear as to how payment is made. This section clarifies any misunderstandings regarding holiday work or extra work beyond that contracted for, that the director may have to undertake. From a practical perspective, directors usually work much longer than they are contracted for and are not paid for overtime. However, in some circumstances, a director may be quite adamant about his pay for non-contracted additional work and therefore clarity is essential.

Producers and directors should also consult well a tax specialist or accountant regarding Value Added Tax (VAT) or other taxes that may be due or payable.

agrees to keep the Company fully and effectually indemnified from and against any liability or expense in connection therewith.]

(3) In the event that the Company makes any payment or incurs any charge at the Director's request for the Director's account or the Director incurs any charges with the Company the Company shall have the right and the Director hereby authorizes the Company to recoup any and all such payments or charges by deducting and withholding any aggregate amount thereof from any compensation then or thereafter payable to the Director hereunder. This provision shall not be construed to limit or exclude any other rights of credit or recovery or any other remedies which the Company may have. Nothing herein contained shall obligate the Company to make any such payments or incur any such charge or permit the Director to incur any such charges.

(4) Should the Company pay compensation to the Director for all or any part of the period for which the Company was not obligated to do so hereunder the Director shall repay said compensation to the Company upon demand or at the Company's election the Company may recoup said compensation by deducting and withholding an equivalent amount from any compensation thereafter payable to the Director by the Company or the Company may recover said compensation by other lawful means.

5 LIABILITY EXCLUSIONS

(1) The Company shall not be liable to the Director or to the personal representatives of the Director for:
   (a) any loss or damage howsoever or by whomsoever caused of or to the Director's property sustained at or whilst in transit to or from places at which the Director shall render the Director's services hereunder; and

5 LIABILITY EXCLUSIONS

(b) (to the extent that the Company can properly exclude such liability at law) for any personal injury, ailment or death arising out of or in the course of the Director's engagement hereunder except to such extent if at all as such injury ailment or death is caused by the Company's negligence and/or the Company may be able to enforce a claim for indemnity against a third party or under any policy of insurance effected by the Company (and in this connection the Company undertakes to effect all customary third party liability insurances).

(2) Notwithstanding and irrespective of any advertisement or announcement which may hereafter be published the Company shall not be liable to the Director for or in respect of loss of publicity, advertisement, reputation or the like due to the Company's abandonment of the production or exploitation of the Film or the Company's failure to use the services of the Director and nothing in this agreement contained shall be construed as to impose upon the Company any obligation to make use of the services of the Director hereunder.

6 WARRANTIES

The Director hereby warrants to and undertakes with the Company:

(1) that the Director has the right to enter into this agreement and to grant the rights herein expressed to be granted;

(2) that all the products of the Director's services hereunder (except for any part or parts thereof which shall contain the works of others included therein at the specific requirement of the Company) shall be original, shall not be defamatory of any third party, shall not infringe or violate any right of any person including (without limitation) any rights of copyright or rights of privacy or any common law or statutory

(2) Producers and production companies should try and exclude themselves from any responsibility for a director's loss of publicity or reputation in the event that the production company does not produce or exploit a film or television programme properly. There have been cases where directors have brought actions against a production company because they did not release a film theatrically. The director could claim that this led to a loss of reputation because the film was perceived to be a failure since it was not released in the cinemas. Therefore, producers should insist on such an exclusion.

6 WARRANTIES

See notes on Warranties in Chapter 4.

rights of any kind and are and shall be solely and absolutely vested in the Director for the full period of copyright and all extensions and renewals thereof it being agreed that in the event of any claim or threatened proceedings against the Company or to which the Company is made a party and which if successful would give rise to a claim against the Director under this subclause the Company shall notify the Director thereof and the Director shall be entitled at the Director's own expense to join in or at the Director's election be kept fully advised thereof and to instruct Counsel to approve and join in any proposed settlement of such claim or proceedings;

(3) [the Director is and shall throughout the term of this agreement remain [a British subject] [and] [a member of good standing of an appropriate [Guild] [Union] or [Craft Organization]].]

7 FORCE MAJEURE

(1) If the Company is unable to make use of the Director's services hereunder by reason of the preparation, commencement, production or completion of the Film being prevented, hampered, stopped, interrupted or interfered with by reason of any act or occurrence beyond the control of the Company or by reason of any fire, flood, earthquake, explosion, accident, war, civil disturbance, Royal Demise, statutory or governmental enactment or order, pestilence, epidemic, national calamity, Act of God, lockout, strike, labour disturbance, or conditions of death, illness or incapacity of the scriptwriter, the individual producer or any of the principal members of the cast of the Film or inability to obtain personnel or materials or facilities or delays of common carriers (each of the aforesaid being hereinafter referred to as an 'event of force majeure') the Company shall be entitled to suspend the engagement of the services of the Director hereunder as hereinafter provided.

7 FORCE MAJEURE

See notes on Force Majeure in Chapter 4.

(2) Any suspension as aforesaid shall commence upon the notification to the Director in writing of the occurrence of such event of force majeure and shall terminate upon the expiration of such period of time subsequent to the cessation of such event of force majeure as the Company may reasonably require to make preparations for the actual utilization of the services of the Director taking into consideration the schedules, plans and commitments of the Company and of the writers, line producers, cast, personnel and equipment desired in the production of the Film or on such earlier date as may be designated by the Company.

(3) If a suspension based upon an event of force majeure shall continue for a period in excess of [eight] weeks the Company and the Director shall each thereafter have the right during the continuance of such event of force majeure to terminate this agreement by written notice to the other and thereby be relieved of all further obligations and liabilities hereunder, provided that, should the Director serve such a notice on the Company, the Company shall be entitled within one week of the receipt thereof to serve a counternotice on the Director terminating the suspension which gave rise to the Director's said notice with effect from a date to be specified and thereafter the provisions of the Director's services shall be deemed to be resumed in all respects with effect from the specified date as if no notices of termination had been given.

8 DISABILITY AND DEFAULT

(1) If the Director shall:

(a) suffer any physical injury or impairment which may materially detract from the Director's ability to perform the Director's services hereunder or if by reason of any mental or physical disability the Director shall be prevented from fully performing or complying with any of the terms or conditions hereof

8 DISABILITY AND DEFAULT

This section of a director's contract is essential since the producer may wish to replace the director if he becomes ill or unable to continue with his role in the production of a film or television programme.

Prior to the start of principal photography of a film or television programme, a director will usually have to undergo a physical

or if the Company and/or the Director shall be unable to obtain membership of any requisite labour organization or any foreign entry permit, visa, passport or other licences, permissions or consents as contemplated hereunder (any such injury impairment disability and/or inability being hereinafter referred to as a 'disability') and such disability shall continue for five (5) or more consecutive days or an aggregate of seven (7) or more days during principal photography or recording of the Film or for consecutive and aggregate periods of ten (10) or more and fourteen (14) or more days respectively during the remaining period of the Director's engagement hereunder; or

(b) wilfully fail, refuse or neglect otherwise than by reason of the Director's disability to comply with any of the terms or conditions hereof or shall fail to give information or shall give false information in respect of any item including any policy of insurance contemplated hereunder (hereinafter referred to as a 'default') the Company shall have the right to terminate this agreement and the engagement of the Director's services hereunder by giving written notice to the Director of the Company's election so to do at or before the termination of any such disability or default. This right to terminate shall be in addition to the engagement during any period of disability or default. The Director agrees that in the event of any claim that disability exists the Director at the request of the Company from time to time will attend and submit to physical examination at reasonable times and at the Company's expense by such physician or physicians as the Company may designate (in the presence of the Director's own physician at the Director's expense if the Director shall so require provided that such physician shall be available when the Company shall so require).

examination in order that insurance will be granted over the production. A physical examination may also be a requirement of a broadcaster or financier.

Producers should have the right to terminate the director's contract in the event of a long-term illness or disability. It is essential that 'disability' is defined so that no confusion arises over what is or is not a disability. Directors will usually ask for the right to be examined by a doctor at the producer's expense in the event of any illness.

Producers will want this clause to be included so that they can continue with their production with a minimum of delay.

(2) If in relation to the circumstances envisaged in subclause (1)(b) of this clause the Company shall by written notice to the Director request confirmation of the Director's willingness to render the Director's services hereunder either generally or with respect to a particular matter or matters and the Director shall fail to give the Company written notice within twenty four (24) hours after the receipt thereof that the Director intends to and will render such services or gives written notice to the Company that the Director will not render such services in whole or in part then the Company if it so desires may deem such action or failure to act an immediate refusal to render such services and consequently an event of default.

(3) If any default or disability shall occur or continue during the period of this agreement the Company shall without prejudice to its rights to terminate this agreement pursuant to subclause (1) of this clause be entitled to suspend the services of the Director as hereinafter provided. Any suspension as aforesaid shall commence upon the notification to the Director of the occurrence of the default or disability and unless this agreement has been terminated prior thereto shall terminate:

(a) if based upon a disability on the third day after the cessation of the continuance of such disability; or

(b) if based upon a default upon the expiration of such period of time subsequent to the cessation of such default as the Company may reasonably require to make preparations for the actual utilization of the services of the Director taking into consideration the schedules, plans and commitments of the Company and of the writers, producers, cast, personnel, and equipment desired in the production of the Film; or

(c) on such earlier date as may be designated by the Company.

9 EFFECT OF SUSPENSION

Upon any suspension of this agreement:

(1) all rights granted to the Company in respect of services rendered by the Director and the products thereof prior to such suspension shall remain vested in the Company absolutely;

(2) the Company need neither pay to the Director nor shall there accrue to the Director's account any compensation for any period of time during which the Director is suspended hereunder whether due to the occurrence of any event of force majeure or the Director's disability or default save for the payment of expenses and sums which have theretofore become due and payable under Clause 5 of this agreement where the suspension is based upon [a disability or] an event of force majeure;

(3) unless this agreement shall be terminated the term of the Director's engagement hereunder shall at the Company's election be extended by a period equivalent to all such periods of suspension and the Director shall not be entitled to any additional compensation therefor;

(4) the Company may if it so desires make payment of any compensation which would have accrued to the Director during any suspension and such payment shall not be deemed to waive any suspension or any of its effects and the amount of such payment may at the Company's election be applied against any compensation thereafter accruing or becoming due to the Director hereunder;

(5) any suspension hereunder shall be deemed to have been lifted for such days if any during the continuance of which the Director shall actually render services to the Company at the Company's request and such days shall not be included in any computation of the duration of such suspension;

(6) during the continuance of any suspension hereunder the Director shall not render service for any person other than the Company in the field of entertainment unless such suspension shall be based upon an event

9   EFFECT OF SUSPENSION

This clause gives the producer the right to stop paying the director in the event that the director is suspended under the terms of the agreement. This clause also gives the producer the right to keep all of the products of the director's services which have already been completed. Producers should always include such a clause in the event that the producer wishes to replace the director. This clause can also be utilized in the event that one of the actors becomes ill and the producer must shut down the production for a specific period of time. However, in these circumstances, insurance for illness may be activated and therefore suspension may not be necessary.

of force majeure and then subject only to the same not interfering with the Director's obligations hereunder;

(7) in computing the duration of any suspension hereunder if the suspension is predicated upon a default both the day upon which said suspension commences and the day upon which it terminates shall be included. If the suspension is predicated upon an event of force majeure or a disability the day upon which the suspension commences shall be included but the day upon which it terminates shall not be included;

(8) save as otherwise expressly provided herein no suspension shall relieve the Director of the Director's obligations and duties hereunder when and as required by the Company except during the continuance of a disability which incapacitates the Director from the rendition of services required by the Company.

10 EFFECT OF TERMINATION

Upon any termination of this agreement:

(a) the Company may abandon or postpone the making of the Film, may substitute another person for and in the place of the Director or may continue the production of the Film or any revised version thereof in any manner that the Company shall in its sole and complete discretion elect;

(b) all rights granted to the Company in respect of work done and services rendered by the Director and the products thereof prior to such termination shall not be affected;

(c) the Company shall pay to the Director the balance (if any) outstanding and unpaid of the remuneration accrued due and payable up to the date of such termination or the commencement of the suspension out of which such termination arose whichever shall be the earlier and thereupon all liability of the Company to the Director hereunder (save for the credit (if any) to be accorded to the Director under Clause 7 hereof and save as is provided in the next succeeding sub-clause) shall cease;

10   EFFECT OF TERMINATION

This clause gives the producer the right to abandon or postpone the making of a film or television programme and also gives the producer the right to substitute another person for the director. Producers should include such a clause in the event that they wish to replace the director.

As a general note, a director will not always get along with actors or agree with the producer. Producers should ensure that they have the ability, as a last resort, to get rid of the director. Sometimes a director may go drastically over-budget or behind schedule and the producer will wish to replace the director with another director in order to complete the programme on time and on budget. From a practical perspective, it is essential that suspension and termination clauses are included in director's contracts.

(d) the liability of the Company in accordance with the provisions of Clause 5 of this agreement shall not (save as is provided in the next succeeding sub-clause) be affected unless termination arises from a default;

(e) unless termination arises from a default and if the Director shall at the date thereof be on location and more than [thirty miles from Charing Cross in London] the Company shall continue to pay the Director's hotel and living expenses pursuant to Clause 6 of this agreement until the date upon which the Company shall provide the Director with the first available travelling facilities (which shall be [first class (where available but not Concorde)] [club class]) for the return of the Director to [   ] and whether or not the Director shall so return the liability of the Company under Clause 6 of this agreement shall cease on such date;

(f) any claim which either of the parties hereto shall have against the other for or in respect of any breach non-observance or non-performance of any of the provisions hereof occurring prior to such termination or out of which such termination shall have arisen shall not be affected or prejudiced by such termination.

11   INDEMNITY

The Director hereby indemnifies and agrees to keep the Company fully and effectually indemnified from and against any and all losses, costs, actions, proceedings, claims, damages, expenses (including reasonable legal costs and expenses) or liabilities whatsoever suffered or incurred directly or indirectly by the Company in consequence of any breach, non-performance or non-observance by the Director of any of the agreements, conditions, obligations, representations, warranties and undertakings on the part of the Director contained in this agreement. The Director hereby expressly acknowledges that this indemnity shall survive the completion of the Director's services hereunder.

11 INDEMNITY

See notes on Indemnities in Chapter 5.

12 INJUNCTIVE RELIEF

It is understood and agreed that a breach by the Director of any of the material provisions of this agreement will or may cause the Company irreparable injury and damage and the Director expressly agrees that the Company shall be entitled to injunctive or other equitable relief to prevent a breach of this agreement by the Director. Resort to such equitable relief shall not be construed as a waiver of any other rights or remedies which the Company may have for damages or otherwise.

13 NO WAIVER

No waiver by either party hereto of any breach of any of the terms or conditions of this agreement in a particular instance shall be deemed or construed to be a waiver of any preceding or succeeding breach of the same or any other terms or conditions. All rights, remedies, undertakings and obligations contained in the agreement shall be cumulative and none of them shall be in limitation of any other rights, remedy, undertaking or obligation of either party.

14 NO PARTNERSHIP

Nothing herein contained shall be construed or deemed to constitute a partnership or joint venture between the parties hereto and save as expressly herein provided no party shall hold itself out as the agent of the other.

15 PARTIAL UNENFORCEABILITY

If any clause or any part of this agreement or the application thereof to either party shall for any reason be adjudged by any court or other legal authority of competent jurisdiction to be invalid such judgment shall not affect the remainder of this agreement which shall continue in full force and effect.

12 INJUNCTIVE RELIEF

See Chapter 5 regarding notes on injunctions.

14 NO PARTNERSHIP

Producers should always state that there is no partnership between the director and the producer's company especially when a director has been very involved in the development of a film or television programme.

SCHEDULE 2

For the purposes of this agreement of which this schedule forms part:

[Net Profits/Producer's Profits/Deferments]

SCHEDULE 2

This schedule should include any net profits/producer's profits or deferments which the director is entitled to. A full definition of how the director is to be paid should be set out. Producers should make sure that any definition of profits does not conflict with any definitions set out in any other profit participants' contracts. (See Appendix B for a sample net/producer's profit definition.)

11 Presenter's agreement

The following agreement is in relation to the use of a presenter in a television programme, series, documentary or other form of programming which utilizes a presenter.

This presenter's agreement is a complete buy-out of rights and is not subject to any union or guild collective bargaining agreements.

It should be noted that the Producers Alliance for Cinema and Television (PACT) has a standard form model contract for presenters.

Presenter's agreement

PRESENTER'S AGREEMENT

THIS AGREEMENT is made the   day of

BETWEEN:

(1) [*Producer's name*] of [*address*]
    ('the Company' which expression shall be deemed to
    include its successors in title and assigns)

(2) _____ of
    [   ] ('the Presenter')

WHEREAS

The Company wishes to engage the Presenter to perform as
presenter in a [*programme*] [*series of programmes*] each of
approximately [   ] minutes in length provisionally entitled
[   ] ('the Series') primarily for television broadcast
which the Company intends but does not undertake to
produce

NOW IT IS HEREBY AGREED as follows:

1 ENGAGEMENT

(1) The Company hereby engages the Presenter and the
    Presenter hereby agrees to make available his/her
    services as a presenter of the Series.
(2) The Company shall be entitled to the services of the
    Presenter hereunder for a period of [   ] (   ) weeks
    commencing on or about the [   ] ('the Engagement
    Period'). Each week of the Engagement Period shall be a
    [ ] day week and the Company shall be entitled to
    nominate such days in any week (including Saturdays,
    Sundays, public and bank holidays). During the
    Engagement Period the Company shall be entitled to the
    services of the Presenter on an exclusive basis.

PRESENTER'S AGREEMENT: NOTES

PREAMBLE

Producers should set out the type of programming which they wish to engage the presenter for. Presenters are usually engaged for a single one-off television programme, a series of programmes or corporate or instructional videos.

1 ENGAGEMENT

It is important to determine whether the presenter is engaged on an exclusive or non-exclusive basis. If the engagement is for a daily television series, then the producer will undoubtedly want the presenter on an exclusive basis.

2 PRESENTER'S SERVICES

The Presenter shall at all times during the term of this agreement promptly and faithfully comply with all reasonable directions, requests, rules, and regulations of the Company and with all rules and regulations in force at such places at which the Presenter is required to render his services hereunder and that the Presenter shall further perform the Presenter's services hereunder diligently, willingly and conscientiously and to the best of the Presenter's artistic and creative skill and ability. The Presenter shall perform such services at the Company's address and at such other places and at such times as shall be notified to the Presenter by the Company.

3 REMUNERATION

(1) In consideration of the performance by the Presenter of his/her obligations and undertakings hereunder but subject thereto and for all rights granted by the Presenter hereunder the Company shall pay to the Presenter [   ] payable in equal monthly instalments in arrears during the Engagement Period.

(2) All payments to the Presenter hereunder shall be deemed to be a complete buy-out and shall be inclusive of and in full consideration for the Presenter's performance in the Series and for all services rendered by the Presenter and all copyright and rights granted hereunder and no further sums shall be required to be paid by the Company in respect of overtime or by way of repeat fees, use fees, residuals, royalties or other payments whatsoever.

(3) The Presenter authorizes the Company to deduct and withhold from any and all compensation payable to the Presenter hereunder all deductions required by any present or future law of any country wherein the Presenter performs services hereunder or the country of residence of any party hereto requiring the withholding

2 PRESENTER'S SERVICES

Producers should try and insist on the warranty set out in this clause since in the event that the presenter does not conform with specific rules or regulations of the production company then it may be easier for the producer to terminate the presenter's services for a specific breach. However the suspension and termination clause of this contract may also provide for this.

3 REMUNERATION

Depending on the type of programme which the presenter has been engaged for payment should be made in accordance with the company's budget for the programme and available cashflow.

Producers should also be clear as to how the presenter will be paid expenses. Producers should insist that no expenses shall be incurred without prior written permission of the company.

or deducting of compensation. In the event that the company does not make such withholdings or deductions the Presenter shall pay any and all taxes and other charges payable on account of such compensation.

(4) The Company shall reimburse the Presenter all reasonable and proper necessary expenses wholly and exclusively incurred in connection with the rendering of the Presenter's services hereunder, provided that the Presenter shall have obtained the prior written approval of the Company and shall provide the Company with receipts in respect of such expenses.

4 DUBBING

The Company shall be entitled to include or procure the inclusion in the Series of recordings in any language of the world of the voice or voices of another person or other persons speaking the lines and making the sound effects of the Presenter's visual and audio performances.

5 COPYRIGHT

(1) The Presenter with full title guarantee by way of assignment of present and future copyright hereby assigns to the Company the entire worldwide copyright and all other right, title and interest of whatsoever nature whether vested or contingent including but not limited to the right to exploit the Series and the products of the Presenter's services hereunder by any and all means and in all media throughout the world in and to the products of the Presenter's services hereunder including without limitation contributions to the scripts of the Series free of all moral rights of the Presenter and all liens and encumbrances to hold the same unto the Company absolutely throughout the universe for the full period of copyright and all renewals and extensions thereof and thereafter in perpetuity.

4 DUBBING

The producer of a television programme or series should be aware that certain presenters, depending on their stature, may object to their voice being dubbed in to another language. Producers should insist on this clause in the event that their programme is sellable outside their own territory.

5 COPYRIGHT

See notes in Chapter 2 regarding copyright.

(2) The Presenter shall do all such acts and execute all such documents as the Company may require to vest in or further assure to the Company the said copyright and all other rights herein expressed to be granted.

6 CREDIT

(1) Subject to the Presenter complying with his/her obligations hereunder and to the Presenter's appearance as Presenter in the Series as exhibited to the public the Company shall accord to the Presenter a credit as Presenter of the Series on the negative and all positive copies of each episode of the Series made by or to the order of the Company and so far as the Company is able and the size, position and style of such credits to be in the absolute discretion of the Company.

(2) No casual or inadvertent failure by the Company to comply with the provisions of this clause and no failure of persons other than the Company to comply therewith or with their contracts with the Company shall constitute a breach of this agreement by the Company. The rights and remedies of the Presenter in the event of a breach of this clause by the Company shall be limited to his/her rights (if any) to recover damages in an action at law and in no event shall the Presenter or any one on his/her behalf be entitled by reason of any such breach to enjoin or restrain the distribution, exhibition, advertising or exploitation of the Series.

7 OPTION

The Company shall have the option but not the obligation to engage the Presenter to provide his/her services as the Presenter for any subsequent series of the Series and for further series on terms and conditions to be negotiated in good faith. The Company may exercise its option on or before 21 days after the Company has been commissioned to produce any subsequent series.

6 CREDIT

If a producer engages a presenter who is not well known, then it may not be necessary to accord any substantial credit.

7 OPTION

It is advisable for producers to acquire the option to engage the presenter for a subsequent series or programmes in the event that a series is re-commissioned or there is a high demand for an additional programme. Although it is difficult to determine whether a further series or programme is desired, producers should state that terms and conditions will be negotiated in good faith. However, if it is certain that there will be another series or

8 WARRANTIES AND INDEMNITY

The Presenter hereby warrants to the Company:

(1) that the facts set out in the recital are correct and that he/she has the right to enter into this agreement and to assign and grant the rights herein expressed to be assigned and granted and has no and will have no contractual obligations to third parties preventing or limiting his/her appearance in the Series;

(2) that nothing under this Agreement shall constitute the Company his/her employer;

(3) that he/she is in such a state of health as will enable the Company to effect insurance with standard exclusions only and at normal rates against loss howsoever caused arising from his/her inability to perform any of his/her services hereunder;

(4) that he/she shall not order goods or incur any liability on the Company's behalf or in any way pledge the Company's credit;

(5) that any scripts or other literary material supplied by him/her for the Series will be original to him/her and that he/she shall be the sole legal owner thereof and nothing contained therein or in other materials shall be defamatory, obscene or infringe or violate the copyright or any other rights of any person;

(6) that he/she shall not without the prior consent of the Company at any time hereafter either personally or by means of press or publicity or advertising agents or agencies make any statement or disclosure or supply any information or photographs to any persons, firm or corporate body (other than his/her agents and professional advisers) or to the public relating to any matter arising hereunder or to the general affairs of the Company or any person connected with the Series

programme then producers should set out in clear terms how the presenter will be paid for work done.

8 WARRANTIES AND INDEMNITY

It is wise to have a warranty that the presenter has no other contractual obligations which may affect his or her appearance. Provisions should also be made if there is an overrun on the production so that the presenter is available on a second call basis subject to any other professional commitments.

It is also important to receive a warranty that the presenter will not engage in any hazardous or dangerous pursuits. For example, if the presenter is an avid parachutist it should be clearly stated that the presenter will not partake in these activities except after the programme or series is finished.

coming within his/her knowledge by reason of the rendering of his/her services hereunder or otherwise howsoever throughout the term of this agreement;

(7) that he/she shall not during the term of this agreement engage in any hazardous or dangerous pursuit;

(8) that he/she shall apply for or assist the Company in applying for and do all such things as may be required in support of any application for his membership of any properly designated labour organization or for any visas, passports, work permits, licences, permissions, consents or other matters necessary or desirable to enable the Company to make use of his/her services in such territory or territories of the world where the Series may be made.

(9) The Presenter hereby indemnifies and shall at all times keep the Company fully and effectually indemnified from and against all actions, proceedings, costs (including reasonable legal costs), claims, damages and losses whatsoever suffered or incurred by the Company as a result of any breach or non-performance of any of the agreements or warranties or undertakings of the Presenter hereunder.

9 EXCLUSION OF LIABILITY

Notwithstanding and irrespective of any advertisement or announcement which may hereafter be published the Company shall not be liable to the Presenter for or in respect of loss of publicity, advertisement, reputation or the like due to the Presenter's non-appearance in the Series and nothing contained in this agreement shall be construed as to impose upon the Company any obligation to make use of the services of the Presenter or permit the Presenter to play any part in the making of any cinematograph film or to include in the public presentation of any cinematograph film any photographs or recordings of the voice of the Presenter made in exercise of the rights herein contained.

9   EXCLUSION OF LIABILITY

It is essential that a producer set out this exclusion. It is possible that the producer may not use the presenter in a series or television programme. This provision ensures that the producer is covered for any loss of publicity or reputation for non-use of his/her performance.

10 CONSENTS

(1) The Presenter hereby grants to the Company all consents required under the Copyright Designs and Patents Act 1988 or any statutory reenactment thereof for the time being in force to enable the Company to make the fullest use of the Presenter's services hereunder.

(2) The Presenter hereby grants to the Company the right at all times hereafter to use and authorize others to use the Presenter's name, photographs and other reproductions of the Presenter's physical likeness and recordings of the Presenter's voice taken or made hereunder and the autograph and biography of the Presenter in whole or in part in connection with the advertisement, publicity, exhibition and commercial exploitation of the Series and subject to negotiation in good faith any music, records or books derived therefrom and in association with the advertisement, publicity and commercial exploitation of any merchandising and other commodities.

(3) The Presenter recognizes that the Company has the unlimited right to edit, copy, alter, add or take from, adapt or translate the products of the Presenter's services and the Presenter hereby irrevocably waives the benefit of any provision of law known as 'Moral Rights' or similar laws of any jurisdiction.

11 SUSPENSION AND TERMINATION

The Company shall be entitled upon written notice to suspend and, if appropriate, to terminate the engagement hereunder in the event of incapacity or default of the Presenter or if the production of the Series is disrupted by any event beyond the reasonable control of the Company. Upon suspension or termination of the Presenter's services, the following provisions shall also apply:

(a) all rights granted to the Company in respect of work done and services rendered by the Presenter and the

10 CONSENTS

Since the presenter is giving a performance the producer must acquire all consents under the Copyright Designs and Patents Act (CDPA 1988). (Producers should familiarize themselves with the CDPA 1988). When engaging American presenters, this clause is essential to protect the producer from certain rights of publicity and privacy that an American presenter can claim under US law.

11 SUSPENSION AND TERMINATION

This clause is essential in case the presenter becomes ill or incapacitated. If this clause is not present, technically the producer may have to wait until the presenter recovers to resume production this gives the producer the ability to replace the presenter.

products thereof prior to such suspension or date of termination howsoever arising shall not be prejudiced or affected;

(b) the Presenter shall not render his/her services to any third party during the continuance of suspension;

(c) the Company shall cease to be liable to make any payments of remuneration to the Presenter during the period of suspension or after the date of termination save for those which have already become due and payable. The Presenter shall not be paid for days taken for sickness unless he/she makes up such days on days approved by the Company.

12 NO WAIVER

No waiver by either party hereto of any breach of any of the terms or conditions of this agreement in a particular instance shall be deemed or construed to be a waiver of any preceding or succeeding breach of the same of any other terms or conditions. All rights, remedies, undertakings and obligations contained in this agreement shall be cumulative and none of them shall be in limitation of any other rights, remedy, undertaking or obligation of either party.

13 NOTICES

Any notices required to be given under the provisions of this agreement shall be in writing and shall be deemed to have been duly served if hand delivered or sent by facsimile or print out communication mechanisms or within the United Kingdom by first class registered or recorded delivery post or outside the United Kingdom by registered airmail correctly addressed to the relevant party's address as specified in this agreement or at such other address as either party may hereafter designate from time to time in accordance with this clause.

12   NO WAIVER

See Chapter 4 notes.

13   NOTICES

See Chapter 4 notes.

14 AGENT

The Presenter hereby authorizes and requests the Company to pay all monies other than expenses pursuant to Clause 3(4) hereof due to the Presenter hereunder to the Presenter's duly authorized agent [   ] whose receipt therefore shall afford the Company a good and valid discharge for the monies so paid.

15 ASSIGNMENT

The Company shall be entitled to assign this Agreement to any third party but any assignment shall not relieve the Company of its obligations hereunder. The Presenter shall not be entitled to assign this agreement in whole or in part.

16 ENTIRE AGREEMENT

This agreement replaces, supersedes and cancels all previous arrangements, understandings, representations or agreements between the parties hereto either oral or written with respect to the subject matter hereof and expresses and constitutes the entire Agreement between the Company and the Presenter in respect of the Presenter's services hereunder and no variations of any of the terms or conditions hereof may be made unless such variation is agreed in writing and signed by both parties hereto.

17 CLAUSE HEADINGS

The clause headings in this agreement are for the convenience of the parties only and shall not limit, govern or otherwise affect its interpretation in any way.

14 AGENT

See notes in Chapter 4 regarding payment to agents.

15 ASSIGNMENT

See Chapter 4 notes.

16 ENTIRE AGREEMENT

See Chapter 4 notes.

17 CLAUSE HEADINGS

See Chapter 4 notes.

18 LAW

This agreement shall be construed and performed in all respects in accordance with and governed by English Law and the parties irrevocably submit to the exclusive jurisdiction of the English Courts.

AS WITNESS the hands of the parties hereto the day month and year first above written

SIGNED by
for and on behalf of
THE COMPANY
in the presence of:

SIGNED by
THE PRESENTER
in the presence of:

18 LAW

See Chapter 4 notes.

12 Location agreement

Film and television producers who shoot on location without securing a proper release could face serious consequences. Producers should always secure releases for every location used. Without such documents, it may be difficult to purchase errors and omissions insurance as well as survive the scrutiny of a distributor's or broadcaster's legal department.

Location agreements should always be sought from the rightful land or home owner when shooting on private property and from the appropriate government entity when shooting on public property. Producers should ensure that the person signing the release has the authority to grant such permission.

Utilizing a location should not cost a great deal of money. In a small town or community, the arrival of a movie or television crew can generate a lot of excitement. Residents of these communities may offer the use of their property for little or no money. On the other hand, in places like Los Angeles, film and television crews have worn out their welcome in many neighbourhoods. Residents become annoyed with traffic congestion and the noise which accompanies a shoot. In some circumstances, home owners have had their property damaged and therefore are aware of how much producers may be willing to pay for locations. They may therefore demand a high sum for each day of shooting.

Producers should realize that when filming in public streets, they may have to get permission from the proper authority responsible for the area in which that filming takes place. In addition, they may need permits from the police if the film or television will affect traffic. Producers should contact the local film commission or the British Film Commission which have been set up to assist film and programme makers identify what consents will be necessary and generally assisting with their production (see Appendix A for a list of addresses).

Shooting a film or television programme without permission amounts to the offence of trespassing. Although trespassing is not a criminal offence, a trespasser can be sued civilly for damages. Therefore, it is always necessary to get a licence from the owner of private property to be present on his or her land or in his or her house. The location contract which follows is in reality a licence which gives the individual producer permission to do something which he or she would otherwise not be legally entitled to do.

LOCATION AGREEMENT

FROM: [Name of Production Company]

TO: [Name of location owner or grantor of permission]

Dear

RE: [Title of Film or Television Programme]

This will confirm the arrangements made between us whereby you have kindly agreed to make available to us the premises at: [location of premises].

('The Premises') for the purpose of filming exterior/interior scenes in connection with the film production provisionally entitled _____ under the following terms and conditions.

(1) The said Premises shall be available to us for a period of [ ] days commencing on or about [ ] and we shall be entitled to make such use of the said Premises as we may require for this period (it being understood that we may require to return at a later date if filming is not completed during the period at terms no less favourable than those contained herein). Our rights to make use of the Premises include (but are in no way limited to) our right to bring onto the Premises such personnel, equipment and props as we require for the purpose of the filming.

(2) You undertake and agree that we shall have the exclusive right and license:

    (i) to enter upon the Premises and make such use thereof as we may require during the period of this licence including in particular the right to rehearse and film scenes for principal photography of the film and to take still photographs for use either in the film or in publicity materials including book publishing or merchandising;

    (ii) to represent the Premises under their proper title or if we so desire to represent them as being

LOCATION AGREEMENT: NOTES

(1) Producers should try and ensure that they have the right to return at a later date. This ensures that they do not have to enter into another location agreement or pay further sums.

(2) It is essential that the producer will have the right to feature both the premises and everything in the premises, including all rights of exploitation of publicity and the right to portray the premises as something else whether it is a fictional place or otherwise. The producer should also ensure that they have the right to make alterations to the premises as long as it is of a temporary nature and will be restored to the original condition. Producers should ensure that no logos or trademarks are used without an added release or consent. (See Chapter 15, Name/Product/Logo Release.)

        another real place or fictional place according to
        our requirements;

(iii) to incorporate the scenes of the Premises in the
final version of the film either as a sequence on its
own or preceded, interlaced or followed by such
other scenes as we may require (including without
limitation scenes of studio sets representing for the
purpose of the film the interior of the Premises);

(iv) to exploit and exhibit the film with or without the
scenes photographed at the Premises by all means
and in any medium either known or hereafter
devised without any restrictions whatsoever;

(v) to make changes, additions and alterations in and
to the said Premises (interior and/or exterior) but
such shall be of a temporary nature only and we
undertake after our final use hereunder to restore
the said Premises to its condition immediately prior
to our period of hire.

(3) We undertake and agree to make good any damage to
the Premises arising directly out of our use thereof
subject to such damage being the direct result of and
caused by negligence on our part, such notification to
reach the production company within 24 hours of the
production vacating the Premises.

(4) In consideration of permission being granted to allow
filming facilities at your Premises, we shall arrange
insurance which will indemnify you up to *[insert amount
of insured value in words and figures]* for any liability,
loss, claim or proceeding arising under Statute or
Common Law in respect of personal injury (and/or
death) of any person and loss or damage to property
caused by negligence, omission or default of this
Company or any person for whom we are responsible in
law provided always that you notify us immediately of
any third party claims.

(5) You agree that should we require to cancel filming at your
Premises for any reason no fee will be due. Should your
Premises have already been altered or changed by us in

(3)(4) The actual amount of insurance should be discussed and
agreed between the Producer and Owner of the premises.
The question of insurance against any loss or damage
caused on the premises and who takes responsibility for that
insurance should be clearly set out in the contract. The
owner of the premises will expect that the producer take
proper care when using the premises and that there is proper
and adequate insurance to cover any loss and damage which
the producer may cause. This will also include individual loss
as a result of personal injury or death. Producers should
insist that the owner of the premises notify them within a
specific period of time (i.e. 24 hours) of any damage.
Otherwise it is possible that 3 months later the producer
could be met with an unpleasant surprise.

(5) Producers should ensure that there is a 'get out' clause in
case the production does not go ahead as planned. This will
save unnecessary expense.

any way, we will restore the Premises to its condition immediately prior to our alteration unless agreed by you.

(6) You grant us the exclusive option exercisable by notice to you on or before the end of the period of this agreement to extend the licence hereby granted for such period at a reasonable fee to be mutually agreed upon at the time.

(7) By your signature to the copy hereof, you warrant and represent that the rights and permission granted to us above reside solely with you and that you are free to enter into this agreement, and that you are vested with all the rights in connection with the contents of the Premises necessary to enable you to grant us the right to film and record any and all contents, designs and insignia in or on the Premises in connection with the film as detailed in clause 2 above. You also confirm that you are aware of the subject matter of the film and the characters involved in the story and neither you nor anyone else claiming through you will make any claim which is in any way related to this situation against us or any third party to whom we license the exploitation of the film.

(8) In consideration of our use of the aforesaid Premises and all rights to which we are hereby entitled we agree to pay you as inclusive compensation therefor the sum of £ (pounds sterling) in full and final payment.

Would you kindly signify your approval of and agreement to the above by signing the copy of this letter enclosed herewith and returning said copy to us.

Yours sincerely

LOCATION MANAGER
FOR AND ON BEHALF OF *[Name of Production Company]*

I hereby agree and accept the terms and conditions as stated above.

SIGNED ....

DATE ....

(6) It is advisable that a clause be inserted which gives the producer the right to extend the use period of the premises in case of delays in shooting. Rather than set out a specific fee it is best to explain that a reasonable fee will be agreed upon if any extension is needed.

(7) Always ensure that a warranty is given by the owner of the premises that he/she is entitled to give all the necessary permissions and consents.

(8) Producers should state that the payment made is in full and final settlement for the use of the premises.

13 Production manager's agreement

Individuals who work behind the scenes on a film or television production are usually represented by trade unions who have negotiated specific agreements with broadcasters such as the BBC or the ITV companies. For the various crew members who work on a film, BECTU (Broadcasting Entertainment Cinematograph and Theatre Union) is the union which represents technical personnel.

If a producer undertakes work for the BBC or an ITV company or that producer is a member of PACT, the producer in most cases is bound to observe the terms and agreement set out in the BECTU agreement. It is rare in the television industry for producers to use non-union talent. However, in film production more and more producers utilize non-union talent in order to keep budgets at a reasonable level. When a producer wishes to utilize non-union technicians, the contracts which are negotiated between the producer and the technicians are usually based on union agreements. What differentiates a union from a non-union agreement is that no reference is made to the specific union and in most cases the producer uses a buy-out clause which ensures that no further payments will ever be made to the relevant technician.

This book does not set out to describe in detail the contents of other union agreements, since the various unions all have different agreements and these agreements are subject to constant changes.

The agreement which follows does not make any reference to additional use fees, residual fees or net

416

profits. Clauses concerning additional payments can be added subject to specific negotiation (see Appendix B for sample definitions of net/producer's profits).

The following agreement is for a production manager, however it can be utilized for different job descriptions on a production.

PRODUCTION MANAGER'S AGREEMENT

THIS AGREEMENT is made the   day of   200

BETWEEN:

(1) [_____] of
     ('the Company')

(2) [_____] of
     ('the Production Manager')

WHEREBY IT IS AGREED AS FOLLOWS

1   ENGAGEMENT

The Company hereby engages the [Production Manager] and the [Production Manager] hereby agrees to render his services throughout the period of this engagement as a [Production Manager] in relation to a [cinematograph film and soundtrack] [television programme] associated therewith based upon [   ] and tentatively entitled ['   '] ('the Film') which the Company proposes but does not undertake to produce.

2   SERVICES

The [Production Manager] shall be responsible for preparing:
(i)   a detailed and comprehensive budget for the Film which shall be a bona fide and informed estimate of all expenditure likely to be incurred in the course of

418

PRODUCTION MANAGER'S AGREEMENT: NOTES

1 ENGAGEMENT

This clause and specifically this contract can be utilized for the various technical and craft jobs on a film or television production. Producers and craftsmen should realize that the various unions have drawn-up 'pro forma' contracts of engagement for use under the various union agreements. This means a producer does not have to draft new agreements each time one is needed and enables both parties to the contract to essentially fill in the blanks. Producers should note that these 'standard form' contracts are quite inflexible and do not leave much room for negotiation. Any specific terms must be agreed between the Producer and the craftsman either by incorporating those terms in the standard form, in a separate agreement or side letter, and such additional agreement or side letter must be cautious not to offend any provisions of a collective bargaining agreement.

2 SERVICES

The job description and the services to be performed by the specific craftsman or technician should be clearly set out in this section. In this example because a production manager, or what is sometimes known as the line producer, plays such a key role in the production of a film or television programme, all of the

419

production of the Film including all fees payable by reference to any use of exploitation of the Film as clearly indicated therein as well as the cost of any completion guarantee and a contingency;

(ii)   a production and shooting schedule for the Film; and

(iii)   a cash flow schedule for the Film and shall deliver each of the aforesaid as soon as reasonably possible but in any event no later than [200].

(iv)   (Other).

3   INDEPENDENT CONTRACTOR

The [Production Manager] acknowledges that his services are being rendered to the Company as an independent contractor and that at no time shall the [Production Manager] become an employee of the Company.

4   TERM

This agreement shall commence on the date hereof and shall continue until completion of the services required of the [Production Manager] hereunder.

5   CONSIDERATION

As full and final consideration for the services to be performed by the [Production Manager] and for all rights in the products thereof granted to the Company hereunder the company shall pay to the [Production Manager] the

production manager's responsibility should be set out in detail. Producers should adjust this section according to the type of responsibilities required by the craftsperson.

3   INDEPENDENT CONTRACTOR

Producers should try and ensure that individuals working on a production are independent contractors. This is for tax reasons and in order to refrain from paying any National Insurance or other contributions which an employer must pay towards an employee. An independent contractor will be responsible for his own tax returns whereas an employee must pay income tax under the PAYE scheme where tax is deducted at source and the responsibility is on the producer to make payment to the Inland Revenue. Producers should also note that when an individual is an employee then they are protected by status regarding certain matters such as unfair dismissal, redundancy, working time, and certain health and safety rules and regulations (see Chapter 10, Director's Agreement, for notes on Loan Out Arrangements).

5   CONSIDERATION

Technicians and craftsmen should try to be paid on a weekly basis. Sometimes a producer will want to pay a certain amount of money up front and the balance on completion of specific services.

sum of [   ] (   ) payable as to [   ] on the date hereof and as to [   ] upon delivery of the last of the items specified in Clause 2 hereof.

6 EXCLUSION

The Company shall have complete control of the production of the Film including but not limited to all artistic controls and the company shall not be obliged to make use of the services of the [Production Manager] hereunder or to include the products thereof in connection with the Film and subject to the company complying with its obligations under Clause 5 hereof no failure of the company in either respect shall give rise to any claim whatsoever by the [Production Manager] for alleged loss of professional standing or opportunity for the [Production Manager] to enhance his professional standing.

7 WARRANTIES AND INDEMNITY

(1) The [Production Manager] hereby, agrees, warrants, represents and undertakes as follows:
   (a) that he is free to enter into this agreement;
   (b) that he will render all the services normally performed by a first class film [Production Manager] conscientiously and to the best of his skill and ability as, when and where required and in accordance with the general requirements of the Company;
   (c) that he will not without the prior written consent of the Company make any statement of disclosure or supply any information to any person, firm or corporation (other than to his professional advisers) in relation to any matter or thing within his knowledge by reason of the rendering of his hereunder;
   (d) that he will not pledge the Company's credit or enter into any commitments or negotiate contracts on its behalf.

6 EXCLUSION

This clause limits the liability of the production company in the event that they do not use the services of the specific craftsmen or technician. For example, if the production company decided to fire a technician there may be the remote possibility that the technician or craftsman could bring an action against the company for loss of professional standing. A technician or craftsman may argue that because they were fired from the job, they may be perceived as incompetent or unable to complete their specific task. This is, however, a rare occurrence and a craftsman or technician would also need the financial clout to pursue such a matter in court.

7 WARRANTIES AND INDEMNITY

This clause puts a significant burden on the technician or craftsman to complete their services under the contract. Producers should ensure that this section is quite strict in case the producer wants to fire the technician for some form of breach or misconduct. Note that in Clause 7(1)(b) that a reference is made to 'the special requirements of the company'. Producers may wish to create standard provisions or rules regarding how freelance technicians must act when engaged by the producer on a project.

(2) The [Production Manager] hereby indemnifies and shall at all times keep the company fully and effectually indemnified from and against all actions, proceedings, costs, claims, damages and losses whatsoever suffered or incurred by the company in consequence of any breach or non-performance by him of any of the agreements, representations, warranties and undertakings on his part contained in this agreement.

8 RIGHTS

In consideration of these presents and insofar as any contributions of the [Production Manager] may give rise to the same the [Production Manager] hereby grants and assigns to the Company exclusively by way of assignment of present and future copyright the entire unencumbered copyright and all other rights of whatsoever nature in and to all products of the services of the [Production Manager] hereunder throughout the world to hold the same unto the company absolutely for the full period of copyright therein including all renewals and extensions thereof and thereafter (insofar as the [Production Manager] is able to grant and assign the same) in perpetuity.

9 FURTHER ASSURANCE

The [Production Manager] shall at the Company's expense perform all such further acts, deeds and things and execute all such further deeds, documents and instruments as may from time to time be reasonably required to vest in or further assure to the Company all the rights herein expressed to be granted and assigned to the Company.

10 CREDIT

Provided that the [Production Manager] shall fully perform all of his obligations hereunder the [Production Manager] shall receive a credit on the positive prints and/or tape of

8 RIGHTS

This clause should be used if any artistic contribution is made by a technician. In many circumstances a technician will have not made any artistic contribution whatsoever. However, it is always wise to include such a clause.

9 FURTHER ASSURANCE

See notes in Chapter 4.

10 CREDIT

Producers should try and confirm in writing what the technician or craftsman's credit will be on a film or television production. This clause gives the producer or production company the right to

the Film and the company shall determine in its sole discretion the manner and size of such credits. No casual or inadvertent failure of this provision shall constitute or be deemed a breach of this agreement.

11 EXPENSES

The Company shall reimburse the [Production Manager] for all expenses incurred by him relating to his services as [Production Manager] and such expenses shall require the prior written approval of the Company.

12 RIGHT TO ASSIGN

The Company shall be entitled to assign this agreement in whole or in part to any third party provided that the Company shall remain liable for all its obligations hereunder notwithstanding such assignment.

13 ENTIRE AGREEMENT

This agreement contains the entire agreement of the parties and may only be varied by written instrument signed by both parties.

14 NO PARTNERSHIP

Nothing herein contained shall be construed or deemed to constitute a partnership or joint venture between the parties hereto and save as expressly herein provided no party shall hold itself out as the agent of the other.

determine the manner and size of any credit to be received. If the production is a union or guild shoot, then the respective collective bargaining agreement will make provisions for credits.

11 EXPENSES

This clause is optional. Note that in Clause 5 (consideration) no reference is made to expenses. Producers may want to include expenses in this clause or refer to them separately. From the producer's point of view, he/she should try and negotiate a fee that is inclusive of any expenses.

Producers should ensure that if they are to include expenses in a technician's contract, then any expense to be incurred must be first approved in writing.

15 GOVERNING LAW

This agreement shall be read and construed in all respects in accordance with and shall be governed by the laws of England and the parties hereby submit to the jurisdiction of the English Courts.

16 CLAUSE HEADING

The clause headings in this agreement are for the convenience of the parties only and shall not limit, govern or otherwise affect its interpretation in any way.

AS WITNESS the hand of the parties hereto the day, month and year first above written.

SIGNED by a duly authorized
representative for and on
behalf of **THE COMPANY** in the
presence of:

SIGNED by the said **PRODUCTION MANAGER** in the presence of:

14 Release from a living person

When producers acquire rights in underlying material such as a book or script, those rights sometimes include life stories of famous individuals or events which evolve around living individuals. When real life characters can be identified in productions such as movies of the week or feature films, producers should try and acquire permission from those individuals who will be portrayed in a production to sign some form of release.

Defamation and privacy laws are different in the United Kingdom and United States. In the United Kingdom, the identification of real persons in a film or television production will only expose the producer to legal action if it is defamatory. However, in the United States the mere identification of a real person may lead to threatened or actual legal action for breach of rights of privacy or publicity. In the United States, a release from a living person is also referred to as a Depiction Release.

An alternative to having a living person sign a release is to fictionalize that person's story. By changing the names of the individuals involved, changing the location and making other alterations so that living people are not recognizable to the public, it may not be necessary to have a release. However, if the story's appeal is based on the fact that it is a true story and you want to be able to use the identities of real people, fictionalization is not a workable alternative. What follows is an example of a release from a living person.

RELEASE FROM A LIVING PERSON – CONSENT AND RELEASE: AGREEMENT

To: [Name of producer/production company]

I understand that you desire to use all or parts of the events of my life in order to have one or more teleplays or screenplays written, and to produce, distribute, exhibit and exploit one or more television programmes and/or motion pictures of any length in any media now known or hereafter devised and sound recordings in any media now known or hereafter devised. I have agreed to grant you certain rights in that connection. This consent and release confirms our agreement as follows:

1 CONSIDERATION: GRANT OF RIGHTS

In consideration of your efforts to produce my story, payment to me of $/£_____, upon the beginning of principal photography of a full-length feature film, and/or $/£_____ upon the beginning of production of a television movie, and/or $/£_____ upon the beginning of production of a pilot programme and a royalty of $/£_____ for each episode, and for other valuable consideration, with full knowledge I hereby grant you, perpetually and irrevocably, the unconditional and exclusive right throughout the world to use, simulate and portray my name, likeness, voice, personality, personal identification and personal experiences, incidents, situations and events which occurred or hereafter occur (in whole or in part) based upon or taken from my life or otherwise in and in connection with motion pictures, sound recordings, publications and any other media of any nature at all, whether now known or hereafter devised. Without limiting the generality of the foregoing, it is understood and agreed that said exclusive right includes theatrical, television, dramatic stage, radio, sound recording, music, commercial tie-up, merchandising, advertising and

RELEASE FROM A LIVING PERSON – CONSENT AND RELEASE: NOTES

1   CONSIDERATION: GRANT OF RIGHTS

In negotiating for life story rights there are a number of important issues that need to be resolved. At the outset, both parties must determine the extent of the rights granted. Does the grant include remakes, sequels, television series, merchandising, novelization, live stage rights and radio rights? Are the rights worldwide? Producers will usually want as broad a grant as possible, whereas the seller may want to retain certain rights.

The producer should also think about other releases that may be necessary. Releases may be needed from the individual, spouse, children, friends, etc. Other questions that should be asked are will these people consent to be portrayed? Will the subject ask his friends and relatives to co-operate? Can some or all of the secondary characters be fictionalized? If the producer is planning to tell the story of the domestic life of a mother, it may not make any sense to purchase her rights without obtaining similar rights from her immediate family.

publicity rights in all media of every nature whatsoever, whether now known or hereafter devised, I reserve no rights with respect to such uses. (All said rights are after this called the 'Granted Rights'.) It is further understood and agreed that the Granted Rights may be used in any manner and by any means, whether now known or unknown, and either factually or with such fictionalization, portrayal, impersonation, simulation and/or imitation or other modification as you, your successors and assigns, determine in your sole discretion. I further acknowledge that I am to receive no further payment with respect to any matter referred to herein. Any and all of the Granted Rights shall be freely assignable by you.

2 PAYMENT OF CONSIDERATION: REVERSION OF RIGHTS

I understand that you shall make the payments mentioned in paragraph 1 only if you begin production of a feature film or television movie or television pilot. In the event that you do not begin such a production within three years of the date this agreement was executed, all rights granted by me under this agreement shall revert to me. I understand that if you do begin production within three years of the date this agreement was executed, all rights granted by me under this agreement shall be perpetual.

3 RELEASE

I agree hereby to release and discharge you, your employees, agents, licensees, successors and assigns from

2 PAYMENT OF CONSIDERATION: REVERSION OF RIGHTS

In some releases from living persons, the contract can be structured as either an option/purchase or an outright sale, perhaps with a reversion clause. A reversion clause provides that if the producer or production company does not exploit the rights within a certain number of years (i.e. a movie or television programme is not made), then all rights revert to the seller (subject).

This clause protects the subject or living person if he/she has sold rights to his/her life story to a producer who is unable to produce a project. With a reversion clause, the subject eventually regains these rights and can sell or option them to another.

Producers should note that in some releases the subject of the release is often paid a fixed fee for consent to the release. A producer could also give the subject a percentage of net profits, a consulting fee and/or bonuses to be paid when the film or television programme is exploited.

3 RELEASE

Producers should be aware that an important part of any release from a living person is that the individual signing the release will

any and all claims, demands or causes of actions that I may now have or may hereafter have for libel, defamation, invasion of privacy or right of publicity, infringement of copyright or violation of any other right arising out of or relating to any utilization of the Granted Rights or based upon any failure or omission to make use thereof.

4 NAME – PSEUDONYM

You have informed me and I agree that in exercising the Granted Rights, you, if you so elect, may refrain from using my real name and may use a pseudonym which will be dissimilar to my real name. However, such agreement does not preclude you from the use of my real name should you in your sole discretion elect and in collection therewith I shall have no claim arising out of the so-called right of privacy and/or right of publicity.

5 FURTHER DOCUMENTS

I agree to execute such further documents and instruments as you may reasonably request to effectuate the terms and

promise never to sue for invasion of privacy, publicity or damage to reputation (defamation).

4 NAME – PSEUDONYM

Once the producer or production company has received a signed release, the producer will have the right to embellish, fictionalize, dramatize and adapt the life story in any way he/she chooses. However, this is a frequent problem in negotiations. The subject who is to sign the release is in most cases delighted to have his/her story told, but when presented with the release they become concerned. The individual realizes that the producer can change their story in any way they like but they cannot sue for defamation or loss of reputation. The individual may demand approval over any scripts or treatments. From a producer's point of view, this would be unacceptable. No producer is going to spend a lot of time and money developing a script only to find that the subject has changed his/her mind or is unreasonably withholding approval. If this situation arises, one form of compromise would be to give the subject approval over the treatment or selection of the writer. Alternatively, the producer may offer the subject a role as creative or technical consultant to the production. Another possible compromise would be to limit the subject matter and period portrayed. The individual to be portrayed may be concerned about an embarrassing incident in his or her life. The release could say that certain incidents (i.e. a divorce) are not to be included in the release. Another compromise would be that the release would only cover limited periods of the subject's life (i.e. only those incidents that occurred before a certain year).

5 FURTHER DOCUMENTS

Producers should try and have the individual agree to execute any further documents which help perfect the consent and intentions of this Consent and Release, and in the event I fail or am unable to execute any such documents or instruments, I hereby appoint you as my irrevocable attorney-in-fact to execute any such documents and instruments, if said documents and instruments shall not be inconsistent with the terms and conditions of this Consent and Release. Your rights under this Clause 5 constitute a power coupled with an interest and are irrevocable.

6 REMEDIES

No breach of this Consent and Release shall entitle me to terminate or rescind the rights granted to you herein, and I hereby waive the rights, in the event of any such breach, to equitable relief or to enjoin, restrain or interfere with the productions, distributions, exploitation, exhibition or use of any of the Granted Rights, it being my understanding that my sole remedy shall be the right to recover damages with respect to any such breach.

7 PUBLIC DOMAIN MATERIAL

Nothing in this Consent and Release shall ever be construed to restrict, diminish or impair the rights of either you or me to use freely, in any work or media, any story, idea, pilot, theme, sequence, scene, episode, incident, name, characterization or dialogue which may be in the public domain from whatever source derived.

8 ENTIRE UNDERSTANDING

This Consent and Release expresses the entire understanding between you and me, and I agree that no oral understandings have been made with regard thereto. This Consent and Release may be amended only by written instruments signed by you and me. I acknowledge that, in granting the Granted Rights, I have not been induced to do

release. This is a precaution in case an issue is not dealt with in the consent and release or in the event that a law changes, etc.

6   REMEDIES

This clause is essential so that the individual cannot injunct or interfere with eventual production of a film or programme.

so by any representatives concerning the manner in which the Granted Rights may be exercised and I agree that you are under no obligation to exercise any of the Granted Rights and agree I have not received any promises or inducements other than as herein set forth. The provisions hereof shall be binding upon me and my heirs, executors, administrators and successors. I acknowledge that you have explained to me that this Consent and Release has been prepared by your solicitor and that you have recommended to me that I consult with my solicitor concerning this Consent and Release. This Consent and Release shall be construed according to the laws of England.

In witness hereof and in full understanding of the foregoing, I have signed this Consent and Release on this day of   .

_____

(signature)

_____

(name, please print)

_____

(address)

Agreed and Accepted: _____

Appendix A
List of addresses

Guilds, unions and associations

USA

Actors Equity Association (AEA)
6430 Sunset Boulevard
Hollywood
CA 90028
Tel: (213) 462 2334; Fax: (213) 962 9788

OR
165 West 46th Street
New York
NY 10036
Tel: (212) 869 8530: Fax: (212) 719 9815

Alliance of Motion Picture and Television Producers (AMPTP)
15503 Ventura Boulevard
Encino CA 91436
Tel: (818) 995 3600; Fax: (818) 382 1793

American Federation of Musicians (AFM)
1501 Broadway, Suite 600
New York
NY 10036
Tel: (212) 869 1330; Fax: (212) 764 6134

OR
1777 North Vine Street, Suite 500
Suite 500
Hollywood
CA 90028
Tel: (213) 461 3441; Fax: (213) 462 8340

American Federation of Television and Radio Artists (AFTRA)
260 Madison Avenue, 7th Floor
New York
NY 10016
Tel: (212) 532 0800; Fax: (212) 545 1238

OR
6922 Hollywood Boulevard, 8th Floor
Hollywood
CA 90028
Tel: (213) 634 8100; Fax: (213) 634 8190

American Guild of Variety Artists (AGVA)
184 5th Avenue
New York
NY 10010
Tel: (212) 675 1003

OR
4741 Laurel Canyon Boulevard
North Hollywood
CA 91607
Tel: (818) 508 9984; Fax:(818) 508 3029

Directors Guild of America (DGA)
7920 Sunset Boulevard
Los Angeles
CA 90046
Tel: (310) 289 2000; Info line (213) 851 3671;
Fax: (310) 289 2029

OR
110 West 57th Street, 2nd Floor
New York
NY 10019
Tel: (212) 581 0370

International Alliance of Theatrical State Employees (IATSE)
13949 Ventura Boulevard, 3rd Floor Sherman Oaks
CA 91423
Tel: (818) 905 8999; Fax: (818) 905 6297

International Brotherhood of Electrical Work (IBEW)
230 41st Street
New York
NY 10036
Tel: (212) 354 6770; Fax: (212) 819 9517

OR
5643 Vineland Avenue
North Hollywood
CA 91601
Tel: (818) 762 4239; Fax: (818) 762 4379

National Association of Broadcast
Employees and Technicians (NABET)
1865 Broadway
New York
NY 10023
Tel: (212) 757 7191; Fax: (212) 247 4356

OR
1918 West Burbank Boulevard
Burbank
CA 91506
Tel: (818) 846 0490; Fax: (818) 846 2306

Producers Guild of America (PGA)
400 South Beverly Drive, Suite 211
Beverly Hills
CA 90212
Tel: (310) 557 0807

Appendix A

Screen Actors Guild (SAG)
5757 Wilshire Boulevard
Los Angeles
CA 90036
Tel: (213) 954 1600

OR
1515 Broadway, 44th Floor
New York
NY 10036
Tel: (212) 944 1030

Theatrical Teamsters
1 Hollow Lane
Lake Success
NY 11042
Tel: (516) 365 3470; Fax: (516) 365 2609

Writers Guild of America (WGA)
555 West 57th Street
New York
NY 10019
Tel: (212) 767 7800; Fax: (212) 582 1909

OR
7000 West 3rd Street
Los Angeles
CA 90048
Tel: (213) 951 4000; Fax: (213) 782 4800

United Kingdom

Broadcasting, Entertainment, Cinematograph & Theatre
Union (BECTU)
111 Wardour Street
London W1V 4AY
Tel: (0171) 437 8506; Fax: (0171) 437 8268
Email: bectu@geo2.poptel.org.uk

British Actors Equity Association (EQUITY)
Guild House
Upper St Martins Lane
London WC2H 9EJ
Tel: (0171) 379 6000; Fax: (0171) 379 7001
Email: info@equity.org.uk

British Film Commission
70 Baker St
London W1M 1DJ
Tel: (0171) 224 5000; Fax: (0171) 224 1013
Email: johnathon@bfc.co.uk (general IT)

British Screen/European Co-Production Fund
14/17 Wells Mews
London W1P 3FL
Tel: (0171) 323 9080; Fax: (0171) 323 0092
Email: info@britishscreen.co.uk

Eurimages, Council of Europe
F-67075
Strasbourg, Cedex
Tel: (33) 88 41 26 40; Fax: (33) 88 41 27 60

Her Majesty's Stationery Office (HMSO)
HMSO Books
PO Box 276
London SW8 5DT (postal enquiries)

OR
HMSO Bookshop
49 High Holborn
London WC1B 6HB
Tel: (0171) 873 0011; Fax: (0171) 873 8247

Producers Alliance for Cinema & Television (PACT)
10 Gordon House
Greencoate Place
London SW1P 1TH
Tel: (0171) 331 6000; Fax: (0171) 233 8935
Email: enquiries@pact.co.uk

Raindance Film Workshop
81 Berwick Street
London W1V 3PF
Tel: (0171) 287 3833; Fax: (0171) 439 2243
Email: info@raindance.co.uk

Writers Guild of Great Britain (WGGB)
430 Edgware Road
London W2 1EH
Tel: (0171) 723 8074; Fax: (0171) 706 2413

Collecting societies

Authors' Licensing & Collecting Society (ALCS)
Marlborough Court
14–18 Hobourn
London EC1N 2LE
Tel: (0171) 395 0600; Fax: (0171) 395 0660
Email: alcs@alcs.co.uk

Design & Artists Copyright Society (DACS)
Parchment House
13 Northburgh Street
London EC1V 0JP
Tel: (0171) 336 8811; Fax: (0171) 336 8822
Email: info@dacs.co.uk

Mechanical Copyright Protection Society (MCPS)
11 Sandyford Place
Glasgow
Lanarkshire G3 7NB
Tel: (0141) 204 4030

Performing Rights Society (PRS)
29–33 Berners Street
London W1P 4AA
Tel: (0171) 580 5544; Fax: (0171) 631 4138

Phonographic Performance Limited (PPL)
1 Upper James Street
London W1R 3HG
Tel: (0171) 437 0311; Fax: (0171) 534 1111

Professional associations and industry groups

USA

Academy of Motion Picture Arts & Sciences (AMPAS)
8949 Wilshire Boulevard
Beverly Hills
CA 90211
Tel: (310) 247 3000; Fax: (310) 859 9619

Association of Independent Commercial Producers (AICP)
5300 Melrose Avenue, Suite 226E
Hollywood
CA 90038
Tel: (213) 960 4763; Fax: (213) 960 4766

Cable Television Administration & Marketing Society, Inc
  (CTAM)
201 North Union Street, Suite 440
Alexandria
VA 22324
Tel: (703) 549 4200; Fax: (703) 684 1167

Casting Society of America (CSA)
6565 Sunset Boulevard, Suite 306
Los Angeles
CA 90028
Tel: (213) 463 1925

International Documentary Association
1551 South Robertson Boulevard, Suite 201
Los Angeles
CA 90035
Tel: (310) 284 8422; Fax: (310) 785 9334

International Television Association (ITVA)
6311 North O'Connor Road, Suite 230
Irving
TX 75039
Tel: (972) 869 1112; Fax: (972) 869 2980

National Academy of Television Arts & Sciences
111 West 57th Street
New York
NY 10019
Tel: (212) 586 8424; Fax: (212) 246 8129

National Association of Broadcasters (NAB)
1771 North Street
North West Washington
DC 20036
Tel: (202) 429 5300; Fax: (202) 429 5343

National Association of Television Program Executives
   (NATPE)
2425 Olympic Boulevard
Santa Monica
CA 90404
Tel: (310) 453 4440; Fax: (310) 453 5258

National Cable Television Association (NCTA)
1724 Massachusetts Avenue
North West Washington
DC 20036
Tel: (202) 775 3550; Fax: (202) 775 3604

Completion bond providers

Film Finances
9000 Sunset Boulevard, Suite 1400
Los Angeles
CA 90069
Tel: (310) 275 7323; Fax: (310) 275 1706

Motion Picture Bond Company
16 Birch Avenue
Toronto
Ontario M4V IC8
Tel: (416) 968 0577; Fax: (416) 960 0474

To register a film title

Non-member title registration agreement

Motion Picture Association of America (MPAA)
1133 Avenue of the Americas
New York
NY 10036
Tel: (212) 840 6161

OR
15503 Ventura Boulevard
Encino
CA 91436
Tel: (818) 995 6600; Fax: (818) 382 1799

British Film Commission
70 Baker Street
London W1M 1DJ
Tel: (0171) 224 5000; Fax: (0171) 224 1013
Email: jonathan@bfc.co.uk (general IT consultant)

New Producers Alliance (NPA)
9 Bourlet Close
London W1P 7PJ
Tel: (0171) 580 2480; Fax: (0171) 580 2480
Email: administrator@npa.org.uk

Raindance Film Workshop
81 Berwick Street
London W1V 3PF
Tel: (0171) 287 3833; Fax: (0171) 439 2243
Email: info@raindance.co.uk

Resources for commissioning and licensing music

Performing rights societies

American Society of Composers, Authors & Publishers
 (ASCAP)
1 Lincoln Plaza
New York
NY 10023
Tel: (212) 621 6000; Fax: (212) 724 9064

OR
7920 Sunset Boulevard, Suite 300
Los Angeles
CA 90046
Tel: (213) 883 1000; Fax: (213) 883 1047

Broadcast Music Inc (BMI)
320 West 57th Street
New York
NY 10019
Tel: (212) 586 2000; Fax: (212) 245 8986

OR
8730 Sunset Boulevard, 3rd Floor
West Hollywood
CA 90069
Tel: (310) 659 9109; Fax: (310) 657 6947

Society of European Songwriters, Authors & Composers
   (SESAC)
421 West 54th Street
New York
NY 10019
Tel: (212) 586 3450; Fax: (212) 489 5699

Selected rights and permissions services

BZ Rights & Permissions
125 West 22nd Street
New York
NY 10023
Tel: (212) 580 0815; Fax: (212) 769 9224

Clearing House Limited
849 South Broadway, Suite 760
Los Angeles
CA
Tel: (213) 624 3927

Copyright Clearinghouse
405 Riverside Drive
Burbank
CA 91506
Tel: (818) 558 3480; Fax: (818) 558 3474

Appendix B

Definition of gross and net receipts/income/profits

The following definitions are only a guide and should not be construed as complete definitions.

Any payments made from the income of a film must come out of receipts at a certain stage. In general, receipts pass first to the distributor who will take a commission and expenses and then to the producer who has to pay off debts in a certain order. Definitions of each stage are made in a number of different ways and it is important to qualify the use of commonly used expressions such as 'producer's net profits' or 'net profits' with a detailed definition. The following are some of those terms with sample meanings.

Distributor's gross

These are the actual receipts which the distributor receives from which any VAT and taxes are deducted.

These actual receipts are the 'base currency' by which profits are calculated. They include income from:

- home video
- television
- non-theatrical uses
- music publishing
- records
- merchandising

With regard to video sales, it should be noted that gross receipts usually only include a royalty. The rest of the revenue is kept by the video distributor, usually a studio subsidiary. Often excluded from gross receipts are income from:

- the sale and licensing of stock footage
- costumes
- photo stills
- publicity posters
- remake, sequel and TV spin-off rights.

Gross participation

A 'gross participant' is entitled to an agreed percentage of the gross receipts before deductions are made for distribution fees and expenses, as well as production costs, although deductions will be made for residuals, taxes and collection costs. There are several forms of gross participation:

- *'First dollar gross'* – this is a blanket percentage of gross receipts as they come in.
- *'Gross after break-even'* – participant only begins to share in the gross after the break-even point has been reached.
- *'Adjusted gross'* or *'rolling gross'* – gross participation minus certain costs (e.g. prints and advertising); this is really more like a form of net profits.

Distributor's net

This is the distributor's gross less any commissions and sales expenses.

Distribution fees

Studios retain a theatrical distribution fee of 30–35 per cent of the US gross receipts and 30–40 per cent of foreign film rentals; this percentage does not relate to the cost of releasing the film. In addition to this, films may also be bound to cover:

- Sub-distribution fees – these are charged when a studio uses a sub-distributor in foreign markets.
- Television distribution fees – these range from 10–40 per cent, depending which television market/network/syndicate the film is sold to. In these distribution deals, 'block booking' may occur, so that revenues are apportioned equally across all films sold even though they were not all successes at the box office.

Distribution expenses

These include the cost of:

- advertising the movie
- striking prints
- holding screenings
- throwing a premier party
- transporting and showing film reels
- dubbing, subtitling and re-editing foreign versions
- shipping
- copyrighting
- insurance
- litigation
- trade association fees
- guild payments
- verifying the accuracy of box office receipts and collection

Other distribution expenses include:

- *Advertising overhead* – this is a blanket fee of 10 per cent of the marketing expenses to cover the cost of a studio's advertising and publicity department.
- *Taxes* – taxes covered by foreign countries are charged as a distribution expense even though American studios get a foreign tax credit for these taxes on their federal returns.

Producer's gross

This the distributor's net as received by the producer.

Producer's net

This is the producer's gross less various costs which the producer must pay off first. These must always be specified and they usually include production costs and interest and overhead charges all of which are usually certified by an accountant.

The costs which the producer must pay off are often referred to as the *'negative cost'*. This includes:

- The cost of producing the picture.
- Any gross participant share of profits.
- *Overhead* – this is a charge of 10–20 per cent of the cost of producing the film.
- *Interests and finance charges* – this charge covers the cost to the studio of tying up its own money in making the film (this is often charged before the funds are actually used, and is often 125 per cent of the bank's prime lending rate).

Producer's net profits

These are the amounts left over after the deduction of those items set out in Producer's Net.

Producers should always try and share producer's net profits with talent and other individuals. This ensures that the producer can recoup the various items set out in the producer's net definition.

It is this term 'net profits' that is most often misunderstood and the source of legal dispute. This is because they are rarely substantial, and are often non-existent. Problems arise when film finance contracts are designed so that the film will never break even.

Recoupment

This is the point at which all negative costs, ongoing distribution fees, interest, financing and distributions costs have been covered and net participants start getting paid. While this works in theory, the recoupment point is continually shifted back, since some income sources are not immediately credited to the film (e.g. non-returnable advances from exhibitors).

Appendix C

Inducement letter/agreement

Author's note: The purpose of an inducement letter is in most cases tax driven. In order that a producer receives some comfort when using a loan out arrangement, they will want to ensure that the talent will abide by the agreement between the producer and the lender of the talent's services. Otherwise, if the (loan out company) breaches the contract the producer will only be able to sue the loan out company.

FROM: *[Name of Director, Writer etc. depending on circumstances]*

TO: *[Name of Production Company]*

DATED: *[Insert same date as agreement with loan out company]*

Dear Sirs

I make reference to the agreement ('the Agreement') which you are about to enter with *[name of loan out company]* ('the Lender') for the assignment and provision by the Lender of certain rights and services to be provided by me as the *[Director/writer etc.]* of the film ('the Film') to be produced by you and provisionally entitled ['   '], a copy of which has been supplied to and read by me.

   In order to induce you to enter into the Agreement I hereby:

1 Irrevocably consent and agree to the signature and delivery of the Agreement by the Lender and to the assignment and provision by the Lender of all the above rights and services under the Agreement.

2 Represent and warrant that there is in force and will throughout the relevant period subsist an agreement between me and the Lender entitling the Lender to assign such rights and to provide such services for all purposes necessary to enable you to produce and deliver the Film.

3 Guarantee and warrant to you as a principal and not merely as a surety the true and binding agreement of the Lender of and to all matters as to which any agreement, representation or warranty on the part of the Lender is contained in the terms of the Agreement.

4 Subject to all the terms and conditions of the Agreement agree to render all of the services required by me and to be bound by and duly to perform and observe each and all of the terms and conditions of the Agreement requiring performance or compliance on my part.

5 Agree that if the Lender should be dissolved or should otherwise cease to exist or for any reason whatsoever should fail, be unable, neglect or refuse duly to perform and observe each, and all of the terms and conditions of the Agreement requiring performance and compliance on the part of the Lender I shall at your sole discretion be deemed substituted for the Lender as a party to the Agreement in place of the Lender provided that in the event that you exercise such discretion you will from the date of such exercise make payment to me personally of all monies that would otherwise be payable to the Lender under the terms of the Agreement and in such event I shall (save where the Lender has been dissolved or has otherwise ceased to exist) procure that the Lender shall acknowledge that any such payments shall discharge you from all liability to make further payments to the Lender under the Agreement.

6 Agree that in the event of a breach or threatened breach of the Agreement by the Lender or by myself of my obligations hereunder you shall be entitled to legal and equitable relief by way of injunction or otherwise against the Lender and/or myself at your discretion in any event without the necessity of resorting to or exhausting any rights or remedies which you may have against the Lender and/or myself and in this connection I hereby submit to the non exclusive jurisdiction of the *[English Courts; or other appropriate jurisdiction]*.

7 Agree to indemnify you fully from and against any breach by the Lender of any of its obligations, representations, warranties and undertakings under the Agreement or by myself under the terms of this letter.

8 As beneficial owner assign to you to the extent of my interest therein if any the entire copyright in the products of my services pursuant to the Agreement (and where such services are as yet unperformed as at the date of this agreement by way of present assignment of future copyright) hereunder and acknowledge that all rights whatsoever throughout the world in the Film and in all photographs and sound recordings taken and made pursuant to the Agreement including all rights of copyright therein and in any written or other material contributed by the Lender or myself shall belong absolutely to you throughout all periods for which such rights may be conferred or created by the law in force in any part of the world and that subject as provided in the Agreement you may make or authorize the use of the same and may exploit the same in any manner and in this connection (recognizing the requirements of film production) I hereby waive the benefit of any provision of law known as the 'droit moral' or any similar law in any territory throughout the world whether now or hereafter brought into force and hereby agree not to institute, support, maintain or permit any action or proceedings on the ground that any use of the products

457

of my services pursuant to the Agreement in any way constitutes an infringement of any 'droit moral' or similar rights or is in any way a defamation or mutilation of the products of my services pursuant to the Agreement or contains unauthorized variations, alterations, adaptations, modifications, changes or translations.

9 Agree:

(a) to look solely to the Lender for all compensation for my services to be rendered under the Agreement and not for any reason whatsoever look to you for such compensations or any part thereof save as provided in paragraph 5;

(b) that if you in your sole discretion elect or give notice to withhold any part of the remuneration payable pursuant to the Agreement by virtue of any ruling or determinations of any body of competent jurisdiction neither I nor the Lender shall challenge the same but shall cause the Lender to provide to you forthwith all such documentation and assistance as you may properly request in order to comply properly with any such ruling or determination;

(c) that if at any time during the term of the Agreement or after the expiry thereof you shall be obliged to make payment of any additional sum to any statutory authority in connection with any payments made to the Lender thereunder, I shall repay the same to you forthwith upon request.

10 Undertake that no breach by the Lender of any of its obligations to me shall constitute or be deemed to constitute a breach by you under the Agreement and accordingly notwithstanding such breach I undertake to continue to fulfil all my obligations hereunder if and so long as you fulfil your obligations to the Lender.

11 Warrant that I am a Director of the Lender and that such Company is incorporated in and validly existing under the laws of *[insert proper country of incorporation]* and that throughout the term of the Agreement I will

not without your consent voluntarily transfer, charge or dispose of any interests in the Lender or resign any office therewith or take any other steps which might diminish my ability to procure the Lender to observe and perform all terms of the Agreement.

Yours sincerely,

....

Name of *[Director, Writer, etc.]*

Appendix D

Standard form licence to reproduce still photographs

THIS AGREEMENT is made the   day of   .

BETWEEN

(1) *[Name of Producer] of [Address]* ('the Producer' which expression shall be deemed to include its successors in title and assigns)

(2) [   ] of [   ] ('the Owner' which expression shall be deemed to include its successors in title and assigns)

NOW IT IS HEREBY AGREED AS FOLLOWS:

1 STILLS

The Owner agrees to make available to the Producer the still photographs described in the Schedule hereto ('the Stills') for the purpose of the Producer selecting therefrom those which the Producer proposes but does not undertake to reproduce in the *[television series] [Film]* provisionally entitled '...............................' [('the Series')].

2 MATERIALS

The Owner agrees to make available to the Producer such positive prints and duplicating material of the Stills in such format as the Producer shall designate for the purposes hereof.

3 RIGHTS

In consideration of the sun set out in the Schedule hereto the Owner hereby irrevocably grants to the Producer, its licensees and assigns the non-exclusive right throughout the universe for the entire period of copyright in the Series and all extensions and renewals thereof and thereafter to copy and reproduce the Stills and to use the same alone or in connection with any other work or works for the purpose of making and producing the Series and trailers thereof and thereafter advertising, publicizing and exploiting the same (including any dubbed, subtitled or other versions thereof) by all means and in all media whether now known or hereafter devised including without limitation the exploitation of the same by means of television (whether free, pay, cable, satellite or otherwise) non-theatrically by video cassette and disc, compact video disc and any other visual or audio visual system whether now known or hereafter devised together with the right to use and to reproduce the names and likenesses of the persons appearing in the Stills for the purposes of advertising and exploiting the Series and the right to broadcast extracts from the Series incorporating the Stills for the purpose of previews and post-transmission comment or review.

4 WARRANTIES

The Owner hereby warrants and undertakes to and with the Producer as follows:
(a) that the Owner is the sole and exclusive unencumbered owner with full title guarantee of the Stills and is fully entitled to enter into this Agreement and to grant the rights herein expressed to be granted and neither the Stills nor the reproduction thereof by the Producer will infringe any rights of any third party (including without limitation rights of copyright, trademark, privacy, publicity or confidentiality) or be in breach of any statute or regulation;

(b) that the performers appearing in the Stills leave granted to the Owner all consents under the Copyright Designs and Patents Act 1988 to enable the Producer to make and exploit the Series in all manner and media throughout the world for the full period of copyright;

(c) that there are no present or prospective claims, proceedings or litigation in respect of the Stills or title ownership of or copyright therein which might in any way impair, limit, diminish or infringe upon the rights herein expressed to be granted.

5 INDEMNITY

The Owner hereby indemnifies and agrees to keep the Producer fully and effectually indemnified from and against losses, claims, proceedings, damages and expenses (including reasonable legal costs and expenses) or liabilities suffered or incurred directly or indirectly by the Producer in consequence of any breach, non-performance or non-observance by the Owner of any of the agreements, conditions, obligations, representations, warranties and undertakings on the part of the Owner contained in this Agreement.

6 SPECIAL CONDITIONS

Any Special Conditions specified in the Schedule hereto are incorporated herein by reference.

7 LIMITATION OF CLAIM

The Owner shall not have the right to injunct or in any way restrain the exhibition or promotion of the Series for any cause whatsoever. Any claim by the Owner in respect of the Materials shall be limited to a claim for damages.

8 GOVERNING LAW

This agreement shall be construed and performed in all respects in accordance with and governed by English Law and the parties irrevocably submit to the exclusive jurisdiction of the English Courts.

AS WITNESS the hands of the parties or their duly authorized representatives the day, month and year first above written.

SIGNED by
a duly authorized representative
for and on behalf of THE PRODUCER
in the presence of:

SIGNED by
a duly authorized representative
for and on behalf of THE OWNER
in the presence of:

Appendix D

THE SCHEDULE

(a) The Stills:

(b) Consideration:

The Producer hereby agrees to pay to the Owner the sum of [   ] (   ) per Still as is actually incorporated by the Producer into the Series upon the date of such incorporation.

Appendix E

Release form (extras)

When producing a film or television programme, it is inevitable that producers will use the services of extras when filming crowd scenes.

It is essential that the producer have the participants' consent to the filming or recording of their voices (if speaking), as well as their performance.

In addition, an individual's consent should be obtained for the exploitation of the Film or television programme in all media and all various formats in which the finished film or programme will be shown.

RELEASE FORM

From: [Producer] ('the Producer')
Address: [Address]

To: [Name of individual]
Address: [Address]

Dear [name of individual]
Re: [name of film or television programme]

We are producing a [film][television programme]
provisionally entitled [   ] ('the Film').

This letter, when signed by you, shall constitute the terms
of your participation in the Film as follows:

1 In consideration of your participation in the Film and
   your agreements and consents the Producer shall pay
   you the sum of [£   ] (receipt of which you hereby
   acknowledge).
2 In consideration of the above fee you hereby irrevocably:
   (a) agree to participate in the Film and consent to the
       filming and recording of you as an individual and
       your voice in your performance and that such
       materials and recordings may be incorporated in the
       Film in whole or in part at the Producer's discretion
       and you hereby acknowledge that the Producer is
       under no obligation to use such materials;
   (b) consent to the exploitation of the Film or any part or
       parts of the Film (including your performance) by all
       means and in all media and formats whether now
       known or hereafter devised throughout the World in
       perpetuity;
   (c) consent to the use and reproduction of your
       performance in the Film and recordings of your
       performance or any part thereof by all means and in

all media throughout the world in perpetuity for the purposes of advertising, publicity and otherwise;

(d) waive and release the Producers from any claim, action or demand arising out of or in connection with the Film.

3 The Producer shall be entitled to assign or license the whole or any part of the benefit of this letter agreement to any third party.

4 You hereby release the Producer, its successors, assignees and licensees, from any and all claims and demands arising out of or in connection with such use including, without limitation, any and all claims for invasion of privacy, infringement of your right of publicity, defamation and any other personal and/or property rights.

5 You hereby understand that the Producer is proceeding with the production, distribution and exploitation of the Film in reliance on and induced by the foregoing consents.

6 This letter shall be governed by and construed in accordance with English Law.

Would you please signify your acceptance of the foregoing by signing and returning to the Producer the attached copy of this letter.

Yours sincerely

.... Date: ....

For and on behalf of [name of Producer]

Agreed and Accepted:

.... Date: ....

[name of participant]

Appendix F
Name/product/logo release

Introduction

Producers should ensure that, when placing any products in their production which include trademarks, service marks, trade names, logos and other materials which are subject to copyright laws, that the proper release is obtained to utilize these materials.

It is possible that any unauthorized use of a name, product or logo, without proper clearance can result in certain scenes being forced to be removed from the film. It is also possible for the owner of a name, product or logo to bring an injunction against the actual release of the film for the unauthorized use of these materials.

The following letter agreement is self-explanatory and sets out the proper form of release.

AUTHORIZATION TO USE NAME/PRODUCT/LOGO

From: [Producer]
Address: [   ]

To: [Name of name/product/logo owner]
Address: [   ]

Dear [name of name/product/logo owner]
Re: [name of film]

This letter will confirm that [   ] has the sole right to grant to the producer (and its successors, assigns and licensees) the right to photograph, record, reproduce or otherwise use the below-mentioned product, including all names, trademarks, servicemarks, trade names, logos and copyrights in connection therewith ('the Product') in the theatrical motion picture tentatively entitled [name of picture] ('the Picture') and in connection with the producing, advertising, publicizing, exhibiting and exploiting of the Picture (in whole or in part) in any and all media now known or hereinafter devised in perpetuity throughout the Universe.

In consideration of your usage of [   ] ('the Product'), the producer shall pay you the total sum of [£   ] payable on signature (receipt of which you hereby acknowledge).

[   ] represents that the consent of no other person or entity is required to enable the producer to use the Product as described herein and in its such use will not violate or infringe upon the trademarks, service marks, trade names, copyright, artistic and/or other rights of any third parties including the rights of publicity and/or privacy.

[   ] hereby acknowledges that nothing herein requires the producer to use the Product in or in connection with the Picture.

The producer shall be entitled to assign or license the whole or any part of the benefit of this letter agreement to any third party.

This letter agreement shall be governed by and construed in accordance with English Law.

Please signify your acceptance of the foregoing by signing and returning to the producers the attached duplicate of this letter.

Yours sincerely

....

For and on behalf of [the producer]

Agreed and Accepted:

....

For and on behalf of [name/product/logo owner]

Index

Account of profits remedy, 12
Acquisition agreement, 62–3
Addresses list:
  collecting societies, 444–5
  commissioning music resources,
    448–9
  completion bond providers, 446
  film title registration, 447–8
  industry groups, 445–6
  performing rights societies,
    448–9
  professional associations, 445–6
  selected rights and permissions
    services, 449
  time variable contingency
    insurers, 447
  United Kingdom guilds and
    unions, 442–4
  United States guilds and unions,
    439–42
Adjusted gross, 451
Aide Au Development fund, 19
Allowable acts, under copyright
  protection, 12
American Society of Composers,
  Authors and Publishers
  (ASCAP), 264
Articles of Association, company, 4
Asssignment of rights, 15–16
Attorney *see* Power of Attorney
Author-Written Sequel, 104, 106

Berne Copyright Convention, 9,
  175
Boilerplate clauses, contractual,
  46, 47

British Screen (agency), 19
Broadcast Music Inc. (BMI), 264
Broadcasting Entertainment
  Cinema and Theatre Union
  (BECTU), 416

Censorship/force majeure,
  Distribution Agreement clause,
  284, 285
Collecting societies addresses,
  444–5
Commissioning music resources,
  addresses list, 448–9
Company formation, 1–2
  Form, 10, 4
  Form, 12, 5
  incorporation documents, 3–5
Completion bond providers,
  addresses list, 446
Confidentiality/Non-disclosure
  Agreement, 311
  typical wording, 312–20
Consent and Release Agreement,
  typical wording, 430–38
Co-Production Agreement:
  typical wording, 214–41
  finance, 218, 219
  insurance provisions, 226, 227,
    228
  production specifications, 223,
    224, 225
  recoupment and profit
    participation, 232, 233
  roles and control, 216, 217
  warranties and indemnities, 234,
    235

Co-productions, 209–10
  check list, 210–12
Copyright, 7, 13
  allowable acts, 12
  categories, 7–8
  Distribution Agreement clauses,
    268, 269, 270, 271
  ownership, 8–9
  Presenter's Agreement clause,
    392
  Purchase Agreement protection
    clauses, 10–11, 120, 121,
    122, 123, 124
  remedies, 12–13
  scope, 7–8
  start/finish, 9–10
  United States provisions, 121,
    123
Copyright, Designs and Patents
  Act (CDPA) 1988, 7, 10, 67
  writer's protection, 175
Council of Europe, Pan-European
  Fund, 221
Credit obligations:
  Purchase Agreement clause,
    124, 125, 126
  under option agreements, 124,
    125, 126, 127
  Writer's Agreement clause, 160,
    161, 162, 163
Cross collateralization, 283
Cutting rights, 348, 349, 350, 351

Damages remedy, 12
Defamation Act 1952, 182
Defamation warranties, 171, 173,
  182
Delivery-up/destruction/seizure
  remedy, 13
Director's Agreement:
  typical wording, 324–85
  credit, 340, 341, 342, 344
  cutting rights, 348, 349, 350,
    351

director's services, 330, 331, 332
remuneration, 332, 333, 334
rights and consents, 345, 346,
  347
Schedule 1 (Terms of
  Engagement) see Director's
  terms of engagement
Schedule 2 (Profits and
  Deferments), 384, 385
Director's cut, 326, 327, 350, 351
Director's employment
  arrangements, 321–3
Director's terms of engagement,
  358–83
  compensation, 362, 363, 364
  disability and default, 370, 371,
    372, 373, 374
  effect of suspension, 376, 377,
    378
  effect of termination, 378, 379,
    380
  expenses and transportation,
    336, 337, 338
  force majeure, 368, 370
  indemnity, 380
  labour permits, 360, 361
  liability exclusions, 364, 366
  restrictions, 358, 359, 360
  services, 330, 331, 332
  union membership, 360, 361
  warranties, 366, 367, 368
Distribution agreement, 242–4
  typical wording, 246–92
  censorship/force majeure, 284,
    285
  copyright, 268, 269, 270, 271
  distributor's default, 286, 287
  E & O insurance, 272, 273
  film exploitation, 275–83
  indemnity, 266, 267
  producer's warranties and
    representations, 258–66
  remuneration, 246, 247, 248, 249
  rights granted, 250–57
  Schedule A, 294, 295

Distribution expenses, 452
Distributor's gross, 249
  definition, 450–51
Distributor's net, definition, 451–2
Droit moral, 108
Dubbing, 392

Equitable remuneration, 131, 133
Errors and Omission (E & O)
    Insurance, 119
  Distribution Agreement clause,
    272, 273
Eurimages funding, 221
European Commission, Media II
    programme, 18
European funding bodies, 220,
    221
European Media Development
    Agency, 18
Exhibitor's gross, 249
Exhibitor's percentage, 249
Exploitation, personal
    responsibilities, 14
Extras release form, 465–7

Film development, 17–20
  control of work, 44, 45
  legal mortgage, 36, 37, 38
  profit participation, 23, 24, 30,
    31
  reporting, 30–32
Film Development Agreement,
    19–20
  typical wording, 22–49
  First Schedule (Title
    Documents), 50–51
  Second Schedule (Development
    Work), 52–3
  Third Schedule (Development
    Budget and Cashflow), 54–5
  Fourth Schedule (Inducement
    Letter), 56–7

Film title registration, addresses
    list, 447–8
Finder/Executive Producer
    Agreement:
  typical wording, 298–310
  confidentiality, 302, 303
  indemnities, 304, 305
  remuneration, 300, 301, 302,
    303
First dollar gross, 451
Force majeure:
  Distribution Agreement clause,
    284, 285
  Option and Literary Purchase
    Agreement, 86, 87
Free television rights, 253
Funding alternatives, 17–19

Gesellschaft fur Misikalische
    Auffuhrungs und Mechanische
    Vervielfaltgunrechte (GEMA),
    266
Grant of rights, 431, 432
Gross after break-even, 451
Gross participation, definition, 451

Indemnities, Finder/Executive
    Producer Agreement clause,
    304, 305
Independent contractor, 420, 421
Inducement letter, as Film
    Development Agreement
    schedule, 56, 57
Inducement letter/agreement,
    typical wording, 455–9
Industry groups, addresses list,
    445–6
Injunction remedy, 13
Insolvency, partner's, 236, 237
Insurance, E & O, 119, 272, 273
Integrity right see Right of integrity
Intellectual property, 99, 101

Japanese Society of Rights of
Authors and Composers
(JASEAC), 264

Legal mortgage, film development,
36, 37, 38
Lending rights, 130, 131
Purchase Agreement, 130, 131
Libel warranties, 171, 173
Licensing rights, 15–16
Literary Purchase Agreement, 80,
81, 94–139
Living person, release form, 429
Loan agreement see Film
Development Agreement
Location Agreement, typical
wording, 410–15
Location shooting arrangements,
408–409

Matching rights see Right of Last
Refusal
Mechanical Copyright Protections
Society, 265
Memorandum, company, 3
Moral rights, 9, 109
Multi-media programming, 99, 101
Music performing rights, 264, 265

Name/product/logo release form,
468–70
Names search, company, 3
Nationality treatment, writer's
protection, 175
Non-disclosure/Confidentiality
Agreement, 311
typical wording, 312–20
Non-theatrical rights, 253

Obscene materials publication,
173, 174, 175
Option agreement, 60–62
consideration, 72, 73
exercise, 76, 77
period, 74, 75

Option and Literary Purchase
Agreement:
typical wording, 64–93
Exhibit A (Purchase Agreement)
see Purchase Agreement
Exhibit B (Short Form Option
Agreement), 79, 80, 81, 140,
141
Exhibit C (Short Form Copyright
Assignment), 79, 80, 81,
141, 142
consideration for option, 72, 73
force majeure, 86, 87
option exercise, 76, 77, 78
option period, 74, 75
option reversion, 84, 85, 86
restrictions, 82, 83
turnaround right, 84, 85
writer's representations and
warranties, 64–71
Ownership of rights, 230, 231

Paternity right see Right of
paternity
Pay television rights, 253
Performing rights societies,
addresses list, 448–9
Performing Rights Society Ltd
(PRS), 264, 265
Power of Attorney, typical wording,
206
Presenter's Agreement, 386
typical wording, 388–407
consents, 400, 401
copyright, 392
credit, 394
exclusion of liability, 398, 399
remuneration, 390, 391, 392
services, 390
suspension and termination,
400, 401, 402
warranties and indemnity, 396,
397, 398
Primary infringements, copyright,
10–11

Principal photography, 229
Producers' Alliance for Cinema and
    Television (PACT), 143
    standard form, 386
Producer's gross, 453
Producer's net, definition, 453
Producer's net profits, definition,
    453
Production manager, 416–17
Production Manager's Agreement:
    typical wording, 418–28
    consideration, 420, 421
    credit, 424, 425
    engagement, 418, 419
    expenses, 427, 428
    independent contractor, 420,
        421
    rights, 424, 425
    services, 418, 419, 420
    warranties and indemnity, 422,
        423
Production specifications, 223,
    224, 225
Professional associations,
    addresses list, 445–6
Profit participation, 23, 24, 30, 31
Protection, personal
    responsibilities, 13–14
Pseudonym use, 434, 435
Public domain material, 436
    United States copyright
        provisions, 121, 122
Publication Rights, 102
Purchase Agreement:
    typical wording, 94–139
    consideration, 110, 111, 112,
        113
    copyright, 120, 121, 122, 123,
        124
    credit obligations, 124, 125, 126
    indemnification, 116, 117, 118
    lending rights, 130, 131
    protection of rights, 118, 119, 120
    representations and warranties,
        112, 113, 114, 116

right to make changes, 108, 109
rights, 126, 127, 128
rights granted, 94–102, 110, 111
rights reserved, 102–107

Radio Rights, 104
Recoupment, definition, 454
Release form:
    extras, 465–7
    from a living person, 430–38
    name/product/logo, 468–70
Remuneration provision:
    WGGB/PACT Agreement, 154,
        155
    Writer's Agreement clause, 196,
        197, 198, 200
Reversion of rights clause, 432,
    433
Right of First Negotiation, 126, 127
Right of integrity, 9, 109
Right of Last Refusal, 126, 127
Right of paternity, 9, 109
Rights and permissions services,
    addresses list, 449
Rolling gross see Adjusted gross

Satellite television rights, 253
Scottish Film Production Fund, 19
Screenplay, development, 24, 28,
    29
Screenwriting Credits Agreement,
    147, 161, 187
Secondary infringements,
    copyright, 11
Security assignment see Film
    Development Agreement
Shelf company, 2
Shooting schedule, 229
Short Form Copyright Assignment,
    79, 80, 81, 141, 142
Short Form Option Agreement, 79,
    80, 81, 140, 141
Slander warranties, 171, 173

Societe des Auteurs Compositeurs
et Editeurs de Musique
(SACEM), 264
Society of European Stage Authors
and Composers (SESAC), 264
Stage Rights, 104
Still photograph reproduction,
standard form licence, 460–64

Tailor-made company, 1–2
Television rights, 253
Terms of engagement, director's,
358–83
Theatrical rights, 252
Time variable contingency
insurers, addresses list, 447
Trade marks index, 3

Union agreements, 416
United Kingdom, guilds and
unions addresses list, 442–4
United States:
copyright provisions, 121, 123
guilds and unions addresses list,
439–42
writers agreement, 145
United States Copyright Office, 61,
62, 67, 79, 203
Universal Convention on
Copyright, 121, 175

Videogram rights, 253, 255

WGGB/PACT Agreement, 143–4
typical wording, 146–206
remuneration, 154, 155
rights and consents, 164, 165,
166, 167, 168
rights to assign, 186, 187, 188,
189
Schedule 1 (Delivery of the
Work), 192, 193, 194
Schedule 2 (Remuneration), 196,
197, 198, 200
Schedule 3 (Short Form
Assignment), 202, 203
Schedule 4 (Net
Profits/Producer's Profits),
204, 205
terms of engagement, 150, 151
warranties, 170, 171
writer's indemnity, 180, 181,
182, 183
writer's services, 152, 153
Writer's agreement see
WGGB/PACT Agreement
Writers Guild of America (WGA),
145, 155
Writers' Guild of Great Britain
(WGGB), 125, 143, 155, 189
blacklist, 155
Writer's turnaround, 169